THE
ROMANCE
OF
BOSTON BAY

BY

EDWARD ROWE SNOW

AUTHOR OF

Storms and Shipwrecks of New England; The Story of Minot's Light;
Castle Island; Historic Fort Warren;
Sailing Down Boston Bay

Edward Rowe Snow

THE YANKEE PUBLISHING COMPANY

72 BROAD STREET

BOSTON, MASSACHUSETTS

FIRST EDITION
DECEMBER 1944

BOSTON PRINTING COMPANY
BOSTON, MASSACHUSETTS
PRINTED IN THE UNITED STATES OF AMERICA

IN MEMORY OF

MY FATHER
EDWARD SUMPTER SNOW

INTRODUCTION

Come with me for a journey to the most romantic and historic sea coast in America, that of Boston Bay. Dotted with countless lighthouses, islands, and forts, its shoreline comprising many attractive towns and cities, Boston Bay is rich in historic lore and legend. The Bay is loved by all who know it. People who have traveled far from home return to Boston Bay to appreciate more fully its beautiful shores and islands.

This volume is written not only for those who have already discovered the charms of this New England location, but for the unnumbered thousands who as yet have not had the privilege of visiting in person the islands and lighthouses of Boston Bay.

Before starting on our journey, I wish to acknowledge the help of many who assisted in planning the trip. Constantly lending her valuable assistance, my wife Anna-Myrle was ever helpful. My mother, Alice Rowe Snow, was always a willing listener. Dr. Robert E. Moody was a continual source of inspiration, while Nathan R. Krock assisted whenever technical difficulties were encountered. Besides those mentioned in the text, I now express my gratitude to the following:

William Alcott, Alice Powers Blackington, Alton Hall Blackington, Dorothy Blanchard, James L. Bruce, Clarence S. Brigham, John Joseph Collins, Madeleine Connors, Herbert E. Dill, Elsie Eastman, Robert J. Egles, Dr. William M. Flynn, Laura Gibbs, Raymond Hanson, Francis F. Haskell, Marion Haskell, Channing Howard, Vincent Holmes, Lawrence W. Jenkins, Honor McCusker, Eleanor Gregory Metcalf, Alba Mann, Franklin Pierce, Irwin Smith, Donald Burnham Snow, Edward Donald Snow, Eunice T. Snow, Winthrop James Snow, Harriet Swift, John G. Weld, and Captain William Wincapaw.

I trust that before we have visited our last fort or lighthouse you will feel, along with me, some of the friendship I have grown to treasure for Boston Bay and its delightful islands.

December 7, 1944   E.R.S.

TABLE OF CONTENTS

PART I
STORIES OF BOSTON BAY

His Majesty, the Sea Serpent 19
The Harbor Freezes Over 25
The Battle of Shirley Gut 35
Increase Mather's Escape 40
The Mysterious Pirate Tunnel 42
The Boston Tea Party 46
Boston's Age of Greatness 50

PART II
THE ISLANDS OF BOSTON HARBOR

The Inner Harbor 57
    Castle, Governor's, Apple, Snake, Noddle's, Susanna,
    Deer, Long, The Pirate Islands, Fort Strong and Fort
    Dawes
Along the Back Channel. 124
    Thompson's, Spectacle, Thimble, Cat, Half-Moon,
    Hangman's, Moon, Nut, and Rainsford's Islands
Hingham Bay 155
    Peddock's Island, Fort Andrews, Bumpkin Island,
    Grape Island, Sheep Island, Slate Island, Fort
    Duvall, Raccoon Island and the Hingham Harbor
    Islands
The Outer Harbor 166
    George's Island, Fort Warren, Gallop's Island,
    Lovell's Island, Fort Standish, Bug Light, The
    Brewster Islands, Calf Island and Green Island

PART III
NORTH, EAST, AND SOUTH OF BOSTON

The Glory of Salem 231
The Misery Islands 239
Baker's Island 241
Marblehead and Race Week 251
Nahant and the Forget-Me-Nots 256
The Chesapeake-Shannon Battle 259
The Thomas W. Lawson 262
An American Army of Two 265

PART IV
THE BEACONS OF BOSTON BAY

Boston Light 271
Boston Lightship 294
Graves Light 296
Minot's Light 301

. . . My soul is full of longing
For the secret of the sea,
And the heart of the great ocean
Sends a thrilling pulse through me.

LONGFELLOW

ILLUSTRATIONS

The Boston Tea Party . . . . End Sheets
Minot's Ledge Light 3
The Boston Lightship . . . . Frontispiece
The Sea Serpent 21
The Britannia Sails 37
Fishermen Walking Across the Harbor 38
Bug Light in Winter 38
Castle Island from the Air 71
The Castle Island Bell 72
Duelist Massie's Grave 72
Deer Island 105
Long Island 105
Scene on the Ice, Boston Harbor 106
Thompson's Island Band 139
William M. Meacham 139
Governor's Island from the Air 140
Garrison at Fort Warren, 1940 173
Nix's Mate from the Air 174
Prisoners at Fort Warren 175
A Dive at Minot's Light 175
John Albion Andrew 175
Donald McKay and the Lightning 176
Gallop's Island from the Air 209
The Building of Minot's Light 209
Scituate's Army of Two 210
The Apple Island Elm 211
Ancient Cannon at Boston Light 211
The America Comes Up the Harbor 212
30-Meter Square Yachts at Marblehead 245
Quincy's Thomas W. Lawson 246
Baker's Island Light 247
Anna-Myrle Snow Climbs Boston Lightship 247
Minot's Ledge Light Off Cohasset 248
Boston Light — Oldest in America 281
Graves Light from the Air 282
Inserted — Map of Boston Bay in Colors

PART I

Stories of Boston Bay

HIS MAJESTY, THE SEA SERPENT

B OSTON BAY, according to the records and statements
of landsmen and sailors of the last three centuries,
has from time to time been visited by that never caught
but often sighted denizen of the deep, the sea serpent. There
are those who claim with haughty disdain that they *know* that
there is no such thing as this mysterious creature of the ocean.
I cannot agree. I believe that we should all look at the possibility with open minds, not necessarily deciding that there must
be sea serpents, but perhaps saying, "Why not?"

Although Nantucket claims a priority whenever the sea serpent is mentioned, "his majesty" really became active along the
north shore of Massachusetts, rather than the far away island.

Around the 1850's, the serpent episodes in Gloucester
and Nahant involved not scores but hundreds of our leading
citizens who saw the great marine snake cavorting up and down
the North Shore. It was considered grounds for possible ostra-
cism from polite society should one venture to suggest that he
or she had been among those along the beach when the sea serpent performed.

There are many today who dismiss with scorn every tale
of the giant monster, but they may as well agree with the ancient
Lactantius, who was so sure of his own scientific knowledge
that he claimed all those who believed in the existence of the
Antipodes were mad. If the recorded information which has
been accumulated throughout the years were merely the scattered reports of ignorant or intoxicated men, we might view
with more caution and deliberation the various statements and
claims regarding the serpent, but such is not the case. In at
least twenty different years, on at least one hundred different
occasions, the sea serpent has been seen off New England shores

by men among whom are included some of the leading intel-
lectuals and practical business men of their day.

The early years of the 19th Century, however, were the
most active for the sea serpent. After his sojourn in and around
Gloucester during the summer of 1817, the serpent traveled to
Boston Harbor where he swam by the sentry at Castle Island
the following summer.

The next year he appeared time after time off Nahant.
The celebrated occasion when James Prince, prominent Boston
resident and Marshall of Massachusetts, observed this sea phe-
nomenon with his powerful telescope should be told by the man
himself:

August 16, 1819

"I will now state that, which, in the presence of more
than two hundred witnesses, took place near the long beach
of Nahant on Saturday morning last. I was glad to find
that I had brought my famous mast-head spyglass with me
as it would enable me from its form and size, to view him
to advantage if I might be so fortunate as to see him. On
our arrival on the beach, we associated with a considerable number of persons on foot and in chaises; and very
soon an animal of the fish kind made his appearance.

"His head appeared about three feet out of water; I
counted thirteen bunches on his back—my family thought
there were fifteen—he passed three times at a moderate
rate across the bay . . . as he swam up the bay, we and the
other spectators moved on, and kept nearly abreast of him;
he occasionally withdrew himself under water, and the
idea occurred to me that his occasionally raising his head
. . . was to take breath, as the time he kept under water was
on the average about eight minutes . . . I had seven distinct
views of him from the long beach so called, and at some
of them the animal was not more than an hundred yards
distance . . . on passing the second beach . . . we were again
gratified beyond even what we saw in the other bay; . . .

We had here more than a dozen different views of him, and each similar to the other; one however so near that the coachman exclaimed, 'Oh, see his glistening eye!'

"I feel satisfied that he is sixty feet long . . . I have been accustomed to see Whales, Sharks, Grampuses, Porpoises, and other large fishes, but he partook of none of the appearances of either of these . . . The water was extremely smooth, and the weather clear . . . I must conclude there is a strange animal on our coast."

Marshall Prince, in watching the animal or fish from a distance of one hundred yards with his powerful telescope, actually brought the picture less than fifty feet away. We herewith reproduce the sketch which the marshall drew at that time.

Thus we conclude that whatever he saw was close enough for him to make careful observations of its physical characteristics. But we have the testimonials of many others who were at Nahant that exciting week of 1819 and saw the sea serpent.

The common explanation of the disbeliever is that the sea serpent was in reality a group of horse mackerel, appearing in a straight line. I doubt if the strongest scoffer could have confronted a certain sturdy Swampscott fisherman, his face tanned and weatherbeaten from the effects of a lifetime at sea, who reported that he, too, had seen the sea snake.

Fisherman John Marston of Swampscott, a veteran sailor, who had seen all of the regular animals and fish along the coast of New England—seals, porpoises, sharks, horse mackerel, and smaller and larger fish of all kinds—made the following statement:

"I saw in the water . . . a singular-looking fish in the form of a serpent. His head was out of water, and he remained in view about twenty minutes, when he swam off towards King's Beach. I should say that the creature was at least eighty feet in length. I saw the entire body, not his wake. It would rise in the water with an undulating motion, and then all his body would sink except his head. This would be repeated. The sea was quite calm at the time. I have been constantly engaged in fishing since my youth, but I never saw anything like this before."

The remarks of Nathan D. Chase of Lynn follow:

"I saw him on a pleasant, calm summer morning of August, 1819, from Long Beach, Lynn, now called Nahant. The water was smooth and the creature seemed about a quarter mile away: consequently we could see him distinctly, and the motion of his body. Later in the day I saw him again off Red Rock. He then passed along about one hundred feet from where I stood, with his head two feet out of water. His speed was about that of an ordinary steamer.

"I saw the creature just as truly, though not as clearly, as I ever saw anything. I have no doubt that this uncommon, strange rover, which was seen by hundreds of men and boys, is a form of snake, Plesiosaurus, or some such form of marine animal."

Amos Lawrence, outstanding Bostonian of the period just before the Civil War, was among those who stood on the Nahant beach that summer of 1819. "I have not any doubt," said this great man, "of the existence of the sea serpent since this morning he was seen off Nahant."

Thomas H. Perkins, who gave Perkins Institute of the Blind to the people of New England, had seen the serpent two years before at Gloucester. His friend Samuel Cabot, great-great-great-grandfather of Senator Henry Cabot Lodge, wrote to Colonel Perkins about the Nahant incident:

"My attention was suddenly arrested by an object emerging from the water . . . which gave to my mind the idea of a horse's head. As my eye ranged along, I perceived, at a short distance, eight or ten regular bunches or protuberances, and at a short interval, three or four more . . . I returned to Nahant, and in crossing the small beach, had another good look of him for a longer time. . . . He moved more rapidly, causing a white foam under the chin, and a long wake, and his protuberances had a more uniform appearance. At this time he must have been seen by two or three hundred persons on the beach and on the heights each side, some of whom were very favorably situated to observe him."

Perkins' own story of his earlier encounter, two years before, follows:

"As he approached us, it was easy to see that his motion was not that of the common snake, either on land or in the water, but evidently the vertical movement of the caterpiller. As nearly as I could judge, there was visible at a time about 40 feet of his body. . . . I had a fine glass, and was within from one-third to half a mile from him. . . . The animal was, as far as I could distinguish, of a chocolate color. I was struck with an appearance in the front part of the head like a single horn, about nine inches to a foot in length, and of the form of a marlin-spike."

Years later, Colonel Perkins, who had been plagued by jokers for such a long time, admitted that he was one of the "unfortunate individuals" who had seen the sea serpent.

The Reverend Cheever Felch of the 74 man-of-war battleship *Independence* then engaged in survey work near Gloucester, saw the serpent on the morning of August 26, 1819, when he was with a group on a schooner. That very afternoon he wrote his account to Major Russell of the *Boston Centinel:*

"William T. Malbone, Esq., commander of the schooner, seeing some appearance on the water, said—

'there is your Sea Serpent', . . . but it proved no joke. . . .
He rose . . . within twenty yards distance of us, and lay
some time on the water. . . . His color is a dark brown, with
white under the throat. . . . From my knowledge of aquatic
animals and habits of intimacy with marine appearances,
I could not be deceived. . . . That there is an aquatic animal
in the form of a Snake, is not to be doubted. Mr. Malbone,
till this day, was incredulous. No man could now convince
him, there was not such a being. The sketch or picture of
Marshall Prince is perfectly correct."

In addition to the above testimonials there are scores of
other affidavits telling of the sea serpent in New England waters.
Hundreds of other locations around the world have been visited
by sea serpents, but never before or since the North Shore
monster made its appearance in the days of our ancestors a century and a quarter ago has there been collected such substantial,
concise, and verified evidence of his actual existence. It is
possible that the reader may still be unconvinced, but at least
he may admit—"Why not?"

BOSTON HARBOR FREEZES OVER

Adventuresome travelers down through the three hundred years of Boston's recorded history have often taken advantage of a cold spell to walk out over the ice for a visit to one of the islands of Boston Bay. Castle Island has been reached in this way at least twenty different years, while Governor's, Thompson's, Deer, Apple, Rainsford's, and Long Islands have all been the destination of many a winter hiker. There are stories of reaching Boston Light itself over the ice, but that feat is not as remarkable as it seems. It merely requires crossing the Narrows on the ice to Bug Light, then proceeding at low tide along the bar to America's oldest beacon at Little Brewster Island.

The Indians probably enjoyed the fun of walking over the harbor in those unusual years when the bay iced over, but they have left no records by which we can judge the severity of the winters before the white man came.

We know that the coldest winter recorded in the Seventeenth Century was that of 1641-1642, as John Winthrop himself describes the unusual condition in his journal. From January 18 until late in February horses and teams drove over the ice "in many places where ships have sailed." The Indians commented upon the severity of the winter season that year, saying that the cold was more intense than at any time in forty years.

On February 17, 1642, Captain Edward Gibbons, a romantic figure in the early Puritanical picture of Boston Bay, gained everlasting fame by riding in his sleigh from his house situated near the end of Winthrop Street in what is now Winthrop right across the harbor ice to Boston itself. This is the first instance of its kind recorded.

It is of interest to observe the effect that the winter of 1654 had on mintmaster John Hull, whose plump daughter, tradition says, was given in marriage with a dowry of an equal weight of pine tree shillings to Samuel Sewall. Hull's remarks follow:

"The frost was extreme and suddenly froze the Bay over, that, in a very few days, it was firm to pass betwixt the town and Long Island, and a constant passage to Charltowne and Noddles Island, etc.; and so continued above a month."

I always enjoy reading Samuel Sewall's Diary for January 24, 1685, where he mentions an incident in church: "Friday night and Satterday were extreme cold, so that the Harbour frozen up, and to the Castle. This day so cold that the Sacramental Bread is frozen pretty hard, and rattles sadly as broken into the Plates." On January 15, 1716, Sewall again observes that the bread froze, but adds that a baptism was performed nevertheless.

In 1733 ice formed in the harbor as far down as Long Island Head, indicating an unusually cold year. Castle Island was visited daily by residents of Boston who walked out over the ice. But it was the winter of 1740-1741 which was outstanding. A solid mass of ice completely stopped all shipping in and out of Boston Harbor, and Deacon John Tudor wrote in his diary that the "Old People" did not remember one of more severity. We may assume that some of the old people were at least eighty years old; therefore the winter which began in 1740 was the coldest for at least three-quarters of a century, or back to around 1665. Tudor goes on to say that "there was a Tent kept on the Ice between Boston and the Castle for entertainment."

The first recorded mention of cutting the ice of Boston Harbor for ship travel was in Tudor's diary for the year 1752:

"Jany. 18. Capt. Atkins and I rode in a sleigh to the Castle, on our return we rode oute to the Channel whare a Number of Men was cutting the Ice to open the Channel way for Vessels to go oute. The ice was 9 inches thick, But they cut with Saws etc. from as low as the Castle up to Clarke's Wharfe in 9 or ten Days and finished January 21st. The next Day a number of Vessells Sail'd."

While it is the first recorded reference to cutting Boston

Harbor ice, we should heed Fitz-Henry Smith, Jr., author of "Some Old-Fashioned Winters in Boston" published by the Massachusetts Historical Society, who says that one "can not presume to say that it was the first time that anything of the sort was done."

The gale of 1778 which caused the *General Arnold* to meet grief in Plymouth Harbor, described in *Storms and Shipwrecks of New England,* was also accompanied by bitter freezing weather. John Rowe of Rowe's Wharf said that particular Christmas Day was the coldest morning in forty years.

Professor John Farrar of Harvard recorded the coldest reading for 27 years as February 14, 1817, when it was 18° below zero. During this cold spell Captain Roustone crossed over to Fort Independence with seven heavily loaded teams, and it was generally agreed that not since 1779-1780 had the ice been so firm and thick.

On December 16, 1835, Boston experienced its coldest day, as never before had the temperature ranged so low from sunrise to sunset. In the middle of the day when it is usually the warmest, the glass read from 12 to 14 below zero from noon to 3 p.m. Bostonians were prepared for the quick freezing of the harbor. Suddenly, however, the weather turned warm and the solid field of ice in the harbor went out to sea with the tide. But the weather forces were merely delaying their efforts. By February 5 the inner harbor was entirely frozen over. A pilot walked on the ice all the way to Boston from Rainsford's Island, a distance of about seven miles. There was fine skating from the city to Fort Independence on Castle Island.

There are characters in Boston Harbor history who somehow keep attracting attention down through the years, and such a man was Dr. Jerome Van Crowninshield Smith, the Port Physician of Boston Harbor, who became mayor in 1854. As we mention elsewhere in this volume, many of his pert inscriptions are still to be seen on the rocks of Rainsford's Island.

Dr. Smith began one of his most remarkable adventures from the shores of Rainsford's Island in 1836 when he walked over the ice to the brig *Cervantes*.

We do not know exactly how far out the brig *Cervantes* was when it was hemmed in by the ice floe, but it was probably nearer to Boston Light than Long Island, judging from all available information. On board the *Cervantes* were several seriously frozen crew members of another vessel, the brig *Regulator*, which had been wrecked off Plymouth. The *Cervantes* had rescued the survivors, all badly in need of treatment, and when a pilot brought word that a doctor was needed, Dr. Jerome Van Crowninshield Smith made plans at once to set out over the ice pack to reach the *Cervantes*.

Starting out on Friday, February 5, Smith began the trip roped to a companion with a good length of line between them so that if either went through the ice, the other could pull him to safety. Although the two men found the snow and water knee deep in many places on their way to the stranded brig, the heroic pair reached the vessel successfully, and Dr. Smith was able to administer to the suffering survivors of the *Cervantes*. Two days later the doctor and his friend returned over the ice to Rainsford's Island. It had been a dramatic episode of Boston Harbor history.

Although when he became Mayor of Boston in 1854 Dr. Smith suffered the same fate that some of our national heroes endured in public office, I cannot pass his picture, now hung in the lecture hall of the Boston Public Library, without a deep feeling of regard for the man who probably loved the harbor as did no other of his generation.

During this same cold spell of 1835-1836 a passage was cut in three days to Central Wharf so that the bark *Highlander* could reach the pier. At that time the ice was one foot thick. Together with the men from the two other vessels, the crew of the *Highlander* ran their hawsers ahead, cut a hole in the ice, toggled the hawser with a hand spike, and then hove at the windlass, the weight of the bark together with the axes and picks of the crew gradually forcing a passage to the wharf.

Perhaps the most interesting ice episode in the entire history of Boston Bay concerns the Cunard liner *Britannia*. One day late in January 1844, the liner arrived safely at her pier in East Boston, and that very night the harbor began to freeze over. With the steamer scheduled to leave soon after February 1, it became embarrassing to the merchants and residents of the city when the ice grew thicker and thicker. Because of the maritime rivalry between the two ports, the people of New York would never let the Bostonians forget it should the *Britannia* be prevented from sailing because of the ice. On January 30 Mayor Brimmer presided at a meeting to decide what could be done. Matthew Hunt was appointed to cut a channel for the liberation of the *Britannia*. When, after working all through the bitterness of a blustery winter's day, Hunt found that the ice was freezing faster than he could cut it, he notified the committee that he could not fulfill the contract. John Hill and Gage, Hittinger & Company then agreed to cut the channel. Professional icemen with much experience on the ponds and lakes of Massachusetts, they recruited a large force of expert ice cutters who soon assembled to begin the work.

On February 1 thousands went out on the ice of Boston Harbor to visit the tents and booths set up there. Boat-Keeper Berry, one of the Boston Harbor pilots, walked up to town from Gallop's Island. Men with ladders charged a cent each for eager harbor explorers to reach the ice from the sidewalk level of the city. These men had cut holes around the public landing stairs to prevent citizens from getting on the ice in their own way. We quote from the *Boston Journal* of February 1, 1844:

"A channel of about sixty feet in width is first marked out, which is then divided into blocks of about thirty feet square. The sections marked are then *ploughed*, by which the ice is nearly cut down to the water. The plough used for this purpose is formed of seven different ploughshares, perfectly flat, and very sharp, which are arranged in a row, nearly similar to what is called a cultivator. After ploughing, the ice is sawed, so as to detach the cakes entirely from each other, after which two grapnels are attached to the cakes and they are hauled under the stationary ice by a gang of about one hundred and fifty men, some fifteen or twenty men standing on the cake in order to sink it sufficiently to make it pass under.

"The blocks of ice on one side only are thus disposed of, thus forming a channel of thirty feet in width. The blocks on the other side are to be detached after this channel has been finished, and will float out to sea with the ebb tide."

The work was kept up hour after hour, and even an injury to contractor John Hill, who hurt himself jumping from a cake of ice, did not delay proceedings. By late the next afternoon the work was completed, and the *Britannia* was ready to sail the next day.

On the morning of February 3 the adventuresome inhabitants of Boston made their way to the waterfront, where they went down on the harbor ice to watch a spectacular event, the sailing of the Cunarder *Britannia*. As she backed away from the pier there were several hundred people who viewed this colorful episode in Boston history. Backing into the slot in the ice cut for the purpose, the *Britannia* turned her paddlewheels until the prow faced the open channel. The incident is illustrated in this volume. Slowly moving her engines, the *Britannia* sailed out through the artificial channel while two hundred cheering enthusiasts walked alongside her all the distance to Castle Island, where they gave the *Britannia* a great farewell. Just where the steamer reached the end of the artificial channel is a hard question to answer, but indications are that the ice cutters did not work farther out than a point opposite Long Island Hospital's present pier.

In 1857, less than thirteen years after the *Britannia* sailed, another Cunarder, the *America*, entered the bay as the ice was forming. The tug *Enoch Train* had been running back and forth to keep a channel open, but on the night before the vessel was expected, the harbor froze solidly. The next day, however, the weather moderated, so when the *America* arrived on January 21, 1857, she came right up to the pier through the broken ice. After the steamer docked the cold returned, and for 36 hours the temperature stayed below zero. The ice became thicker and thicker.

Since the *America* was scheduled to sail within a few days the Boston citizens were faced with the 1844 situation all over again. A committee, quickly formed, concluded arrangements for opening a channel. Rapid progress was made this time, so that by five o'clock on January 27 there remained a section only 1¼ miles long to finish cutting. Trouble developed, however, when the *America* tried to back away from her pier the next day. She could not swing for the seaward turn, so the *Enoch Train* again maneuvered in the channel, breaking up the ice so that the *America* could make a fresh start. But it was the following morning before the *America* sailed, accompanied by many people part of the way down the harbor on the ice.

Booths and tents were again present down the bay, but there was activity of a different nature between Boston and East Boston, where the ferry ran. On the evening of the coldest night the ferry became jammed fast in the ice, and everyone aboard was forced to spend all night in the middle of Boston Harbor, with the ice crunching and shifting around them as the great bay froze. When morning came one of the prominent Boston banks failed to open its vaults, because the cashier was aboard the stranded ferry with the keys to the vaults in his pocket.

An immense hawser, brought out to the ferry, was made fast to a temporary bowsprit, and a long line of husky men, at least 130 in number, slowly pulled the ferry across the harbor. We reproduce the incident in this volume.

Albert F. Newhouse, later a prominent Boston truckman, was a boy at the time. When interviewed in 1909, Newhouse said that there was a solid sheet of ice in 1857 stretching away down to Boston Light, and that he had reached Boston Light over the frozen surface. Newhouse drove a pair of horses pulling an ice cutter for the *America's* channel. He said that the *America* sailed out to sea at 11 in the morning of January 29.

Newhouse participated in a weird experience off Shirley Gut during the same freeze-over. He and a group of other boys took their sleds out over the ice from East Boston, and by standing on the sleds and opening their coats, they would sail along in the wind.

"It was great fun. One time when I was away ahead of the rest I ran into the legs of a man with rubber boots on, his pants tucked in the boots, sticking out of a large hole in the ice that had been made by somebody who had been spearing eels just off Point Shirley, near Shirley Gut. I called to the rest and we soon found that the man had fallen into the hole and drowned, the body being under the ice while the legs stuck out. It was the body of John Bradshaw, who was steward on the pilot boat *Phantom* that was frozen in down below Deer Island."

Although there were many cold winters during the Civil War, our next story is about the year 1885. Sunday, February 15, 1885, was not exceptionally cold, but it did come at the end of almost a week of steady zero temperatures which froze Dorchester Bay solidly. The people of South Boston planned a great week-end carnival on the ice off City Point. Nearly 5,000 persons went out over the frozen harbor that Sunday, many on skates, scores on bicycles, and several on tricycles.

An outstanding event of the day occurred when John Manning, the Boston safe mover, drove out over the frozen wastes with his friend Richard J. Walsh and Walsh's six year old son, now Judge Richard M. Walsh of the Dorchester Court. It was eleven o'clock in the morning, but the temperature was steadily rising toward the melting point. Manning's horses were a fine pair, and he drove them with speed and efficiency all over the area between Thompson's Island and the mainland, and then disappeared toward Squantum. Shortly before noon he was observed returning from the direction of Squantum, and as he passed over Dorchester Channel, which went up to the Dorchester gas house, the team plunged through the ice. Both horses passed under the surface together with the sleigh, but all three occupants of the sleigh escaped. They were rushed ashore to McElroy's Seaside House and given first aid treatment. During the afternoon parties tried to grapple for the horses and sleigh, but they were not found. It was said at the time that a Mr. Lally had lost a horse and buggy near the same location exactly ten years before.

The winter of 1917-1918 was colder than any other in the entire history of the Boston Weather Bureau. On January 2, 1918, the steamer *Canopic* was frozen in the harbor, while three men of the crew of the fishing schooner *Rex* walked over the ice from the middle of the harbor where their schooner was caught to Tea Wharf. Captain Joseph I. Kemp, illustrious Boston pilot, forced his government tug through ice thick enough to walk on all the way out to the *U. S. S. New Orleans*, then caught in the ice below the Lower Middle. On the other side of the harbor the tugs *Henry Gillen* and *Grover Cleveland* were wedged firmly in Hingham Bay.

The winter of 1933-1934 was our last extremely cold winter. Ice formed around the entire fringe of Boston Harbor, but the activities of engine-propelled craft proved more than a match for the cold weather, which reached a low mark of 17 below zero on December 29, 1933, the coldest in the history of the Boston Weather Bureau. Less than a month and a half later, however, the glass dipped again, not stopping this time until a record 18 below was officially recorded at 4 a.m., February 9, 1934. During this cold spell I walked to several of the harbor islands with a friend. We took the precaution used by Dr.

Jerome Van Crowninshield Smith 98 years before, that of rop-
ing ourselves together for safety.

The winter of 1942-1943 included several extremely cold
days with temperatures far below zero, but the writer spent
that period in an Algerian base hospital in North Africa, so
any personal observations are lacking. However, in general,
the winters every so often are extremely cold, and on the
average seem to refute the observations which our parents and
grandparents are so apt to make, that the winters of today are
not as cold as they were fifty, sixty, and seventy years ago.

THE BATTLE OF SHIRLEY GUT

The Battle of Shirley Gut was fought in May 1776. On the 17th of that month Captain James Mugford was cruising aboard the privateer *Franklin* in the outer harbor, watching for a powder ship he had reason to believe was on the way from England. As the American forces desperately needed powder, the ship's capture would be an important victory. Late that afternoon he sighted the vessel, the ordnance ship *Hope* of Bristol, England. She was no match for brave Captain Mugford who boarded and took her in plain sight of the British fleet at Nantasket Road. With the capture of the vessel, Mugford ran for Shirley Gut, a dangerous thing to do at that time of day because of the fast ebbing tide, but there was no alternative. All went well until he reached the western end of Shirley Gut; there the *Hope* grounded. Mugford sent to Boston for aid to unload the valuable powder and anchored the *Franklin* close at hand.

Within an incredibly short time a great fleet of scows, sloops, schooners, and barges reached the powder ship, and the cargo was unloaded. The *Hope*, floating off at high tide, sailed triumphantly into Boston.

All of this activity rankled in the hearts of Commodore Banks and the other officers of the British fleet anchored near by, and they swore vengeance on Mugford. Two days later on Sunday evening, May 19, when Mugford sailed the *Franklin* out toward Shirley Gut, they watched the Continental cruiser as she proceeded toward the treacherous waters. Then the unexpected happened—Mugford ran aground just as the *Franklin* entered the Gut. The accompanying ship, *Lady Washington*, in command of Captain Cunningham, stood by to render assistance.

The two men, awaiting the incoming tide, went ashore at Deer Island to observe the British fleet. They found that the English had watched the stranding of the *Franklin* and were even then loading thirteen whaleboats to be sent in an attempt to capture the privateer. Hastening back to their respective vessels, the two American leaders prepared their ships to repel boarders. The *Franklin* was swung so that her broadsides would sweep the straits; the lower lanyards were cut and the shrouds were soaped so that no boarder could secure a hold. Boarding nettings were spread fore and aft on the cruiser and the long pikes ground sharp and tallowed halfway from point to grip. A dramatic sight thrilled the onlookers at Shirley Gut in the late afternoon light that May Sunday in 1776.

Just as the last rays of the sun were disappearing, an alert lookout shouted, "Boats coming, sir!" All hands went to quarters except those manning the windlass bars which kept the *Franklin's* broadsides facing the enemy.

"Boats, ahoy," cried Mugford, "keep off or we fire into you."

"We are friends," came the answer. "We are on our way to Boston." But the regular cadence of the oars as the man-of-war stroke hit the water revealed a different story.

"Keep off, or I fire," was Mugford's final warning.

"For God's sake, don't fire. We are going to board you," said a British voice, but it was swallowed up almost at once in the roar of the *Franklin's* broadsides as they crashed into the oncoming whaleboats. This first gun fire destroyed the artillery of the enemy. The survivors, nevertheless, came steadily on, throwing grapnel hooks and boat hooks aboard in a vain effort to gain the deck of the *Franklin*. But the Americans were too strong for them. It is said that one Yankee speared nine Britishers in succession as they attempted to climb aboard. In the entire engagement not a single Englishman set foot on the decks of the *Franklin*. It was a great show of the fighting effectiveness of the Americans.

At the very height of the battle, however, with the contest still in doubt, Captain James Mugford was fatally wounded in the side. Dropping his sword, Mugford shouted out, "I am

THE BRITANNIA SAILS THROUGH THE ICE, FEBRUARY 3, 1844

DESCRIBED ON PAGE 30

FISHERMEN WALKING ACROSS THE HARBOR, JANUARY 1918

BUG LIGHT IN WINTER
REACHED BY ICE FROM BOSTON, 1857

a dead man, but do not give up the vessel. You will be able to beat them off."

The most successful feat of the Americans showed the ingenuity of the Yankees. The patriots seized the tall masts of the boarding craft with lengthened boat hooks, careening them violently so as to swamp the British boats. The occupants, thrown into the water, were soon pulled under by the swirling current of Shirley Gut. Time and again this maneuver was repeated, until finally the surviving British forces saw the battle was lost and gave up the fight.

As Mugford lay on his deathbed, the sound of the oars of the retreating Britishers was sweet music to his ears, and he passed away happy in the knowledge that the Battle of Shirley Gut had become an American victory. Mugford's remains were taken to his home in Marblehead.

The morning after the battle, two children were walking along the beach near what is now Sunnyside, Winthrop. Suddenly one of them observed an overturned British whaleboat to which they both ran. The horrified children found the body of a British marine near the boat with a pike wound in his breast. He was later identified as Thomas Dwiffe and buried on the shore.

The funeral of Captain Mugford occurred in Marblehead, May 23, 1776, and a monument was later erected to the memory of the only American who lost his life in the Battle of Shirley Gut.

INCREASE MATHER'S ESCAPE

Many incidents have occurred around Boston Bay which have shown the ingenuity or alertness of the true Boston "Yankee" of the Seventeenth and Eighteenth Century. Increase Mather of the famous Mather "dynasty" was a man of this type. When Sir Edmund Andros took over the reins of New England's government in 1686, the people soon came to feel that his rule was far too harsh. At a secret meeting held in protest, Increase Mather was chosen to return to England on the ship *President*, then in Boston Harbor, to complain in person to the king about Sir Edmund.

When Mather was asked to make the journey, he replied, in true Puritan fashion, "If you say to me, Stay, I will stay; but if you say to me, Go, I will cast myself on the Providence of God, and, in His name, I will go." There were many obstacles in his way, however, for the secretary of Governor Andros, Edward Randolph, had a warrant to prevent Mather from leaving the country. Learning of the warrant in time, Mather hid away in disguise.

Thwarted in his attempts to seize Mather, Sir Edmund Andros ordered Captain Tanner of the ship *President* to sail at once before Mather could get aboard the vessel. Tanner obeyed, but as soon as he had reached the outer harbor, he dropped anchor, and then by prearrangement awaited Increase Mather's arrival. Mather had already escaped from Boston, stopping for the first night at his friend Colonel Phillips' home in Charlestown. From there he journeyed to Winissimett, now Chelsea, stopping with Thomas Pratt. All this time the soldiers of the governor were scouring the countryside in search of him, but the ingenious Puritan covered his tracks well. Using Snake Creek, Mather sailed by Newgate's Landing, where a boat was awaiting him. He was soon negotiating the twisting channel of the Old Crooked Lane Passage, which ran between Hog Island and the mainland, coming out into the harbor proper at the present location of the bridge from Winthrop to Orient Heights. Mather could then see the masts and spars of the *President* showing over Deer Island, and he felt that the worst of the journey was over.

Cutting inside of Apple Island, Mather finally reached the gut between Deer Island and Pullen Point, later known as Shirley Gut. Here he found a confederate awaiting his arrival, with a small fishing schooner ready to sail. After transferring to the fishing craft, Mather was aboard the *President* within an hour. Captain Tanner ordered all sails set and the *President* was soon on the way to England, with the man whom Governor Andros had tried to prevent sailing. After a wait of several years Increase Mather returned to America with the new charter. Increase Mather's escape from Andros was told and retold by the freedom-loving Americans for generations afterwards as a symbol of rebellion winning out against tyranny.

THE MYSTERIOUS PIRATE TUNNEL

One of the most unusual places in the North End of Boston is the ancient Commercial Street Tunnel, remnants of which can still be identified in the building having its entrance at 453 Commercial Street. The account of the way in which it was built and its subsequent history form one of the interesting stories of Boston Bay.

In the year 1745 a strange but singularly attractive character arrived in Boston, Captain Thomas Grouchy. There were those who believed him to be a privateer, and others were so bold as to place the word pirate alongside his name. He purchased the fine Governor Phips mansion at the northeast corner of Charter Street, and joined the Old North Church, where his persuasive talk and polished manners soon gave him an important position in the church community.

Meanwhile, obviously unknown to the other parishioners, he participated in activities of a different nature. While we cannot vouch for the story about him that has come down through the years to the present generation, we believe what follows is essentially correct.

Late one autumn rumors came from the North End waterfront that unusual activities were taking place. During the high spring tides two ancient hulks were brought up on the beach, and floated into two previously prepared depressions in the shore there, so close that their taffrails touched. Then a gang of seamen rowed ashore, and began building a wooden barrier around the ships so that none could see the work. But the people of the neighborhood soon learned what transpired. The seafaring laborers were gradually excavating under the hulls of the vessels, building a tunnel between the ships which they continued across what is now Commercial Street and Henchman's Lane. This tunnel, fourteen feet wide, was lengthened until it reached the Governor Phips mansion which Captain Grouchy then occupied. With the completion of the tunnel, the gangs of sailors left the harbor.

Mysterious vessels entered the bay during the darkness of the nights, anchoring off Captain Grouchy's tunnel to send their cargoes ashore in open boats, which at high tide could be guided right into the tunnel itself, to be unloaded later in leisurely fashion.

Several articles given to the Old North Church by Captain Grouchy probably made their way ashore through the tunnel. Some fine chandeliers were presented to the church by the captain and it was the statement of a Mrs. Crocker that the chandeliers were captured by Grouchy's men from a Spanish vessel, thus ultimately finding their way to an American church instead of to some Spanish cathedral to which they were originally consigned to go. Several cherubic figures, still in the Old North Church today, were also gifts of the notorious Grouchy.

The social life of the bold captain was active and varied. Grouchy entertained in a lavish fashion, and his parties were well attended. Many outstanding festivities were held in the old mansion, which had a fine ballroom, guest chambers, and servant's hall, with stables and coach houses, all of which were surrounded by gardens, terraces, and shade trees.

Suddenly in 1758, at the height of his popularity, without warning the captain vanished. There were whispers that Captain Grouchy had been caught and killed at sea, but no definite news was ever heard. So far as we know the date of his death is unknown, he left no children, and there was no will. He simply disappeared. The fine colonial mansion on Charter Street was sold to his creditors, and Captain Thomas James Grouchy, mariner extraordinary, disappeared from the annals of Boston Bay. To this day speculations are still being made about this Dr. Jekyll and Mr. Hyde of Bostontown.

Captain Grouchy's tunnel, however, remained. In later years historian Shaw visited the location, and asked "an aged friend" about the tunnel. His informant told him that the tunnel had been owned by one of the ruling elders of one of the churches in the North End who had been suspected of having activity in the smuggling trade. Drake, however, is more definite. He tells us that "this privateering merchant built an underground arch of brick, leading all the way from his house to the beach; and on the first night after a vessel dropped anchor, his boats, loaded with valuable booty, pulled with muffled oars to the shore, where the goods were taken by the sailors up to the captain's house through the arch, lighted by flaring torches." Horace E. Scudder, in *Boston Town*, takes his grandsons down to 453 Commercial Street for a visit to the tunnel.

Some years ago, on first hearing of the tunnel, I went up to the location, now the Nathan Tufts Meter Company, and ran the gauntlet of ridicule by claiming the existence of such a passageway under the building. I had my records with me, however, and one by one the workers there admitted the possibility of my statements. One of them suggested I return at five o'clock, when the eighty-year-old watchman came on duty. At five he made his appearance, and I queried him about my quest. He was my man.

"Yes," said the aged Bostonian, "I have been in this building for over half a century, and have seen part of the tunnel exposed when they were laying new pipes in Commercial Street, somewhere between 1875 and 1890. The tunnel was of brick, about fifteen feet across, and I can take you to a part of it right now."

My heart was strangely excited when he led me into another section of the building, where a heavy manhole cover protected an area below the floor. "I don't know that anyone has been down there for thirty years," he said as we strained to pull the cover away.

Kneeling down to peer into the hole, I noticed hundreds of heavy, thick cobwebs barring my way, but we placed a ladder down and I squeezed my 200 pounds through the opening. Lower and lower I descended until my feet touched the floor. There, screened by scores of cobwebs, was a severed section of the original Captain Grouchy tunnel, showing the original arch. It could not be a mistake, for the arch was of the proper width, and in the right location, diagonally across the street from Henchman's Lane. I went home that evening, my clothes covered with dirt from the hundreds of cobwebs I had encountered, but with a feeling of satisfaction. I was the first person in the twentieth century to visit what was left of the ancient smuggler's tunnel of Captain Thomas James Grouchy, erstwhile mariner of Boston Bay.

THE BOSTON TEA PARTY

Although most of us remember the story of the Boston Tea Party, few of us know as much as we should about one of the important events which led to the American Revolution. The struggles between the colonists in America and their mother country in England came to a crisis when the Boston Tea Party took place on the night of December 16, 1773. The event is pictured in the end sheets of this volume.

Perhaps the reader will recall the efforts of the East India Company to send tea to America and the energetic refusal of the Americans to accept the tea because of the tax. By the spring of 1773 so much tea had accumulated in the English warehouses that the Company appealed to Parliament for some means of getting rid of it, and the English Government responded with an act empowering the Company to export tea to America without paying the usual English duty. This, the British thought, would allow the company to sell the tea in America, the price being so low that the threepence tax in America would not be noticed. But when the Americans found out what was transpiring, they refused to accept the British proposal, as the tax was still on the tea.

On the night of November 1, five hundred Bostonians assembled at Liberty Tree, where Washington and Essex Streets meet today, and formed a committee to visit the tea consignees and ask them to resign their appointments. Their mission failed, however, for the tea merchants refused their request. A legal town meeting was then held on November 5, with John Hancock acting as moderator. A series of eight resolves was drawn up, and the merchants again unsuccessfully appealed to.

A vessel reached Boston on November 17 with the news that the tea ships would arrive at any hour from England. A legal meeting was called for the next day, and at that meeting word was again sent out to the consignees to resign their positions. When the tea merchants refused for the second time, the town meeting was declared dissolved at once. Historian Hutchinson later said that this sudden dissolution struck more terror into the hearts of the consignees "than the most minatory resolves."

On November 28, 1773, the first of the three vessels scheduled to arrive with the tea appeared off Boston Light. Captain Hall had on board the *Dartmouth* 114 chests of the hated commodity. Although the day was Sunday, a mass meeting was called. Thousands of patriots assembled at Faneuil Hall, and so intense was the interest that the gathering had to be moved to the Old South Meeting House to accommodate the large number of people. It was said that even the pirate executions of two generations before had failed to attract as great a crowd. A decision was agreed upon by all present that the tea should be returned to England without unloading, and that a volunteer watch of twenty-five men be placed at Griffin's Wharf to prevent the landing of any tea.

Sheriff Greenleaf now appeared at the meeting with a message from Governor Hutchinson, demanding that the gathering disperse. Hutchinson's proclamation was greeted with hisses and catcalls. Copley, the artist, who was son-in-law of tea merchant Clark, agreed to visit the consignees at Castle Island and act as mediator. Owner Rotch of the *Dartmouth*, together with the two other owners of the vessels which had not arrived, the *Eleanor* and the *Beaver*, promised that the tea should return to England without touching land.

When the *Eleanor* and *Beaver* reached Boston, they were moored off Griffin's Wharf, now the corner of Atlantic Avenue and Pearl Street a short distance from South Station. The situation reached a stalemate, for the law prevented the vessels from clearing port until their cargo had been discharged, and the townspeople would not allow the ships to be unloaded. To further complicate matters, on the twentieth day after arrival the ships would be liable to seizure. Governor Hutch-

inson issued a decree forbidding the sailing of any vessel without his personal approval, while Admiral Montagu of the
British Navy stationed two warships to guard outer Boston
Harbor. Although every Bostonian was anxious for the tea
to be returned to England peacefully, he was also determined
not to accept the tea with the tax. The showdown was close
at hand.

Thursday, December 16, arrived, the twentieth day after
the *Dartmouth* reached port, and Captain Hall either had to
sail or have his ship held liable to seizure. Owner Rotch now
made formal application for permission to sail, but he was
refused. The Governor, to be as inaccessible as possible, left
for his country seat on top of Milton Hill, so when Rotch per-
sonally applied to him later for a special passport to sail by
Castle Island, it required a considerable journey.

Meanwhile, every Bostonian who could come appeared at
the Old South Meeting House. It was estimated that by three
o'clock the largest crowd ever to assemble in Boston up to that
time had gathered at the meeting house. 7,000 persons were
present. Many prominent people spoke that afternoon including Samuel Adams, Josiah Quincy, and John Rowe, whose
question, "Who knows how tea will mingle with salt water?"
was received with loud applause.

At six o'clock owner Rotch returned from his interview
in Milton with Governor Hutchinson, who had refused to grant
him a pass. No sooner had Rotch made this announcement
at the meeting than Samuel Adams jumped to his feet shouting, "This meeting can do nothing more to save the country."
Instantly a war whoop was heard, and fifty men, evidently
prepared in advance for the Governor's refusal, rushed by
the door in full Indian costume and started off in the direction
of the harbor. Hundreds followed after them.

Guards had been placed around Griffin's Wharf so that
the Governor's spies could not intrude, and the "Mohawk
Indians" soon reached the vessels, the *Eleanor*, the *Beaver*,

and the *Dartmouth.* Then began the hard physical task of throwing into the harbor the contents of 342 boxes of tea on the three vessels. The chests were emptied with dispatch and efficiency while the great crowd stood silently by around the shore and on the wharf, watching by moonlight as the strangely costumed figures dumped chest after chest into the bay. All who were present knew that what transpired might lead to open warfare, but possibly only a few expected the fighting would start as soon as it did sixteen months later at Concord and Lexington.

It was three hours before the last chest of tea splashed into the bay. One heavy container fell into the harbor by accident before its contents were thrown out; it later floated ashore at Dorchester to be brought back to Boston Common and publicly burned. The "Indians" of Boston had done their task well. In later years there was much discussion as to how many people had actually participated in the affair. No names were revealed until after the Revolution ended, but about 140 people took part, while over a thousand watched on the wharf itself. The last survivor of the episode, Captain Purkett, died in 1846. A vial of the tea, shaken out of the boots of one of the "Indians" and carefully saved by the Melville family, is still preserved by the Bostonian Society at the Old State House, where it will remain for future generations to view. One of the tea chests is on exhibition at the Royall House in Medford.

BOSTON'S AGE OF GREATNESS

Mercantile, literary, and maritime Boston grew side by side in the stirring days halfway through the Nineteenth Century. Directly contrary to the predictions of many hopeful New Yorkers, the City of Boston did not at this time fall behind as a seaport, but actually forged swiftly ahead. Between 1790 and 1800, an average of 570 ships annually reached Boston, while by 1840 almost three times as many vessels yearly sailed in by Boston Light, bound for the wharves of New England's largest port. Coastwise trade also increased, arrivals doubling from 1830 to 1850.

Three men are outstanding in their contributions to this period—Robert Bennet Forbes, Father Edward Taylor, and immortal Donald McKay.

Robert Bennet Forbes made his first sea voyage at the age of six. A captain at twenty, he was master of his own ship at 26. Years later, envisioning the eventual eclipse of the sailing vessel by the screw propelled steamer, Forbes built the first ocean-going tugboat, appropriately named the *R. B. Forbes*. There is a fine drawing now in the Old State House, which shows the *Forbes* assisting in the liberation of the liner *Cambria* from the Truro beach. Captain Forbes was also the hero of the terrible Irish famine of 1847, when he sailed into Cork Harbor, fifteen days out from Boston, to bring relief to the starving people of Ireland.

Father Edward Taylor was a maritime figure of such great importance during this period that his influence extends even to this day and age. The outstanding preacher of the years from 1833 to 1870, he completely dominated his audiences in the Sailor's Bethel in Boston. During an era which produced great Boston literary and political figures, it has been suggested that his name was better known than any other from Boston. Those coming under the spell of his voice never forgot him, for he was truly a wonderful speaker. Walt Whitman mentioned his personal electricity, calling Father Taylor the only essentially "perfect orator" he had ever heard. Father Taylor's death in 1871 was mourned by thousands the world over.

Donald McKay is the third great figure of this period. Boston ships and sailors from earliest times have been engaged in all the profitable American enterprises as they developed— fur trading, slave-running, whaling, commerce with China, India and other parts of the world—and when the need for clippers developed, Boston produced its first in 1850. Samuel Hall built the *Surprise* in 1850, which under Captain Philip Dumaresq broke all records from New York to San Francisco, but it was not until a Nova Scotia Scotsman named Donald McKay moved to Boston that the Athens of America began her greatest period of maritime mastery, the Clipper Ship Era.

Producing clipper after clipper from his yard at East Boston, McKay quickly assumed a commanding lead which was never taken from him. In 1850 he became the first to build a clipper of more than 200 feet, the *Staghound*. The *Flying Cloud,* launched in 1851, showed her ability by sailing to San Francisco from New York in 89 days, shattering all previous marks. Her captain was Josiah Cressy of Marblehead.

The *Sovereign of the Seas,* which made her appearance in 1852, was larger and better than anything McKay had built to that time. When no one dared to accept the responsibility for such gigantic proportions, McKay constructed the vessel for his own interests. Placing his brother Lauchlan McKay in charge, Donald McKay watched with pride as this beautiful ship left Boston. The *Sovereign of the Seas* soon demonstrated her power by sailing 411 miles in a 24-hour period, a new world's record. Reaching Cape Horn in the midst of a severe Antarctic winter, the ship sailed steadily on, through hurricane and mountainous seas, losing spars and masts with disheartening regularity, but reached San Francisco in 105 days, record time for a winter rounding of Cape Horn.   The worth of large ships had been proved.

By this time East Boston, South Boston, and Medford were turning out ships as fast as they could be built, and Boston was soon the chief port of the Clipper World.   The sun never set during that period on Boston-built clippers.   Edward and Henry Briggs of South Boston launched many famous vessels, the leader of which was the *Northern Light*, which sailed from San Francisco to Boston's Narrows in 76 days 5 hours, a record made by this South Boston vessel which still stands. Robert E. Jackson of East Boston, who built the *Blue Jacket*, and Lapham, Curtis, Magoun, and others on the Mystic River, all contributed to the great maritime activity of the day.

With so many builders turning out such a large number of fast clippers, why were the ships of Donald McKay usually supreme?   I think the answer can be found in McKay's own words:

"With all my care, I never yet built a vessel that came up to my own ideal; I saw something in each ship which I desired to improve."

All of McKay's ideals were combined in the majestic ship which slid into Boston Harbor on October 4, 1853.   The 335-foot *Great Republic* was the world's largest sailing ship when launched, with the top of the ship's mainmast 276 feet above the deck.   Donald McKay rightly believed that all records would be at the mercy of his dream ship, but it was not to be. At her pier in New York when a disastrous fire broke out nearby, the *Great Republic* burned to the water's edge.   Cut down and rebuilt, the vessel later made a fine record, running from New York to San Francisco in 92 days.   She reached the equator in the record-breaking time of fifteen days eighteen hours. Arriving off San Francisco in 89 days the *Great Republic* was fog-bound for three more days, or she might have equalled the fastest time ever made between the two ports.   It is believed that Donald McKay never recovered from the shock of the burning of the *Great Republic*.

When James Baines ordered several ships for the Australian run, McKay built the *Lightning*. This was the world's fastest ship, logging 436 miles on March 1, 1854. The *Donald McKay*, logging 421, was not far behind, while the *James Baines* ran from Liverpool to Australia in 63 days.

Donald McKay, the peer of clipper ship builders, constructed over fifty vessels of different types, and was active until 1877, when he retired to his farm at Hamilton, Massachusetts, where he died in 1880. The inscription at the base of the Castle Island monument to the memory of McKay and his clippers does not exaggerate when it says that McKay's genius "produced ships of a beauty and speed before unknown which swept the seven seas, made the American clipper famous the world over, and brought renown and prosperity to the city of Boston."

Before saying farewell to the clippers, let us go aboard one of the great sailing champions, far at sea. Encountering a storm, the towering ship moves through the white-capped surface water at a speed of better than twenty knots, her bowsprit plunging under as the seas sweep the decks. Huddling in the lee of the deckhouses, the members of the crew are ordered aloft, climbing and fighting their way one and even two hundred feet above the decks and sea to the top of the bending, swaying masts, where they clamber out on the elongated spars to furl the fluttering, snapping, canvas sails. Breaking spars and cracking masts deter them not. On, on, and on the clipper sails, heeding nothing, until the goal is attained. Countless scores of brave men have fallen with a groan or cry into the ocean, never to be seen again, sacrificed to the jealous God of Speed which countenances no rival. Yes, it was a cruel, bitter fight which our grandfathers, the greatest sailors of all times, carried out, ending in death for many, but the exhilaration of the contest spurred them all on, officers and men alike.

Just as the end of the War of 1812 was the beginning of Boston's greatest shipping period, likewise the Civil War warned of its conclusion, and Boston's preeminence as a seaport soon was over. John R. Spears says that the shipping of America declined because of natural causes, but Boston lost more than its proportional share, to New York's subsequent profit. This was in spite of the fact that Boston is many miles nearer to Europe, Asia, Africa, and South America than is her larger rival.

Perhaps Boston will regain her leadership by means of the airplane. When the world sky trails of the future are planned, the advantageous position of the Hub of the Universe may be realized, with new glory coming to the city which Donald McKay made famous. The levelling of historic Governor's Island should gladly be accepted by all Bostonians if it brings a great American plane base here as a result. Then Boston again would be the port of a century ago, exchanging her white wings of the Clippers for the silver wings of the air.

The finest creation of American genius, the Clipper Ship, has gone forever. Even those children who watched the last of the beautiful sails as they disappeared off Boston Light during the fifties and early sixties have passed on, except for a scattered handful, but the thoughts inspired by Boston's *Flying Cloud, Sovereign of the Seas, Lightning,* and the other clippers of the Bay will never die.

PART II

The Islands of Boston Harbor

THE INNER HARBOR

CASTLE ISLAND

A HOPEFUL band of twenty Puritans led by Governor Thomas Dudley sailed across Boston Harbor on the twenty-ninth of July, 1634 and landed at what is now Castle Island, looking for a good site for their proposed fort. They climbed to the top of the cliff and were so impressed with the commanding view its twenty acres offered that they decided Castle Island best suited their needs. Dudley and each man present subscribed five pounds for the fortification, and the group elected Deputy-Governor Roger Ludlow to take charge of the actual construction.

None of the first three commanders of the fort stayed long at the Castle. Nicholas Simpkins, who was given the honor of being the first to command the defense, became involved in financial difficulties within the year, and resigned his position. He was succeeded by Lieutenant Edward Gibbons of Pullen Point, whose many enterprises forced him also to relinquish the office. Richard Morris became the next commander.

It was while Morris was at the Castle that the first tragic incident took place. In the summer of the year 1637 three ships sailed into the Harbor from Ipswich. When the Castle boat ordered the vessels to stop, two of them dropped anchor, but the third sailed by. The gunner at the Castle sent a warning shot across her bow, but the wet powder delayed the firing of the gun just long enough to kill a passenger in the rigging of the vessel. The next day the coroner and a magistrate, after boarding the ship and viewing the dead body, rendered the verdict that the poor man "came to his death by the Providence of God." Probably this decision eased the minds of the good Puritan villagers, but it was of no use to the unfortunate victim.

Richard Morris believed in the doctrines of Ann Hutchinson, and for this reason lost command of the Castle. He was banished from Boston in September 1638, and Captain Robert Sedgwick took his place on the island. The Court told Sedgwick to hire a gunner and an assistant, giving them for pay three hundred bushels of corn a year.

Affairs in New England were so quiet in 1642 that the General Court decided the Castle was no longer needed for protection, and in May 1643, gave orders to abandon the island. These instructions had hardly been carried out when the colorful La Tour, fresh from his struggles with D'Aulnay, sailed into Boston Harbor. His ship, the *Clement*, carrying 140 people, fired a friendly greeting as it neared the Island; but there was no answering gun from the deserted fort. A short distance away La Tour saw a small boat, piloted by a woman. Mrs. Gibbons, wife of the former commander at the Castle, was taking her children down to their farm at Pullen Point. La Tour had a boat lowered and started to overtake them, but she became frightened and made for Governor's Island, where John Winthrop was then living. Governor Winthrop, hearing the cannon shot, had come down to the beach to find out the cause of the disturbance. Mrs. Gibbons was able to land on the shore before La Tour caught up with her. When the Frenchman reached the beach, he explained that it had merely been his intention to ask Mrs. Gibbons a few questions about the settlement at Boston. Meanwhile, the harbor was filling with boats of all descriptions, manned by loyal colonists who feared their governor was in danger. The citizens were soon reassured by Winthrop and returned to their homes. But Winthrop, writing in his journal, believed that "if La Tour had been ill-minded towards us . . . he might have gone and spoiled Boston."

After this incident the good people of Boston Bay realized that the Castle would have to be refortified. The General Court arranged with the towns to have the fort rebuilt, agreeing to pay one hundred pounds for maintenance. Richard Davenport was commissioned commanding officer in July 1645.

Davenport was constantly troubled by money matters, especially in 1654, when the towns were asked to send men and supplies to the Castle to help out with expenses. Boston did what it could by giving the Castle a great bell, and later sent a substantial supply of gun powder.

This bell has an unusual history. One of the few actual treasures from John Winthrop's period, it was probably captured by Spanish pirates from a Scandinavian ship in the early part of the 17th century. A little later Captain Thomas Cromwell, commissioned by the Earl of Warwick to go after the pirates, captured at least four of these Spanish ships. Having become a rich man, he settled at Boston in 1646. The Suffolk Records contain his will mentioning six bells which he gave to Boston. The bells were distributed for various purposes, but the one in which we are interested was sent over to Castle Island in 1655 for the use of Captain Davenport. We know that this bell was in continuous service at the island until 1831. It may now be seen on a window ledge at the Old State House, the lettering telling us that it originally belonged to the ship *Patrioten*.

The troubles of Captain Davenport were soon to be ended. One hot day in July 1665, deciding to forget for a time the cares of office, he lay down on his cot beside the powder magazine. A thunderstorm came up, and a bolt of lightning struck the room, killing Davenport and injuring several of his men. It was a miracle that the Castle was not blown to pieces, since the magazine was only a few feet away.

Two important events are connected with the term of office of the next commander, Roger Clap. His account of the great scare of 1665, preserved in his memoirs, tells of the gigantic fleet which was sailing on Boston under De Ruyter, the Dutchman. Fortunately, contrary winds forced the Dutch commander to Newfoundland, where he bombarded the coast and inflicted terrible damage. Clap also tells of the disastrous fire of March 1673, which destroyed practically all the buildings on the island. Governor Bellingham had just died, and due to the confused state of his will the shrewd colonists voted to use his money for the erection of a new fort, sixty feet square. There were only six men in all at the island to man the thirty guns eventually installed there. Clap, who landed at Nantasket from the *Mary and John* in 1630, had fourteen children growing up at the Castle. The names he gave them sound unusual in this generation. Experience, Wait, Hopestill, Waitstill, Preserved, Thanks, Desire, Unite, and Supply were some of the titles he bestowed. Supply, the favorite son, rose to be a lieutenant under his father at the fort. He was killed by the accidental explosion of a cannon and was buried on the island. When James II sent Sir Edmund Andros to be governor of what was termed the Dominion of New England, Clap resigned his position rather than serve under this hated baronet.

John Nelson of Long Island received word that the Prince of Orange had landed in England. Nelson at once headed a group of citizens who overthrew the Andros government and imprisoned the unfortunate governor at the Castle. Andros almost escaped by dressing in women's clothing, but the guard detected the military boots showing under his skirts. Extremely indignant, Andros tried various means of escape, and at one time reached the shores of Rhode Island before being captured and brought back to Castle Island. After eight months of confinement he was finally released and left these inhospitable shores forever.

In 1691, the new charter decreed that the Lieutenant or Deputy-Governor of the colony should automatically become the commander at Castle Island. Lieutenant-Governor William Stoughton therefore became the new official at the island. Stoughton Hall, at Harvard College from which he graduated in 1650, was named for him. He was chief justice in the court which tried the witchcraft cases, Samuel Sewall being his colleague.

Stoughton noticed the Castle was in a wretched condition,

partly due to a disastrous fire twenty years before, and reported it to his superior in England. Nothing was done to repair the crumbling fortress until the turn of the century, with the arrival of Colonel Wolfgang William Romer. This chief military engineer of all the British forces in North America surveyed the situation carefully. He decided the old Castle was beyond repair and ordered it torn down. In 1701 the actual construction of what was to be known as Castle William began. Commander Stoughton was not to see the completion of this edifice, since he died the same year Romer started his work.

Samuel Sewall began to hear rumors concerning the vocabulary of this famous builder of North American forts, and rowed over to the island to obtain first hand knowledge. He landed at the Castle and walked up to the fortifications. Sewall noticed the fine construction with pleasure, but on hearing Romer admonishing his workmen he was worried. His loyal Puritanism could not countenance this builder who swore, but he realized the man was a great engineer. After thinking the situation over carefully for a few days, he advised the men to turn a deaf ear to the cursings of Romer, but to listen attentively when he spoke concerning the actual construction of the fort. Under the doubtful advantage of Sewall's conscience-satisfying plan, the new fortress was pushed to completion.

Three years later the entire harbor was aroused by news flashed up from Hull that a vast armada was sailing on Boston. By the time the fleet reached the Road, every able-bodied man was armed, and the Castle was alive with excitement. It was an English fleet, fortunately, and Sir Hovendon Walker's squadron of sixty-one ships with five regiments from Marlborough's army soon anchored off the Castle. It was the largest fleet that had ever floated on the waters of Boston Harbor. Walker's squadron remained here a few weeks and then sailed for the disastrous expedition into Canada.

William Tailer, who had succeeded Povey, noticed a change in the soldiers at the Castle. Many Sunday afternoons the rattle of muskefire could be heard by the good folk of Boston, possibly trying to sit through the second hour of one of Cotton Mather's sermons. Because of the disturbance from the fort, a law was passed forbidding the shooting of guns on the Lord's Day. It is indeed fortunate that some irreligious invader, taking advantage of the Sunday edict, did not sail by the silent fort and capture the town single-handed.

Since their Sunday shooting had been banned, the soldiers visited Boston in their spare time. Soon the commander at the Castle heard that his soldiers were head over heels in debt, even bartering their good uniforms in exchange for life in the village. Therefore, another law was passed forbidding the soldiers to barter their clothing or to contract for more debts than they could pay.

October 19, 1716, Lieutenant-Governor William Dummer assumed control at Castle Island, which was now recognized as the most important fort in British North America. John Larrabee, being senior officer, really was more in charge than Dummer, who spent much of his time at his Newbury farm. The colonial legislature discovered that Dummer had been using three soldiers from the fort to work on his farm at Newbury.

In 1753 splendid new barracks three hundred sixty feet long were erected at the island for the troops of Shirley and Pepperell. The regular garrison, of course, was kept in the citadel itself. William Pepperell, the hero of Louisburg, became commander of Castle William in 1757. He was succeeded the same year by Governor Pownall, whose fine sketch of the Castle of that period still exists.

In 1761 Governor Pownall was appointed to South Carolina, Governor Francis Bernard of New Jersey succeeding him in Massachusetts. Bernard was blamed for most of the pre-revolutionary trouble in the period of his governorship and surely was confused time after time in deciding his problems. With the passage of the Stamp Act in 1765, however, he was clever enough to have the offensive packages of stamps landed at

Castle Island. Of course the vigorous American opposition to the Stamp Act soon caused the law's repeal, with the return of all the stamps to England in the course of the following summer.

In this struggle between England and America, Massachusetts stood foremost, Boston the center of attack and resistance, and Castle William "a key to be grasped by the strongest hand." With the public mind still upset by the misunderstandings between Governor Bernard and his legislature, affairs were further complicated when a vessel belonging to John Hancock was seized by the officers of the custom house. The revenue commissioners responsible were insulted and threatened. They fled aboard the *Romney*, British Man-of-War, which landed them at the Castle.

The poor refugees immortalized by Longfellow in his *Evangeline* arrived in Boston Harbor while Bernard was at the Castle. After a hasty consultation it was decided that the ships should leave the harbor without landing. But hundreds of these poor folk had already been distributed around the bay, and they stayed here for several years. According to the correspondence of Governor Bernard they grew quite contented with their new homes, and were heartbroken when forced to leave Massachusetts.

When Governor Bernard left Boston Harbor in 1769, a short period of calm was enjoyed, but it was only the lull before the storm. Lieutenant-Governor Hutchinson was now the commander of the Castle. Colonel John Montresor of His Majesty's Engineers in North America put the two hundred ten guns at the island in fine condition, but we read that the Bostonians were reluctant to help him. Perhaps they felt that the guns might at some time in the near future be used against them, as did turn out to be the case.

In 1770, the Boston Massacre occurred. The 14th and 29th regiments were forced to leave Boston as a result of this tragic event. The enraged citizens had become so hostile that the men were removed to the Castle to avoid further trouble.

While at the island, one of the soldiers composed the following prophetic ditty:

Our fleet and our army will soon arrive
Then to a bleak island you shall not us drive.
In every house you shall have three or four
And if that does not please you, you shall have half a score.

Although it is claimed that the Castle never participated in an actual engagement, it was under fire in the month of March 1776. On the fifth of the month, Lord Percy planned to attack the Americans at Dorchester Heights, but a terrible gale came up which drove his transport ships far ashore at Governor's Island. In the Battle of Dorchester Heights the Castle batteries directed a withering fire against the various American emplacements on the mainland, but the Continentals answered shot for shot. This engagement was the only serious battle in which the fort ever participated. Strangely enough, the guns were directed against the very Massachusetts people they were constructed to protect.

With the Americans firmly entrenched at Dorchester Heights, the British knew they would have to leave Boston, and Admiral Shuldam took charge of the departure. As they were passing down the harbor, they stopped at Castle Island and started the task of destroying the fort. Dr. Warren tells us that they left the island ablaze on March 20, as they sailed for the outer harbor. After many skirmishes on the other islands, the fleet left Boston, blowing up Boston Light as a final gesture.

We are fortunate in having the actual account of the destruction of Castle Island, as written down in the diary of Archibald Robertson, a young officer in the Royal Engineers. A few paragraphs from his important account follow:

"March 17, 1776.—Got to Castle William about 10 and in an hour saw the Rebels on the heights of Charles Town.

[March] 18. In the Morning went to Castle William.

19. Went to the Castle; found the mines all loaded but 12, which were again unloaded as the General wanted them not to be ready for some days.

20th. Waited all the morning at Nantasket for want of a Boat. Got my Baggage taken out of the *Glen*. Between one and two found the Rebels had begun a new Work on Dorchester Point opposite Castle William. We fired at them from the Castle and by a Gun bursting had 7 men wounded. About two we observed about 21 Whale Boats set out from Dorchester Neck and row across to Thompson's Island, where they landed a small Cannon and pull'd it to the point and fired on our working Partys on Spectacle Island. At 3 o'clock Colonel Leslie came to the Castle from the General with orders to load the mines. We began immediately and had 63 done by 7 o'clock. The Boats lay off until the mines were fired. The Barracks and other houses were then set on fire and at 9 the Rear Guard consisting of 3 Companies, the Artillery, etc., Embarke'd and we got all safe on board the Transports. We got under way about 11 and went down near the Admiral in King Road."

Washington now sent a company of men across to the Castle to start refortifying the island. That ace of versatility, Paul Revere, spent some time in charge at the Castle and was successful in repairing most of the damage done.

Richard Gridley, the hero of Louisburg, supervised the erection of the new fortress in 1778 and added to the defense many guns taken from the wrecked British frigate *Somerset*. John Hancock assumed control of the Castle in 1779.

Hancock relinquished the title of commander at the fort in 1781 to Lieutenant-Governor Cushing. It was under Cushing that John Howard's famous prison reform system was tried in Massachusetts, with Castle Island as the location for this experiment. A small group of prisoners was sent from the mainland to what was to be the first state prison in Massachusetts. They were not the first prisoners at the Castle, however, for in the earlier days Indian prisoners helped build the Castle, and King Philip had complained of it. Indian hostages confined at the Castle in 1721 escaped from the island, causing an uproar in Boston before being caught. Edmund Andros had been able to get away for a brief time; but the man whose escapades became famous was Stephen Burroughs, a former Dartmouth College student. Robert Treat Paine had prosecuted him and Burroughs had been imprisoned in western Massachusetts. Very successful in escaping from the jails on the mainland, Burroughs considered the island a logical challenge to his ability. Once at the Castle, of which he gives a very thorough description in his memoirs, he began to plan for an early release. The chimney wall offered the more practical escape as the walls of the prison itself were five feet thick. Securing an old rusty nail, he scraped away night after night. When he had made a hole large enough for escape, he waited for the next stormy evening, whereupon he and seven companions climbed out of the opening into the pouring rain. They made their way down to the dock, where they overcame the sentry and started with him in the Castle boat for the Dorchester shore. The others wanted to drown the poor soldier, but Burroughs persuaded them to take the man along and leave him tied up on the beach.

Landing at Dorchester Point they reached a barn and hid under the hay. They were captured the next morning and brought back to the Castle. As the fort was still a military reservation, the men were subjected to the regular court-martial. They were sentenced at evening parade, stripped, and given one hundred lashes. Burroughs tells us that the lashes were laid very lightly on his back because he had saved the life of the sentry. Three of the others were punished very severely, "the flesh flying off at every stroke."

Early in 1788 the authorities believed Burroughs had repented and released him. He had been brought to the Castle in

1785. His exploits while at the Castle were told as legends for generations.

In the year 1799 the changing of the old name to Fort Independence was accomplished. President John Adams participated in the ceremony held in August 1799. George Washington died December 14, 1799, and the officers at the Fort wore crape on their left arms for the next six months.

The work of rebuilding Fort Independence was now started, the first stone of the new structure being put into place May 7, 1801. Before many months had passed a fine five-bastioned fortress was nearing completion. Lieutenant-Colonel Tousard was the constructing engineer. When the fort was completed, Nehemiah Freeman, the commander, named each of the five bastions. He called the east bastion, Winthrop; the southern bastion, Shirley; the north bastion, Dearborn; the northwest bastion, Adams; the western bastion, Hancock.

The most unusual story connected with Castle Island took place over a century ago. In 1817 Lieutenant Robert F. Massie of Virginia, 21 years of age, became an officer at Fort Independence. On Christmas Eve he was playing cards with the men in the barracks when an older officer suddenly accused him of cheating. The table was overturned and Massie was challenged to fight a duel. He accepted. It was agreed that the two men were to meet at dawn on Christmas Day.

Christmas morn was clear but bitter. The men with their seconds left the fort at daybreak and walked around to the Dearborn Bastion, where a vain attempt was made by the aides to reconcile the principals. The duel began. The older officer, an expert swordsman, soon had Massie at a disadvantage and ran him through. Fatally wounded, the Virginian dropped to the ground and was carried back into the fort. Massie died that afternoon, and his death was mourned by his friends. A fine marble monument was erected to his memory, and placed over his grave at the scene of the duel.

Feeling ran high for many days against Massie's opponent, and suddenly he disappeared. Ten years went by, and in May 1827 a young man enlisted in Battery H in Boston, and was sent to Castle Island. Although he signed the register as Edgar A. Perry, he was really Edgar Allan Poe, destined to become one of America's greatest writers of atmosphere and mystery. One day he saw the marble monument and, after asking the soldiers, obtained the story of the duel. Not satisfied with the explanation of the disappearance of the other officer, Poe continued his questioning until he eventually learned the truth.

According to the story Poe finally uncovered, Massie's adversary was so detested by the other men that a group of officers decided on a terrible revenge. Visiting the man one night, they drank with him until he became intoxicated, took him down into the lowest dungeon at the fort, and forced him into a small subterranean casemate. There they shackled him to the floor. Then walling up the narrow opening to the windowless casemate, the men left the victorious duelist to his fate.

Poe promised never to repeat the story, but years later he wrote the *Cask of Amontillado*. It is a similar tale, but names and places are so changed that Castle Island is not suggested as the scene of the story.

In 1905, eighty-eight years after the duel, when workmen were repairing a part of the old fort, they came across a section of the cellar marked on the plans as a small dungeon, but only a blank wall greeted them. On closer examination it was found that a small part of the wall had been bricked up, so the men broke through at this point. Obtaining a lantern, they penetrated the gloomy interior, and found a skeleton on the floor with fragments of an 1812 army uniform clinging to the bones. After an unsuccessful attempt at identification, the remains were given a decent burial in the cemetery.

Outside the walls of the fort, Massie's grave was not allowed to remain in peace. His skeleton and the monument were taken over to Governor's Island in 1892, and again in 1908 they were moved down to Deer Island. As if this seeming sacrilege were not enough, his remains and the monument were sent over to Fort Devens, Massachusetts, in 1939. Thus we have the strange story of the roving skeleton of Boston Harbor, or the duelist whose remains were buried four times in four different locations in 122 years.

On the 3rd of May 1808, Lieutenant Sylvanus Thayer, fresh from Dartmouth College, was sent over from Castle Island to erect water batteries on the shore of Governor's Island. After the completion of the shore defense, he was put in charge of building the enclosed redoubt at the top of the hill. This young lieutenant did work of such promise at Governor's Island that his superiors sent him to France to study under the great experts of that country. After many years away from home, he returned to take charge of the Military Academy at West Point. His achievements there can best be summarized by the inscription on his statue at the school—"Father of the Military Academy." Thayer left West Point in 1833, coming to Boston Harbor, where he began simultaneous operations at George's Island, Governor's Island, and Fort Independence.

In 1857 an unknown writer visited Castle Island, and left the following description of that period.

"We wave our handkerchief and attract a boat over from Castle Island where we soon land and find ourselves literally trampling on the dust of centuries. In order to enjoy the full tide of beauty, we must ascend to the ramparts. Behold the Charles River winding as it were out of the clouds, and pouring through forests of masts with Boston looking down from its triumvir throne; the State-House—how beautifully it sets, lending a coronal finish to the scene! The heights of East Boston on the right, and the misty Blue Hills in the distance. Then at the mouth of the harbor, see the splendid lighthouse; glance at the long, low, straight and emphatic line of Fort Warren; now the Long Island Head Light and Hotel; again the Back

Channel with the water gleaming in between the island on
your right and the seawall below; the Farm School on
Thompson's Island. . . . Deer Island Hospital, the grand-
est building of them all, with its windows illuminated by
the setting sun, and you will have accomplished the circuit
of prominent points in Boston Harbor."

Henry Lawrence Eustis was born at Castle Island in 1819.
The son of General Abraham Eustis, he attended Harvard Col-
lege, graduating with the class of 1838 which included such re-
nowned men as James Russell Lowell and Charles Devens.
Eustis followed the military traditions of the family by attend-
ing West Point, where he was a classmate of Ulysses S. Grant.
Eustis graduated from the military academy at the head of his
class. In 1843 he was placed in charge of construction work at
Lovell's and George's Islands, leaving to join the faculty of
Harvard College. He left Harvard to become a colonel in the
Tenth Massachusetts Infantry. Gaining fame for his heroism at
Salem Heights, he fought valiantly until sickness forced him
to return north. With the end of the war he went back to Har-
vard as an instructor and died a few years later.

The Fourth Massachusetts Battalion was quartered for
some time at the Castle, and among its honored members were
Charles Francis Adams and William Francis Bartlett. In his
Autobiography Adams describes his life as a soldier at Castle
Island. He did garrison duty at Fort Independence as a member
of the Fourth, starting April 24, 1861. He tells us:

"A pleasanter or more useful five weeks, in the educa-
tional way, I do not think I ever passed than those during
which I played soldier at Fort Independence in April and
May, 1861. The first night down I was in the guard detail.
The guard room,—long unused and very damp,—was aw-
ful."

William Francis Bartlett enlisted on April 17, 1861. As a
child he had roamed the shores of Winthrop with the great
Garibaldi, and later visited the famous soldier in Italy. He left

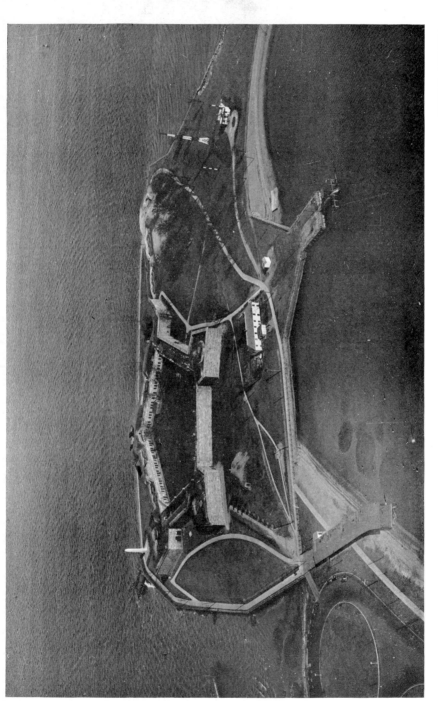

CASTLE ISLAND FROM THE AIR

THE McKAY MONUMENT IS OVER THE UPPER LEFT BASTION. NEAR THE LOWER LEFT BASTION THE MASSIE DUEL WAS FOUGHT.

EDWIN T. RAMSDELL

THE CASTLE ISLAND BELL
E. R. SNOW SHOWING GEORGE R. MARVIN THE ANCIENT LETTERING

DUELIST MASSIE'S GRAVE NOW AT FORT DEVENS

the Junior Class at Harvard to train at Castle Island, staying at Fort Independence from May 25 until June 25. Bartlett was very happy during his month at the Castle, declaring it "the pleasantest and most fruitful that I remember." He was given a captain's commission in the Twentieth Regiment. A month later in the thick of the war, while watching the enemy with his field glasses, a bullet shattered his left knee so badly that the leg had to be amputated.

Sent north, Bartlett was able to return to the battlefield less than a year later, this time distinguishing himself at Port Hudson. Because of the loss of his leg, the colonel rode into battle on horseback. The only mounted officer, he was an easy target for the Southern marksmen. The Confederate officers cried to their troops not to shoot such a gallant man, but the enemy finally brought him down. Recovering from his wounds, he joined the army in time to be captured at Petersburg and taken to the prison camp. He never fully recovered from sickness contracted in the Confederate prison.

The year 1876 brought him to the end of his career. John Greenleaf Whittier honors this brave youth in verse:

> *As Galahad pure, as Merlin sage,*
> *What worthier knight was found*
> *To grace in Arthur's golden age*
> *The fabled table round?*

The Fourth Battalion became the Thirteenth Massachusetts Infantry, and when Stonewall Jackson threw the entire North into panic the regiment was rushed down to the scene of war. During the draft riots of 1863, the garrison from Castle Island was hurried to Boston.

In the year 1879, Fort Independence was given up as an active commissioned defense, in order that the garrisons might be concentrated at Fort Warren, and Ordnance-Sergeant Maguire was left in charge of the island. A few years before the fort was decommissioned, his son Joseph was born at the Castle.

Joseph Maguire began at a very early age to show ability as an oarsman. He had plenty of practice rowing back and forth from the Castle to school. When he grew older he was so outstanding that John Wray took an interest in him, and under Wray's tutelage he rose to great heights. He won the championship of the United States in 1894 at Saratoga.

In 1891 a bridge was built from Marine Park to the island, the Castle thus becoming identified with the mainland and South Boston.

All Boston celebrated June 29, 1896, as Farragut Day. Thousands crowded the streets of South Boston, and hundreds of children walked out on the pier to Castle Island. Many of the boys and girls wore Farragut Day buttons, which read as follows: "South Boston Historical Society, Farragut Day, June 29, '96." This badge entitled the children to a free ride on the two little boats, the *Ella* and the *Pearl*, which ran from the island to the City Point Landing. Arrangements had been made with Captain Walker of Station 12 to have a squad of policemen at the island at three o'clock.

So many children had gathered at the float by two p.m. that the first boat trip was started at that time. This proved a fatal mistake, as the police had not reached the island. Officer Pickham of the Park squad was at the Castle, but was unable to handle so many children. At 2:30 the *Ella* left City Point Landing for the island, loaded with children. As it neared the Castle, the boys and girls at the landing started a rush for the float, and Officer Pickham was swept aside. The children ran down to the raft and crowded the runway. Suddenly the float turned turtle, with the runway collapsing, throwing the boys and girls into the water. Several heroic rescues were made. John Haley, a one-legged man, leaped into the water; Kate Ward joined in the rescue; Officer Pickham threw off his outer clothing and plunged in; Ordnance-Sergeant McGrath rushed to the scene. All but four children were saved through the combined efforts of these people. The dead were all boys.

When the Spanish War broke out in 1898, the United States took the fort away from the city, and made it into a mine and torpedo station.

On July 22, 1898, five hundred engineers and friends gathered at Castle Island to see two of the mines blown up. Colonel Mansfield had invited them to Fort Independence to witness the unusual sight. The mines were anchored one thousand feet from the easterly side of the island and were marked with red flags. The cable had been connected with the switch ashore, and all was in readiness. Sergeant Hart moved the switch, and a two hundred foot column of water shot into the air. A moment passed before the sound of the explosion reached the island. Everyone present came away from the exhibition firmly convinced that mines were something to be handled very carefully.

Just how delicate the mines were was demonstrated in a tragic manner not quite five months later. On December 6 of that year, the engineers were moving the mines to the south-eastern side of the island. Suddenly, without warning, a great explosion rocked the city. When the smoke and dust had cleared there was a gaping hole in the seawall. A minute or two before three men had been unloading a wagon on the spot. They were Engineer Hiram Vaughn; Peter Brennan, the driver of the wagon; and a civilian James Ryan. Not only were these three men blown to pieces, but Ordnance-Sergeant Maurice McGrath, three hundred feet away, was killed. Sergeant Hart, who had been standing behind the powder magazine, escaped injury. The explosion was probably due to one of the mines rolling against the seawall.

With the Spanish War now over, the island was turned back to the city, and once more the residents of Boston enjoyed their precious view from the ramparts of Fort Independence.

In 1899 Sergeant John Gorham took charge at the fort, and his young son, Arthur J. Gorham spent much of his time exploring there. Early one morning in the spring of 1900,

Arthur was walking around the eastern battery outside the fort itself when he noticed that the door near the powder magazine could be pushed open. As he had never been there before, he went inside and felt his way around in the darkness. There was a strong odor which he could not understand, so he lighted a match. He saw three planks, a small bottle of pills, a .22 calibre revolver, and the body of a dead man. The police were called, but no satisfactory explanation of the body has ever been discovered. It was deemed impossible for the man to have arranged bottle and pills in the manner found. Murder was suspected, but nothing further was ever done.

One day Arthur astonished his mother by paddling across the mainship channel on an ice cake, but he returned safely to the Castle Island shore. This was only one of his many exploits. Later he joined the army, serving for some time at Fort Warren, where he distinguished himself in track and football.

In the spring of 1911 Miss May Kinnear, a clairvoyant of Campello, dreamed of a treasure on a Boston Harbor island. In her dream, bearded, fiery-eyed men were burying gold by the light of a huge fire. Accompanied by her brother, George Kinnear, she spent some time touring the Harbor, and decided Castle Island was the isle of her dream. Mr. Kinnear purchased picks and shovels, and with the assistance of his friend, Fred Harrington, dug for many weeks. The location they chose was near the old life-preserver on the glacis. After many days of unsuccessful labor, they abandoned their work and left the island.

In 1911 the summer school was started at the island. The sick children from four schools in South Boston marched two by two over the long planked bridge leading to Castle Island, and attended classes inside the fort. The school was continued for several years.

The strandway to Castle Island was built in 1925, and in May 1932, an automobile roadway was opened to the public.

According to an old legend, there is a curse on all who dare to visit Castle Island. Regardless of its authenticity, it is interesting. Some time before the Revolution, as the story goes, an English gentleman lived on the island with his charming young daughter. She was in love with a young American boy. Her father, however, had other plans and determined that she should marry a British officer, also in love with the girl. The two suitors agreed to fight a duel for the young lady, and the American was killed. The girl, determined to join her lover, committed suicide. The British officer, heartbroken, rushed down to the dock and plunged into the channel, crying as he went that he would put a curse on all who ever came near the island. Some sailors still believe that the numerous shipwrecks near the Castle are to be blamed on this curse. There have been many other suicides on the island in the last few decades. In 1903 a man jumped from the wharf into the ocean, and his body was never recovered. About fifteen years ago a Somerville man was found in one of the casemates with a bullet in his head. In spite of the story's romantic appeal, there is very little historical foundation to the tale. It may have been spun by the old minstrel Rochford.

In the spring of 1933, a commanding monument fifty-two feet high was erected in front of the fortress to commemorate the life of Donald McKay, the famous East Boston ship builder. Standing proudly on the esplanade, this graceful shaft built of Maine granite greets the various ships coming up the Harbor. The profile of McKay is set in relief on the northeastern panel, and as the inscription states, his genius "produced ships of a beauty and speed before unknown which swept the seven seas." These graceful ships will never be replaced in the memory of the true sailors of America by the modern steel giants. Designed by Aldrich, the monument was given to the people of Boston without ceremony, as the committee in charge believed the ship builder would not have wished a dedication.

As I write these lines, I have just returned from a final visit to the Castle. By permission of William P. Long, the courteous head of the Park Department, I was allowed to roam at will around the old fortress. My thoughts, of course, were of the many outstanding characters of history and romance who had lived there: the Puritan Dudley; the financially incompetent Simpkins; the unfortunate Davenport; astute-minded Clap; Romer, the blasphemer; impatient Edmund Andros; Massie, the duellist; engineer Thayer; and gallant Bartlett. All had trod the ground where I was standing. As I walked around the island I pictured the scenes enacted there during the three centuries of activity which the fort has enjoyed.

So we leave the venerable island, trusting that for countless generations it will be cherished by the people of Boston. Castle Island should remain a treasured possession of all New Englanders.

GOVERNOR'S ISLAND

Governor's Island has had without question more unofficial visitors than any other Boston island in the past generation, as hundreds of boats from South Boston, Charlestown, East Boston, and Winthrop call here every year. As far as casual visitors are concerned, it is safe to say it is the best known island in all New England.

In scarcely five minutes as we make our way up the harbor, we are close to the green, hilly shores of the isle, and its beauty holds our attention. As we round the southern point, we notice the demilune battery on the shore, and drop anchor near the ruined granite wharf. Then we row ashore, land on the sandy beach, and walk up to the old well. We are now near the site of the home of John Winthrop, the first Puritan occupant of the island. Let us sit down on the old granite blocks and think back three centuries, when these 70 acres were known as Conant's Island.

Roger Conant owned the island while he was a resident of Nantasket. Although we have no actual record to prove that he lived on the island, it is reasonable to believe that he spent some of his life here.

The struggles of the Court of Massachusetts concerning

the leasing of the island to John Winthrop form a unique part of the records of Massachusetts Bay. Before Winthrop was awarded the property it had been appropriated for "publique benefits and uves" on July 5, 1631. A month later the ship *Friendship* ran aground here on its way to the Christopher Islands. In 1632 the island was "demised to John Winthrop, Esq., the psent Goun^r, for the terme of his life, for the ffine of fforty shillings." John Winthrop promised to plant a vineyard and an orchard here, and in return his heirs were to be allowed the island for 21 years, provided they paid one-fifth part of all fruits and profits to the Court.

Certain changes were made in the agreement between Winthrop and the Court on March 4, 1635, whereby the rent was made a "hogshead of the best wine that shall growe there, to be paid yearely, after the death of the said John Winthrop, and noething before." The vineyard did so poorly, however, that the Court decided to take no chances with the future, so on May 12, 1640, the rent was again changed, this time to two bushels of apples every year. As this was to be paid during his lifetime, John Winthrop made the first payment on the 7th of October, 1640. The Winthrop family probably continued this yearly payment until 1683, for at that time Adam Winthrop petitioned to be allowed to make a final cash settlement. The Court granted his request, allowing him to send "fiue pounds money forthuith, by the first opportunity, to our agents in England."

Ann Winthrop became heir to Governor's Island shortly after 1700. Although Sweetser tells us that in 1696 an eight-gun battery had been constructed on the southeastern point and a ten-gun battery erected on the southwestern point, no batteries were actually built there till much later. Ann Winthrop was notified in 1744 that the Government had decided to erect a battery at the eastern shore.

On October 19, 1744 a bill for this purpose was passed, and five days later five hundred pounds was appropriated for a block house and two batteries to be placed at Governor's Island. Three acres of the land were purchased for the fort.

The Revolutionary War came and went without disturbing the tranquil sleep of the island which Roger Conant once owned, and only one incident of note can be connected with the birth of our nation. On March 5, 1776, five of Lord Percy's transport ships were driven ashore at Governor's Island in a great gale which completely thwarted the British in their plans for overcoming the Americans at Dorchester Heights. After the evacuation of Boston, the island was too near the city to be used for cannonading the British fleet lying in Nantasket and President Roads.

But more eventful days were at hand. Ten years after the Treaty of Paris the Massachusetts Historical Society, at the invitation of James Winthrop, held a regularly scheduled meeting near the site of John Winthrop's house.

On the ninth of April 1808, the Government purchased from James Winthrop one acre of land at the southern point and three acres on the summit, together with a road 40 feet wide between the two for $15,000. The fort was named for Joseph Warren.

On May 23, 1808, the demilune battery was begun on the southern point by Lieutenant Sylvanus Thayer, who is known as the "Father of West Point." Thayer also erected the four-star fortress at the top of the hill and the dungeon keep which was built on the same spot prior to the Civil War. The genius of this young officer has never been fully appreciated by the residents of Massachusetts, and it is believed that the greatest engineer which the army has ever produced should have some recognition for his work. In addition to the battery, a brick guard house and a small powder magazine were built. The powder magazine still stands today, but all we can find of the guard house which once stood on the southern end are the crumbled walls. The shore battery has been completely ruined by the sea which has taken at least an acre of land from this point in the last hundred years.

Another demilune battery was erected on the shore half a mile nearer Boston, and this lunette stands practically as it was originally built except that the guns have been removed. The only damage to this demilune was from the great explosion which rocked Boston on September 7, 1902. These two demilune batteries were established on the beach so that they could give a raking fire to hostile warships coming up the harbor. Fortunately they were never called into action although they were occupied during the War of 1812 by a plucky band of Bostonians.

On the wall of the Bostonian Society office at the Old State House there is a view taken from Beacon Hill. This sketch shows the home of the Sea-Fencibles, a low one-story building erected over the water of what was formerly Back Bay. This organization, which included many prominent Bostonians, possibly caused the British to give up the idea of capturing Boston. The Sea-Fencibles arranged giant furnaces on the demilunes at Governor's Island for heating iron, shot, and tar to be thrown onto the British ships by mortars.

But the 1814 Treaty of Ghent ended our last war with England, and Governor's Island lapsed into the pastoral state it normally enjoyed. Even the announcement in 1833 that it would lose the name of Fort Warren to George's Island farther down the harbor did not seem to matter, especially when the new title would honor the first governor of Massachusetts, John Winthrop.

The relatively modern fortifications at Governor's Island were commenced shortly before the War between the States, Sylvanus Thayer again being the chief engineer in charge. The zig-zag stairway going down to the demilune battery was installed in 1852, and the dungeon keep was begun about the same time. The keystone of the arch placed over one of the short tunnels gives us the date when the works were finally completed—1872.

Sometime before 1892 the graves of the soldiers at Fort Warren were transferred to Governor's Island, and in that year the graves of the men at Castle Island were also brought to Fort Winthrop. The graveyard stood on the northern slope of the hill, possibly two hundred yards from the keep. Every grave was again moved in 1908, this time to Deer Island.

After an attempt at garrisoning the fort had been made during the Spanish-American War, the island returned to the caretaking status it usually enjoyed. Caretaker Shaw had come to Governor's Island from Castle Island in May 1901, bringing his wife and two sons with him. Nothing unusual took place until September 1902. On the seventh day of that month, a Sunday, there were several hundred people visiting the island. The other resident of the island had taken a trip to the mainland; Shaw was quite busy warning people away from the various stores of powder hidden in the earthern mounds.

Late that afternoon, three men landed from a fishing boat at the demilune battery located near the bottom of the zigzag stairway and matched coins to see which of them would stay to watch the boat. The three men were Albert Cotton of Somerville, and Joseph Wakefield and Christian Knudson of South Boston. Knudson lost the toss, stayed behind to watch the boat, and thereby saved his life. The other two men climbed the stairs leading up to the path which winds about the entire southern side of the upper level. Soon Knudson could see them near a powder magazine. Cotton sat down on top of the mound and started to smoke his pipe. Wakefield went around to the front of the magazine, and that was the last time he was ever seen. In a moment there was a terrific concussion and Boston felt its worst explosion. Knudson saw Cotton being blown through the air. The whole top of the island seemed to rise. Bricks, granite blocks weighing tons, earth, and stones were scattered all over

the island. Knudson was struck by a rock and knocked unconscious.

There had been 18,000 pounds of gunpowder stored in
regular hundred-pound barrels inside the powder magazine, and
in some way it had been ignited. Wakefield was blown to pieces,
only a part of his body ever being found. Cotton was found
many yards from the scene of the explosion, frightfully muti-
lated, and died without regaining consciousness. All over the
island various groups had miraculous escapes from the giant
stones which landed among them. The Saint Joseph's A. A. of
the West End had been picnicking when the blast went off, and
the debris landed all around them. When they discovered that
no one was seriously hurt, the entire group knelt in grateful
prayer on the slopes of the hillside.

The explosion did considerable damage on the island, and
even out in the harbor two boats were struck by rocks from the
blast. The old castle itself was struck by two granite slabs which
can still be seen at the base of the fortress. Four girls, who were
trapped in the short tunnel that stood at the head of the zig-zag
stairway, were horribly frightened when several huge granite
rocks came tumbling in beside them, but they were not hurt.

Sergeant Shaw's residence was down on the lower plain of
the island between the wharf and the 1808 shore battery. His
younger son, Hugh, who was playing the piano at the time of
the explosion, was thrown to the floor by the shock. The boy
rushed out of doors to see that the explosion had actually
pushed the tide away from the beach scores of feet, and that a
heavy black smoke hung over the entire island.

On the way to the scene of the explosion, Hugh found ter-
rorized groups huddled together in various parts of the fort,
wondering what the next moment would bring. The boy hurried
on and reached the scene of the blast. He saw Cotton's body and
started to help the others look for Wakefield. Another man was
found, apparently badly hurt, but after examination it was seen
he was only extremely intoxicated. Shaw told the writer in July

1935, that he could never understand why at least a dozen people were not killed by the blast with so many passing and repassing the powder magazine. He also spoke of the terrible feeling he had the next day when his father had him go into the adjacent powder magazine to count the barrels of gunpowder. Shaw was relieved when he completed his count and came out into the sunlight again.

Although it was believed by the investigators that either Wakefield or Cotton set off the explosion, it is only recently that a new version of the story has appeared. Twelve boys from East Boston had broken into the powder magazine to take three hundred-pound kegs of explosives. Breaking open the small barrels, they sprinkled a trail of powder along the path over to an empty magazine, where the boldest boy scratched a match and applied it to the trail. The method was quite similar to that employed by the British when they blew up Boston Light in 1776. According to this story, the boys, amazed to find that the powder blazed up, were panic stricken. Terrified by the thought of what they had done, they rushed to the back of the abandoned magazine. Meanwhile the blaze was eating its way along the trail, and in a moment the terrific concussion threw the boys against the walls. A few minutes later they dragged their way down to their boat, and soon left the scene of their crime.

The fort was soon afterwards practically abandoned. Thus closed the active part in the history of Governor's Island. Although Sergeant Shaw remained at the island some time longer, the task of keeping hundreds of people in order was too much for any one individual, and in March 1905 the Army removed the caretaker.

In 1912 work began on a long flight of broad granite stairs and a gravel walk leading up from the dock. The wide, granite stairs were completed, and then the entire plan was abandoned because of friction with the Government.

Between the time that the Government removed the ordnance-sergeant from Governor's Island and the year the new stairs were put in, two individuals had gained a somewhat dubious possession of the seventy acres of terrain. They were John Barnacle and Sala Brown, who were staying at the Island in a "quasi-hermitical" state. Although they lived separately at first, each occupying a deserted powder magazine on different sides of the island, they later decided on a merger and moved into an archway having two small powder storerooms. Barnacle and Brown lived on the clams from the flats and fish from the water with an occasional dinner of vegetables. Once a month one of them took the dory and rowed to East Boston with two bushels of clams which he exchanged for a bag of potatoes and other supplies. When in 1912 the Park Department began their active work on the island, these two men were forced to seek another location to carry on their peaceful pursuit of happiness.

The islands in winter are always astonishing revelations of Jack Frost at his best. We have visited many of the deserted islands just after a heavy snowstorm when the scenery itself was well worth a long journey from the fireside on a winter's day. Perhaps the most enjoyable trip we ever made was on February 1, 1935. At that time we walked across the ice from the East Boston Airport and up the slopes of Governor's Island. Two boys were skiing down the side of the island. Over by the southern powder magazines, we found a drift 18 feet high and 20 feet wide. At one place, right under the keystone of the arch which reads "1872", the passageway was almost buried from view.

Governor's Island also has its legends and ghost stories. The legends tells us that at one time a chain stretched across the harbor from Castle Island to Governor's Island. Several small boys have recently assured me that there is still in existence a tunnel which goes under the harbor from Governor's Island to Castle Island. Of course, there is no truth in either story. We must blame John Winthrop for one of the ghost stories. On the eighteenth of January, 1644, three men sailing into Boston saw weird lights arise out of the water between the city and Governor's Island. The lights shot out sparkles and flames and then took the form of a man. A weird voice was heard calling: "Boy, boy, come away, come away." Winthrop believed that it was the spirit of the sailor who had blown up Captain Chaddock's pinnace, as the sailor's body was never found.

Now that we have brought our history and romance up to date, we shall continue our journey around Governor's Island. Climbing the Park Department's wide granite stairway, we cross a path, flanked by massive green mounds, which leads in both directions around the island. Reaching the top of the granite stairway, we go through fields, underbrush, and shrubbery until we stand near the old dungeon keep itself. I always like to call it a "castle," as it was formerly entered by a drawbridge over a moat and surely is picturesque enough to be classed with the strongholds of ancient times.

We go down the granite stairs on each side of the two hundred foot tunnel, noticing the original entrance to the old castle high above the level of the dry moat. The only way we can get into the fort today is through the western side of the cellar, where two of the musketry loopholes have been widened. While squeezing our large frames through the broken musketry loopholes, we think of the Civil War days at Fort Warren when six men forced their way out of similar holes which had not been widened at all!

We are now in the dark cellar, and if you haven't brought your flashlight, you would be wise to go up the stairs to the upper level at once. Stalactites point down from the ceiling; a cool, damp atmosphere pervades the entire cellar. We who have lights will explore the various ghostlike chambers of the lower level, visiting one small room in particular. It is a dungeon hard to find and we must follow directions carefully to reach our goal. First we make sure that we are in the outside room of the northern side of the dungeon keep. Then, with our faces due south, we walk straight ahead out of the doorway and should soon find the entrance to the dungeon. Inside it is always pitch dark, so we must be cautious. The granite upright in the middle of the dungeon was the post around which prisoners were hand-cuffed, and after a few days spent here the most hardened criminal was probably willing to behave.

Continuing our explorations, we notice the great brick cistern where the water supply was kept. Let us go up the circular granite staircase, the pride of its builder, Sylvanus Thayer. Stopping at the courtyard on the first floor, we view with mingled feelings the ruin caused by the vandals of Boston. These lovers of destruction have done a thorough job of tearing down the inside of the building, but most of its charm can still be appreciated. Where officers and men formerly paraded we now see only pitiful piles of granite and brick, forever separated from their former grandeur and usefulness. Resuming our climb, we reach the second floor. In 1927 the thrill seeker could work his way around the entire story, balancing on beams and jumping from one window ledge to another. But now there is only a small part of the floor left, comprising the hallway and a small apartment facetiously designated "Mabel's Room," thereby dating the time of this christening as contemporary with the farce, *Up in Mabel's Room*. A dangerous opening in the floor of the hallway makes us careful as we step across to stand at the old entrance. As a boy was killed here in 1930, we shall be very cautious as we move about.

We now ascend the next flight and reach the top of the keep. Here we notice the 16 emplacements where formerly the great guns overlooked the harbor. A wall six feet wide surrounds the roof of the fortress where at one time the huge Parrott guns were sentinels. The roof was for many years covered by a wooden shelter built to shield the big guns. We jump up on the wall, keeping a respectful distance from its sloping edge and look out over the harbor. One of the prettiest views of the bay is from the top of this castle. Eighteen towns and cities can be seen from this vantage point, while over fifty localities can easily be identified with the aid of a telescope.

Ocean liners sweep majestically by on their way to Europe, small crafts run in and out among the neighboring islands, and sturdy tugs with their barges puff along down the bay. The drone of an airplane high above the castle is in striking contrast to the peaceful scenes on the island itself. Castle Island is directly across the harbor, its green banks sloping to the bay. There the white monument of granite to Donald McKay and his clipper ships stands out distinctly against the duller gray of Boston's oldest fortress. To the right we see the giant drydock where formerly the *Leviathan* was annually overhauled. The Custom House, the Federal Building, and the Shoe Machinery Building are prominent in Boston's skyline, while around in the northwest Bunker Hill monument adds its silhouette. Off to the east the Winthrop water tower and the Deer Island prison are outstanding land marks, and far in the distance Graves Light and Boston Light are seen. Around to the southeast Long Island Light and the buildings of the Long Island Hospital add their beauty, while the incinerator at Spectacle Island gives a somewhat dubious note to the vista. Thompson's Island, the home of the Farm and Trades School, completes the delightful view from the top of the old castle. But the sun is getting low in the west, and we must soon leave.

We begin our trip back to the beach by passing through the long tunnel, making a right turn, and walking by three of the empty powder magazines. The third magazine was the one in which young Hugh Shaw counted the powder barrels on September 8, 1902. We now reach the scene of the worst explosion in the history of Boston, and descend to the water battery on the beach. After walking along the shore until we are back at the ruined wharf, we get into our tender and row to the ship. And so we say goodby to Governor's Island, and steer our way out into the harbor.

During the summer of 1941 the island was joined to the mainland at East Boston, and is now being cut down to enlarge the airport. The writer was the last person to navigate a craft

through the waterway between Governor's Island and the mainland, the event taking place on the morning when the island
was joined to the shore.

APPLE ISLAND

The tree at Apple Island is exactly a mile from the castle
at Governor's, but our route by boat is much longer. We must
stay in the main channel, sailing about three miles before we
are able to anchor in "Apple Island Road," a point between the
Cottage Park Yacht Club and the island. Although the flats
around Apple Island make it a dangerous place at low tide,
proper observance of the buoys will prevent a disastrous ending
to our trip. The landing should be made on the Winthrop side,
near the site of William Marsh's wharf opposite old Chelsea
Point.

The first prominent owner of Apple Island was the Honorable Thomas Hutchinson, father of Governor Thomas Hutchinson, who wrote an admirable history of early Massachusetts.
In 1724 Hutchinson sold the island to Estes Hatch for the equivalent of $1000.

We shall now change the scene of our story to Germantown, Quincy. William Marsh and his family came to live in
Germantown about the year 1812. He was a quiet Englishman,
called by many a "remittance man," as he received money from
home at regular intervals. Something turned the inhabitants
against Mr. Marsh and his family, so that he was requested to
leave town. Marsh had always loved the water, and during his
sojourn at Germantown had grown to admire our beautiful harbor. When his neighbors asked him to leave, he bought a ten-
ton sail boat and left Germantown with all his worldly posses-
sions aboard.

Marsh purchased the boat about the first of May, 1814, and
cruised all about the harbor, stopping at Hog Island until John
Breed requested him to leave. Among other places which he
visited was Apple Island. When the chilling blasts of the No-

vember winds made him think of a home for the winter, he remembered the snug colonial mansion located on top of this
island, so he landed and took possession of the uninhabited
house. By the time spring came he was firmly established, and
since he was contented in his new home, he tried to buy the
island. It was not until many years had passed that this could be
accomplished. Marsh agreed to pay $550 for the island, and on
January 15, 1830, the final papers were passed.

Marsh visited Boston once a year, appearing on State Street
to discuss the various events of the period. Quite often he was
seen at Point Shirley, where he purchased most of his needed
provisions. But wherever he went, his manner and bearing were
mysterious, and to his death he was looked upon as a very odd
character. He died on the island on November 22, 1833, and
was buried on the western slope near his old home. His mansion was destroyed by fire on November 11, 1835.

Oliver Wendell Holmes was inspired to write his *Island
Ruin* about William Marsh of Apple Island. I quote a few lines
from the poem:

> *They told strange things of that mysterious man;*
> *Believe who will, deny them such as can;*
> *His birthplace England, as his speech might show*
> *Or his hale cheek, that wore the red streak's glow*
> *He lived at ease beneath his elm-trees' shade*
> *Did naught for gain, yet all his debts were paid;*
> *They said his house was framed with curious cares,*
> *Lest some old friend might enter unawares;*
> *That on the platform of his chamber's door*
> *Hinged a loose square that opened through the floor;*
> *Touch the black silken tassel next the bell,*
> *Down with a crash, the flapping trapdoor fell;*
> *Three stories deep the falling wretch would strike,*
> *To writhe at leisure on a boarder's pike.*
> *Why tell each idle guess, each whisper vain?*

Enough; the scorched and cindered beams remain.
He came, a silent pilgrim to the West,
Some old-world mystery throbbing in his breast;
Close to the thronging mart he lived alone;
He lived; he died. The rest is all unknown.

Apple Island was sold to the city of Boston by Edward T. Marliave on May 21, 1867, for $3,750. Many ships have been burned on the shores of the island, including the *Ontario*, the *Baltic*, the *James Adger*, the *Coyote*, and the *Hen and Chickens Lightship*. The remains of three vessels are still on the Apple Island Flats, but they have rotted away to such an extent that they are not dangerous to the boats sailing over them at high tide.

When the Portuguese settlers were forced to leave Long Island, they scattered all over the harbor, two or three families choosing Apple Island on which to establish their homes. Joseph King, one of the Portuguese who moved there, was soon made the official representative at the island of the Board of Street Commissioners of Boston, under whose jurisdiction the property remained. Unfortunately for King, the belligerent element of the city soon found that Apple Island was an ideal place to engage in fistic combats, and the neighboring town of Winthrop protested against the uproar which could be heard there every Sunday. The city of Boston sent Patrolmen Emil S. Liemann and T. T. McCarthy down to the island on August 25, 1901, to maintain order, and soon the residents of nearby localities were allowed to spend their Sundays in peace.

When we walked across the ice to Apple Island on February 1, 1935, the cliff on the eastern side was breaking away in huge slabs and slipping into the sea. It was a most impressive sight, with the great pieces of earth, 30 inches thick and sometimes 15 feet square, lying diagonally against the cliff. Unless a seawall is erected, the island will gradually wash away and in 50 or 60 years will be reduced to six or seven acres.

The Apple Island legend is a tragic one. Some ten years before Marsh landed there for the first time, it is said that a beautiful young girl, a descendant of one of the royal governors, was missed from home, and a few weeks later her lifeless body was recovered from the waters off Apple Island. Since a band of robbers was living on the island at that time, the young girl's sweetheart at once suspected that the men were the cause of his lady's death. Nothing was heard from him for weeks, until a friend finally disclosed that he had gone to the island and joined the robber band in order to find out the details of the girl's death.

One day a fisherman was sailing by the island, and as was usually the case, looked at the tall elm at the top of the island to get his bearings. From the lower limb of the elm there hung a body! On reaching Boston he notified the authorities who dispatched armed men to the spot. When the body was cut down, it was found to be that of the young man who had tried to avenge his sweetheart's death. There was not a robber left on the island, and they never again returned to the scene of their double crime. The ghosts of the two were said to be still walking up and down the shores and around the great elm in 1900, but not for years have they been either seen or heard. The elm, landmark for over a century in Boston Bay, was cut down in 1938 by hoodlums.

SNAKE ISLAND

Between Apple Island and the Winthrop shore lies an island of 3.36 acres called Snake Island, the goal of scores of children as well as older folk from Winthrop. Here they play pirates or dig in the sand, spending many happy hours in the peaceful locality. Snake Island was so named because its shape resembled a coiled serpent.

In the early days of the Revolutionary War, Snake Island was mentioned in a resolve of the Committee of Safety for May 14, 1775, as follows: "*Resolved*, as the opinion of this Committee, that all the live-stock be taken from Noddle's Island, Hog Island, Snake Island, and from that part of Chelsea near the sea-coast." James Lloyd Homer speaks of an unsuccessful treasure hunt at Snake Island around 1830. Perhaps the treasure still awaits some romantic person who is willing to dig up the entire island to find the buried gold which has so far eluded all searchers. Two seekers recently dug here unsuccessfully.

The Treworgy brothers from Winthrop lived on Snake Island in 1900 in the cabin of the deserted steamer *United States*. They tended about 150 lobster traps around the harbor. Although they did not stay on the property the year round, they came to the island about the first of March and left around the middle of November. One of the brothers was drowned from his boat off the island a few years later, and the other brother finally gave up the lobster business and left the island.

The island had passed into the possession of the Tewksburys and the Belchers and was sold for tax claims to Captain Samuel G. Irwin for $12. O. E. Lewis had purchased the land late in the nineteenth century from Captain Irwin. The shack on the south side of the island was the home of James Adams. The cabin occupied by Horton D. Fullerton was next in line, while the residence of Bill Carey, whose Portuguese name did not at all resemble his new American one, came next. The latter's hut boasted the only flagstaff on the island, from which the Stars and Stripes floated on the breeze Sundays and holidays. Next door was John Green, over whose door the sign "Welcome to Guests" somewhat surprised the casual visitor. Judson G. Fullerton lived nearest Winthrop's shore in a small shack. Another man by the name of Hunt made his home there at this time. Each man was in the lobster-trapping and clam-digging business.

The Winthrop Board of Health finally decreed against the occupation of Snake Island, and gradually the inhabitants moved away to less deserted shores. It has been many years since a house has stood on Snake Island, and probably many more will pass before some venturesome person again dares to locate there.

NODDLE'S AND SUSANNA ISLANDS

In January 1629, John Gorges conveyed to Sir William Brereton, among other parcels of land, two islands which are today known as East Boston and Orient Heights. They were then called Brereton's Island for William Brereton, and Susanna Island for his daughter.

Brereton's rights were denied him in February 1629, and William Noddle comes into this account of East Boston three hundred years ago.

We will never know exactly when Noddle came to the island which was to bear his name, but he was probably living there when it was owned by Brereton. Noddle, who is among the list of freemen included in the 1631 Colony Records, was drowned in the ocean the following summer while carrying wood in his canoe. This original "Noddle-Islander" probably died without children, for we can find no further mention of the name Noddle in the early history of the settlement.

Noddle's Island was included in 1631 with the islands appropriated for public uses, but the sole privilege of catching the waterfowl and pigeons there was given to Jobe Perkins. The island at this time, with its hundreds of birds, was surely a "happy hunting ground" for the alert Perkins. Samuel Maverick, who was living in the vicinity when the Puritans came into Boston Harbor, was quick to realize this fact, and saw to it that he was given the permit for 1633. Maverick was allowed by the Puritans to stay on Noddle's Island provided he made an annual payment of "either a fat wether, a fat hog, or 40s in money." The great John Winthrop visited Maverick at his humble home in June 1630. Prince's well-known chronology of that year tells us that "on this island, with the help of Mr. David Thompson [of Thompson's Island], he had built a small fort with four great guns to protect him from the Indians." Maverick also owned land in Maine, according to the York Records.

John Josselyn, he who "voyaged to New England," arrived at Boston on July 3, 1638. Going ashore on Noddle's Island, he found that Samuel Maverick was the "only hospitable man in all the country." Josselyn's story of his interview with Maverick's servant girl is perhaps a little questionable for discussion here, even in this supposedly modern age, but the details are mentioned in his account of the visit. The same afternoon Josselyn went for a walk in the woods. He came upon what he believed to be a large pineapple plated with scales, and took hold of the object." "No sooner had I touched it," he tells us, "but hundreds of Wasps were about me." Stung repeatedly, his face was so swollen by the time he returned to the house that Maverick could only recognize him by his clothes.

Maverick rose to prominence in spite of opposition on all sides, and in the closing years of his life even the King honored him. The manner of his death has always remained a mystery, but we do know that Samuel Maverick wrote a letter on October 15, 1669, which is still in existence. That letter is the last known trace of the man whom Captain Edward Johnson of Woburn calls a man of "very loving and courteous behavior."

Sir Thomas Temple bought most of Noddle's Island August 4, 1664, and three years later became sole owner. The new proprietor of Noddle's Island had come to New England in 1657 and later gave Harvard College £100. While on a visit to England, he interviewed the King, talking with Charles about coining money. Temple told his majesty that he thought it no crime for the New Englanders to make money for their own use, and taking a pine tree piece from his pocket, presented it to the sovereign. Looking the coin over very carefully Charles noticed the pine tree, and asked Temple what it represented. Temple, alert, replied that it was the royal oak in Boscobel Wood which had protected Charles' life after his defeat.

On June 24, 1711, Boston saw a great flotilla sail into the

harbor. Its sixty-one ships constituted a larger fleet than Nelson
had at the Battle of the Nile. Leaving their sick at George's
Island, the officers sent the men to Noddle's Island. Scores of
tents were soon scattered about the former residence of Samuel
Maverick, and headquarters were established near the present
location of Belmont Square. Ever since, the slope on which they
camped has been known as Camp Hill. Two great reviews were
staged by these picked regiments of Marlborough's finest, and
Sumner has given us a vivid picture:

"On the gentle slopes of the hill, and on the broad
green fields, thousands of the best disciplined troops of
which the world can boast, with gay uniforms and glistening bayonets are performing their evolutions to the sound
of martial music which rises, swells, and dies away on the
passing breeze. . . . Far down the beautiful bay is seen the
mighty fleet quietly riding at anchor among the islands in
Nantasket Road. . . . Never before had there been such a
splendid display upon our shores as the island that day
exhibited; and since that time it has seldom exceeded, if
indeed, it has ever been equalled."

The expedition to Canada ended in disaster, many of the
ships being wrecked in a gale on the Saint Lawrence River. As
soon as the last white sail had disappeared beyond the horizon,
the inhabitants of Boston resumed their everyday pursuits.
Christopher Caprill, a tenant at the island, complained to the
Province that the soldiers had stolen his vegetables and apples
and had trampled down his hay, but the Province claimed the
damages were the direct concern of the English Government and
had nothing to do with the Massachusetts Colony. Caprill never
collected.

Henry Howell Williams, in 1765, purchased the stock and
farming outfit on Noddle's Island where he probably had been
living as a tenant since 1762.

The second battle of the Revolution was fought near Noddle's Island, May 27, 1775. General Stark and 300 men went

there to clear out the live stock. They engaged the British marines but fled from the regulars coming from Boston. Although General Gage sent a schooner of sixteen guns and eleven barges of marines up Chelsea Creek in hopes of cutting off the raiders, Putnam came to the colonists' rescue. The battle lasted all through the night, and when the British finally deserted their schooner, the Americans set fire to it.

During the time of the Boston siege, many of the younger ladies crossed over to Noddle's Island and lived in the Williams mansion. William Tudor made many trips across to visit his lady love. He would walk to Chelsea, where he undressed and tied his clothes on his head. After swimming over to what is now East Boston, he would hurriedly dress and then call on the young lady. The couple were later happily married.

After the British left Boston, the sight of the English ships lingering in the harbor made the Bostonians desire adequate protection, and Noddle's Island was fortified, all the citizens aiding in the project.

The account of the launching of the *Constitution* in 1797, is an extract from the Williams family diary.

"Saturday, 21st October, Wind east and rather cold. Papa and the boys went to Boston. At twelve o'clock we all paraded up the hill to see the ship-launch, as she was to make tryall for the third time. . . . At half-past twelve she went, and I think that every one that saw her must be gratified, as it was impossible for anything to go better, or look prettier."

During the War of 1812, New England's opposition to the administration was determined and open. Since Governor Caleb Strong would not cooperate in any way with the national Government, the United States retaliated by removing most of the men from the forts around Boston. The British fleet was anchored in Castine Bay and seemed to have the whole of the northern Atlantic Coast under control. Boston awoke with a start and determined to protect herself, being too proud to ask

the Government for aid. Afraid of a repetition of the blockade
of 1776, the Bostonians met on August 30, 1814, and settled
upon Noddle's Island as the logical place to build a fort to defend the city. Camp Hill on Noddle's Island was the ideal location, having a covered way to the water battery. Loammi Baldwin was chosen engineer.

On the twenty-fourth of September, 1814, it was announced
that the work was nearing completion. Volunteers totalled five
hundred on October 2, and the *Gazette* of October 3 tells us that
a few days more of work "by the same number of men, will
complete the fortifications." The "Fusiliers," the "Rangers" and
the "Boston Light-Infantry" all served here in October 1814.

The English actually landed on the outer islands during
the War of 1812, but did not venture to come into the harbor
itself. The new fortification was officially named Fort Strong on
October 26, 1814, but with the subsequent declaration of peace
on February 17, 1815, it fell into disuse and was dismantled and
abandoned. The only reminder of the fort today is the old
well, still under the sidewalk, about 75 feet from the northeast
corner of Belmont Square.

The duel of Noddle's Island occurred four years later. In
1815 Lieutenant Francis B. White and Lieutenant William
Finch were serving on the *Independence*, and Finch so insulted
White that White never forgot it. When the two met at the
Charlestown Navy Yard in September 1819, White immediately
sent his second, a Mr. Godfrey, to Finch with a challenge. Finch
accepted, and the time and place of meeting was agreed upon—
Saturday, September 25, at Noddle's Island, between two great
elms near what are now Meridian and Border Streets. White re-
ceived a mortal wound, and his body was buried from the Navy
Yard the following day. He had been the only surviving son of
Major Moses White of Rutland, Massachusetts.

Donald McKay's famous clipper ships were of course built
at the East Boston ship yards. The *Flying Cloud's* great 89-day
record to San Francisco still stands. *The Sovereign of the Seas*

also made a wonderful run of 411 miles in 24 hours.

Susanna Island, joined quite firmly not only to Noodle's Island but to the mainland as well, is known at the present time as Orient Heights. On the first of April, 1634, the Orient Heights of the future was granted to Boston "for euer for the yearly rent of iij£ [3 pounds] but the rent was reduced to iiij *s* [four shillings] before a year had elapsed."

Probably the best known of all the owners of Hog or Susanna Island was Samuel Sewall. Sewall took possession of Hog Island May 2, 1687, performing an elaborate ceremony with two columns of witnesses watching the proceedings. Sewell tells us his friends "watched my taking Livery and seised of the Iland by Turf and Twigg and the House." On July first he returned to Hog Island and made plans for building a pier or "Causey to land handsomly." At this time there were some fine cherry trees growing at Orient Heights, for Sewall brought home a basket filled with the fruit. The fourteenth of October Sewall landed the lumber for a pier and began work the middle of the next month. A few days later he spent his first night on the island when he and his cousin Savage worked so hard that nightfall caught them before they could leave. The following spring Sewall laid out many scores of trees, mostly of the chestnut variety.

On April 2, 1698, he went to Susanna Island by a method common for Boston Harbor—John White took him there in a birch canoe. He had come for serious business, however, as the tenant's horse and many of the sheep had died the previous week. While on the island, canoeist White killed an eagle on the wing and also brought down a sheldrake.

Governor Joseph Dudley was the guest of Samuel Sewall at Hog Island on October 13, 1702. An illustrious company was gathered there for this festive occasion, including Captain Cyprian Southack, Colonel Townsend, Mr. Thomas Richards, Colonel Povey, and Jeremiah Dummer.

Sewall's trips to Hog Island grew less frequent, and he

last mentions going there in 1717, at which time the tenant told him he had not been seen for five years. The pier had fallen down, and other repairs were necessary. Some time after Sewall's death in 1729, the island passed from Oliver Wendell to Jonathan Jackson.

It is interesting to note that there was not a person living at Hog Island when the census survey of 1798 was made. The island was listed as Belle Isle, as Russell preferred that name to any other. The name is still perpetuated in Belle Isle Inlet, located between Hog Island and the mainland. This inlet was for many years known as "Crooked Lane."

Around 1813 Russell sold the island to John Breed, an Englishman of means who had come to America to forget his grief over the loss of his bride. In 1814 Breed was visited by William Marsh.

Breed built a wonderful stone mansion on the southern slopes of Hog Island Hill. It was two hundred feet long and one story in height; its beautiful garden was a pleasure to behold. John Breed was granted permission in 1816 to construct a bridge with a suitable draw across to Chelsea; this bridge was completed the following year. Until 1838, when the Eastern Railroad built the tracks across the island, this bridge was the only connection with the mainland, and Breed lived here in a kindom of his own. Soon afterwards a causeway road was constructed from Noddle's to Breed's Island, with a bridge built to Winthrop in 1839, making three connections with the mainland. In his history of Charlestown, Timothy Sawyer tells us of the treasure hoard kept by Breed in a cave on the hill, which was guarded by an Indian named Gossum. Breed died suddenly in 1846, and when his relatives visited the island they found $5,000 in silver stored in the cave. Two great horse pistols, which, according to legend, never left his side, were found near his body. His will gave most of the property to his brother Richard, then living in England.

The island was sold in 1872, and the railroad was put

through to Lynn and Revere three years later. In 1877 the branch line to Winthrop was opened, and Breed's Island became known as Winthrop Junction. With the turn of the century Orient Heights came into its own and today there are many thousand people living in the section. It is indeed a prosperous community, with its library and churches.

Some years ago, in excavating for the radial highway which passes over Breed's Hill, the shovel brought up John Breed's old pump log. Sections of the long timber have been preserved in the Orient Heights Library and the Deane Winthrop House for the sight of future generations.

And so we leave the two islands which together have a present population of 70,000. Greatly changed from the days when the two Samuels, Maverick and Sewall, walked their shores, they now play a prominent part in the development of Boston.

DEER ISLAND AND LONG ISLAND

There are two islands in our harbor which have become small towns in themselves. Deer Island and Long Island, with a combined area of four hundred acres, have a population of three thousand. This population is made up mostly of people under care of the city of Boston, the county prison being located on Deer Island and the almshouse and hospital on Long Island. Deer Island is no longer an island, a road being connected to the mainland. Long Island, located across President Road from Deer Island, is more isolated.

DEER ISLAND

We shall now visit Deer Island, boarding the *Michael J. Perkins* at Sargent's Wharf, Eastern Avenue, Boston.

Deer Island is over a mile in length and contains 183 acres. It is divided, as was Gaul, into three parts, the United States Government, the state of Massachusetts, and the city of Boston each owning a share. According to the latest survey, the national Government owns one hundred acres, while the city of Boston owns the larger part of the remainder. The United States Army's Fort Dawes is here, while the Navy has a radio compass station at Deer Island. The House of Correction for Suffolk County is situated near Shirley Gut, and the Pumping Station for the Commonwealth of Massachusetts, North Metropolitan Sewerage District, is on the western side of the island.

Three hundred years ago Deer Island was overrun by the animals from which it gets its name. William Wood, writing in 1634, tells us that the "Iland is so called, because of the Deare which often swimme thither from the Maine, when they are chased by the Woolves: Some have killed sixteen Deare in a day upon this Iland."

In 1655 James Bill, a resident of Pullen Point, was barred from cutting wood at Deer Island since the authorities believed there was only enough to supply a farm. A little later John Shaw leased Deer Island, renting it in 1663 to Sir Thomas Temple who was reputed to be a direct descendant of Lady Godiva.

When the King Philip War broke out in 1675, hundreds of friendly Indians were forced to move to Deer Island. A few months later, old Ahatton and other Indians petitioned for the right to visit other islands to get clams and fish, as the redskins were starving to death. Many did perish from hunger before a boat was provided for the unfortunate men. On the 19th of April, 1676, Jonathan Fairbanks asked possession of a certain little Indian girl who at that time was a member of a tribe on the island, but it is not known if his request was granted. Later in the war the colonists changed their attitude; Deer Island Indians were pressed into duty against the victorious tribes, and helped turn the tide for the Puritans.

After thus aiding the New Englanders, these Indians brought forward some of their old claims, and Charles Josias, alias Wampatuck, grandson of the great Chicatawbut, demanded the island. His claims were settled by compromise, and a group of prominent Bostonians including Capt. Shrimpton and Simon Lynde paid him 19 pounds for his rights.

During 1688 Governor Sir Edmund Andros was trying to collect a tax from all landowners. When Shrimpton failed to pay him, Andros sent his High Sheriff, James Shurlock, down to Deer Island. Shurlock took John Pittom, the tenant, with his family, and turned them adrift in a small boat, leaving two men on the property to see that Pittom did not come back.

During the Revolution Major Greaton of the Continental Army landed at Deer Island and removed several hundred sheep and a number of horses from under the eyes of the British fleet anchored less than a mile away. Another incident of more tragic import was the Battle of Shirley Gut on May 19, 1776.

The celebrated lifesaver, William Tewksbury, moved to Deer Island shortly after the Revolution, making his first rescue in 1799. In December of that year he saved an English sailor who had fallen from a vessel anchored in the harbor.

On May 26, 1817, Tewksbury made his most outstanding rescue, one which made him known from Boston to Baltimore. At four o'clock the afternoon of that day, he and his son Abijah were collecting ballast near the present site of the Winthrop water tower when a boy from Point Shirley came running up the beach to tell them that a pleasure boat had upset somewhere between Deer and Long Islands. Tewksbury and his son rushed to their canoe, hoisted sail, and soon reached Shirley Gut. As Tewksbury could not see the wrecked boat, he stood for Long Island until he saw his wife and children running along the beach in the direction of Money Bluff. He then changed his course to run parallel to theirs.

The canoe was a small lap-streak model, a heavy sea was running, and Tewksbury's wife and children were watching him from the shore. He realized that his own chances of reaching safety were small, but he took in his sail and managed to get seven of the eight survivors into the frail canoe. The eighth man was anxiously awaiting his turn when Abijah called to him, "Father, the canoe is sinking, we shall all perish." Tewksbury had not noticed the water steadily creeping up the sides of the boat; by the time the seventh man was aboard the water was within three inches of the gunwales. Therefore he had to start for Deer Island without the last man, who was holding onto the jolly boat tied to the sunken pleasure craft. The canoe with its nine occupants safely made shore, but when Tewksbury returned for the lone mariner, he had vanished. Evidently the tide had risen just enough to submerge the jolly boat so that it was of no use to the unfortunate sailor. Three others had perished before Tewksbury arrived. The Reverend Mr. Brown describes the final scene in this unusual rescue:

> *The suff'rers they at length receiv'd,*
> *Then hasten'd to the shore;*
> *In hopes that those might be reliev'd,*
> *Who seem'd to breathe no more.*

> *And ere the sun had sunk below*
> *The surface of the main,*
> *They felt their grateful bosoms glow*
> *With life and health again.*

For his heroism Tewksbury was rewarded with a gold medal from the Massachusetts Humane Society. Up to 1825 the Tewksbury family had saved 31 lives, and had received numerous medals.

In the 1830's there was a peculiar tragedy at old Pullen Point when a baker, apparently in the last stages of alcoholic insanity, drove down to the Point in his buggy and shouted that he was going to cross the Gut at high tide. Whipping up his horse, he drove into the swirling current where horse and man quickly drowned. It was remarked at the time that the loss of the man was not serious, but it was to be regretted that he had taken along a dumb animal in his folly.

DEER ISLAND ALMOST A CENTURY AGO
SHIRLEY GUT AND POINT SHIRLEY IN BACKGROUND

MEN LOADING BALLAST AT LONG ISLAND
EUTAW HOUSE IN BACKGROUND

SCENE ON THE ICE, BOSTON HARBOR

CITIZENS HAULING THE FERRY-BOAT

DESCRIBED ON PAGE 31

The signal station at Deer Island was attended in the year 1819 by Frederick William Augustus Steuben Brown, wandering poet of Boston Harbor. His summer there must indeed have been a fascinating one, and his visits doubtless occupied most of his spare time, for his poetry has the factual background which could have been acquired only after careful research. He is reputed to have been one of the founders of the Methodist Church in Winthrop, and was often seen in the company of Sturgis the salt manufacturer.

His poem on Deer Island is quoted in part:

> *Here superstition often tells,*
> *Of a ghost, that's heard to screech,*
> *And utter dismal piercing yells,*
> *At midnight on the beach.*

> *For oft I've heard the story told,*
> *How a ghost without a head;*
> *Here guards some thousand pounds in gold,*
> *By some strange fancy led.*

James Lloyd Homer visited Deer Island in 1845, spending many happy hours bowling on the green and swinging young ladies in the picturesque swing by the trees. He tells of a curious treasure hunt that turned out to be unsuccessful. Captain Tewksbury, Mr. Brown, and Captain Crooker went down to Money Bluff where they dug silently for several hours, but did not find even one coin. Captain Crooker blamed the failure of the expedition on some of the party who talked after promising to keep silent. It had broken the spell!

When the terrible ship fever raged among the Irish immigrants in 1847, Dr. Moriarty was placed in charge of the temporary quarantine established at Deer Island. Hundreds of immigrants stricken with the fever died there and were buried in nameless graves. The Quarantine Station at Deer Island was made permanent in 1849. In the same year plans for a new almshouse were drawn, and this building, completed in 1852, is in use at the present time as part of the prison.

Paupers of the city and commonwealth were soon removed to the new building at Deer Island, and on January 25, 1854, it became the House of Industry. Before the year elapsed, the Massachusetts poor were sent to Rainsford's Island, and on July 1, 1858, the inmates of the House of Reformation together with those of the almshouse school connected with it were sent to Deer Island. In 1869 a farmhouse was built and a house for pauper girls was also constructed.

The bar which runs out from Deer Island was the scene of a shipwreck in 1886. At daybreak on January 9, the schooner *Juliet* crashed against Fawn Bar. Heavily coated with ice, she rolled over on her beam ends, with the men trying desperately to hang on. Three of the crew, Hollis Munson, Philip Truesworthy, and Winnie Milliken, having lashed themselves to the mast, were forced to watch the other three gradually lose their holds and be swept off the ship. The breakers, 20 and 30 feet high, rushed over the vessel, engulfing everything for four or five seconds at a time. The first to be lost was Charles Truesworthy, the mate; the next to die was one of the crew, James Dunn; and the last to lose his life was Captain Leach. At nine a.m. the sea had gone down enough to permit the tug *Samuel Little* to come to the aid of the survivors. Four inmates of the prison assisted in the rescue of these men.

The Suffolk County House of Correction was moved to Deer Island in 1896, while Master James R. Gerrish was in charge. The previous year the reformation department had been transferred to Rainsford's Island. The Hill Prison and the power plant were built while Gerrish was master at the island. Gerrish is said to have advised against the location, believing it too near the water. When Gerrish resigned in 1907, James H. Cronin became master. In 1910 a new seawall was built near the Hill Prison, but three years later it was badly in need of repairs. In November 1920, a storm destroyed 450 feet of the wall, and Commissioner Johnson secured an old barge which he floated up on the beach for protection. Emergency repairs were made in 1925, and a permanent wall was later constructed.

Major George F. A. Mulcahy, a Dartmouth graduate and World War veteran, was appointed master of the Deer Island House of Correction on September 16, 1926. He is now on leave of absence in the service of his country, with Deputy Andrew McCarthy in charge at the prison.

A prison break was attempted on August 14, 1933, when four prisoners drove across the Gut at low tide, using one of the island trucks. Making the wrong turn at Point Shirley, they abandoned the car and hid. The writer happened to be at the Point, and his car and services were commandeered by four guards, two of whom rode on each running board with riot guns in their hands. All the prisoners were finally captured and returned to prison.

Shirley Gut started filling up years ago. The *Constitution* sailed through this narrow passageway in 1812. As late as 1916 the Gut was navigable by the Nahant boats, but around 1920 the depth at high tide was only six feet. Ten years later it was only half that depth, and by the summer of 1935 only a few inches of water were to be seen except at the highest tides. Automobiles cross at any time of day. Thus for the first time in history Deer Island is connected with the mainland.

FORT DAWES

Fort Dawes, named for William Dawes of Revolutionary War fame, was commissioned January 10, 1941. Located at the end of Deer Island, it was built around the area formerly known as Resthaven Cemetery. An interesting event took place late one stormy evening at the fort when two officers, each in separate quarters, heard a woman's scream coming from the beach. Rushing to the shore, they met each other, but after searching for a considerable time, gave up their efforts. The headless ghost mentioned in the poem was blamed for the disturbance.

DEER ISLAND LIGHT

We shall now visit Deer Island Light, located five hundred yards from Deer Island, and a thousand yards from Long Island. This lighthouse has had its share of romance and tragedy. Keeper Wesley Pingree spent his honeymoon here with his bride, the former Josephine Horte, in 1895.

One winter Sunday in 1916 Keeper Joseph McCabe had left the light to help his fiancee at Deer Island address their wedding invitations. In the afternoon the temperature dropped, and a howling northwester sprang up; when McCabe reached the shore at the island he found his boat frozen to the beach. As it was low tide, he borrowed rubber boots and started to walk along the bar to the light. Jumping to a large rock while approaching his goal, he slipped and fell into the ocean. Watchers on the shore quickly launched a dory, but they reached the spot too late. His body was never found.

Judson B. Small became the assistant keeper of Deer Island Light in 1923 and has continued in that capacity ever since. Merrill B. King was keeper when Small started his service, and during the gale of December 27, 1930, was at the light alone. At four p.m. that day breakers 40 feet high were sweeping right across the area between Deer and Long Islands; every time a sea hit the lighthouse the whole structure would shake. King had previously calked cotton in all the cracks through which water might seep. Being alone in such a storm was a fearful experience, but when morning came the blow was over and the sea subsided by noon of the next day.

Judson Small's brother Tom had been keeper at Bug Light until the fire of 1929, when he was transferred to Duxbury Pier in Plymouth Harbor. Merrill King left Deer Island Light in June 1931, being succeeded by Tom Small.

The last civilian keeper at Deer Island Light was Fred Bohm, who transferred across the harbor from Spectacle Island Range Lights. Now retired, he has a fine record to look back on.

LONG ISLAND

Leaving Deer Island Light, we cross over to Long Island, the longest of all the islands in Boston Harbor, although it does not have as much shore line as Peddock's.

Let us delve a little into the Suffolk Deeds of this period. Joseph and Elizabeth Rock owned at least 40 acres of Long Island in 1669 and mortgaged this land in 1671 for 200 pounds.

Other property owners at Long Island were James Woodward and Thomas Stansbury. Stansbury, a shopkeeper of Boston, held his property longer than any of the other tenants, whose land was gradually bought up by John Nelson, relative of Sir Thomas Temple. Nelson's daughter married Robert Temple of Noddle's Island, and their granddaughter was the mother of Robert C. Winthrop.

On April 18, 1689, Nelson headed a band of colonists at Fort Hill and ordered Sir Edmund Andros to surrender himself and the fort. This revolution led to the imprisonment of Andros at Castle Island. When William was firmly established on the English throne, the colonists who had participated in this first outburst against authority probably breathed more easily. What would have happened to them had James II returned to power is another story.

John Nelson became so prominent an owner that by 1720, 31 years after the storming of Fort Hill, Long Island was still known as Nelson's Island. In the meantime, Nelson had started on a voyage in 1692, was captured at sea by the French, and imprisoned at Quebec. While in prison in this northern settlement, he discovered that the French were plotting against the New England people, so he secretly dispatched a messenger to Boston to warn the colonists. When the French learned of Nelson's trick they sent him to France where he was locked up in the Bastile. Only after years of effort by Sir Purbeck Temple was he released. When he finally returned to Long Island, he was given a wonderful banquet to celebrate his arrival. He had been away ten years, and the celebration was so important that fragments of the table cloth used at the feast were still preserved in 1880!

In 1819 Long Island Lighthouse was built. The tower, erected on the highest part of Long Island Head, was 22 feet high and could be seen for 15 miles. It has been moved twice since its erection in 1819.

When James Lloyd Homer visited Long Island Light in 1845, he found Captain Charles Beck, already with many years of service, in charge of the lighthouse there. Beck explained to him that when a pilot boat in the harbor had run out of pilots, the captain hoisted a blue and white ball as a signal, whereupon Captain Beck raised a black ball from his mast to let the officials in Boston know of the situation in the outer harbor.

The first regiment to be quartered at Long Island was the famous "Fighting Ninth." This regiment was recruited by Thomas Cass, formerly commander of a Massachusetts Militia organization known as the Columbian Artillery. Composed almost wholly of men of Irish birth, six of the companies were from Boston, and one each from Salem, Marlboro, Milford, and Stoughton. After a long tedious stay at Faneuil Hall in Boston, the soldiers were taken aboard the *Nellie Baker* May 12, 1861, and soon arrived at Camp Wightman, Long Island. The camp was named in honor of Mayor Wightman of Boston. Pickets were set up along the shore to prevent desertion and interference from sailing craft, and the soldiers soon began to feel they were actually in the army.

When Colonel Cass learned one evening that some of his officers were missing from camp, he had the countersign changed while the officers were still out. The colonel heard the officers returning and walked down to the sentinel they would have to pass, keeping in the background. The guard, knowing the colonel was close at hand, changed to "charge bayonets" and loudly called "Halt! Who goes there?" This so astonished the returning officers that they halted and ceased talking. One of them called out that they were friends with the countersign, and tried to give the word. He failed, of course, and when Colonel Cass stepped forward, the officers knew the game was up. They were each inspected by the colonel, and after a severe scolding, were dismissed.

At two p.m. on June 26, 1861, the Ninth Regiment sailed from Long Island. Friends and relatives had come down to make their final farewells, and as the boys marched up the gangplanks and on the three steamers there was no cheering; the occasion was too serious. The *Ben de Ford*, the *Cambridge*, and the *Pembroke* were the three ships selected to carry the 1022 men to Washington, and as the transports sailed into the channel and passed Long Island Light, a last view of the deserted tent city was presented. For many of the men it was the last view of Boston Harbor.

Some of the adventuresome conscripts at Long Island believed that they could escape to the mainland, one such attempt taking place on the night of Sunday, September 13, 1863. Four conscripts deserted in a small boat and, by skillful navigation, managed to go part of the way to another island before their makeshift craft sank in the channel. Two were drowned, but the other two men were successful in reaching Jeffries Point, East Boston. They were soon captured and brought into court, where nearly $1000 in money was found on them. When the bodies of their companions were picked up, $408 was taken from their pockets.

At the end of the war Long Island returned to the peaceful pursuits of former years. In 1867, however, an important change was effected when Fort Strong, Noddle's Island, was moved down the Harbor to Long Island Head.

The island gradually became the place for Sunday prize

fights, and many fistic encounters were witnessed at old Camp Wightman. The police finally had to stop the pugilistic activities of Sunday visitors, and on June 29, 1873, when a riot squad of 40 husky policemen landed on the shore, there was a great run for the boats. Some escaped and some were captured; at any rate this put an end to the Sunday prize fights for many years.

The Portuguese families had been quietly living at Long Island since 1850, but the city of Boston decided to take over the island, except for the 50 acres owned by the Federal Government, and made the purchase in 1882. In 1887 the city of Boston was forced to evict the 30 Portuguese families then living at the island; they took up new abodes around the harbor. The male paupers from Rainsford's Island were moved to Long Island in 1895, and the female inmates of the almshouse at Rainsford's Island were also moved there.

In the year 1899 extensive plans were made by the Government, and 15.24 acres were purchased from the city. These plans necessitated moving Long Island Light, and the work was begun on September 13, 1900.

With the advent of the World War, about 1500 men were quartered at Fort Strong, mostly those from the 55th Artillery. Captain Augustus L. Hodgkins had many a trying experience running the *Batchelder* around to the forts during the terrible winter of 1917-18.

On January 8, 1918, Edwin Tarr, keeper of Long Island Light since 1909, died while sitting in his chair looking out over the water. He was the light's last keeper. The beacon was lighted by custodians until 1929, at which time it was made automatic.

The Medical Director at Long Island Hospital is Dr. James V. Sacchetti, who succeeded Dr. Charles L. Clay in 1940.

Dr. James V. Sacchetti's residence is to the left of the pier, with the various buildings of the institution situated south of his home. The institution building, the men's dormitories, the women's dormitories, the men's hospital building, the women's hospital building, the chapel, the power house, and the splendid recreation center which has come to be known as the Curley building are among the edifices on the island. The custodial division and the hospital division are under the same general management, only minor differences being made between them. The Long Island Hospital is used for chronic diseases only.

An unusual scene along the shore at Long Island is the number of small huts and camps made from driftwood washed in from the ocean. Many of the inmates of the almshouse occupy their leisure moments building and taking care of these huts which seem to take them away from the realities of life.

Much has been done to make the life of the inmate a pleasant and useful one. An occupational therapy shop has been opened where the inmates learn embroidery and rug-making. Those who have special talents are encouraged in their efforts to carve, weave, make ship models, weather vanes, and other objects. Some evenings entertainments are given, and once a week moving pictures are shown. At other times the radio supplies music, drama, and news accounts in the modern auditorium. In the recreational center there is a barber shop, a smoking room, a library, and a reading room.

NIX'S MATE AND BIRD ISLAND

There are two islands down the harbor which have long stood for tragedy and terror in the history of Boston Bay. Several notorious pirates have been buried on Bird Island and Nix's Mate, and many an honest sailor has been startled by the skeleton of a buccaneer hanging in chains on one of these islands. Due to the inroads of man and nature, both islands have practically vanished from the harbor. While a small part of the original Nix's Mate Island still remains, Bird Island, which was possibly named after Goodman Bird, is but a memory.

At low tide we may see a pile of granite stones marking the site of Bird Island, but the rocks are usually covered at high tide. With the gradual abandonment of Bird Island Passage the island has been practically forgotten by the mariner of today.

Governor Winthrop tells an exciting story of several men who were frozen in at Bird Island in 1634. When they were coming up from Deer Island, the passage became so difficult that they were forced to stop at Bird Island for the night. The group must have suffered terribly; it was so cold that the harbor froze over before morning and they were able to walk over to the mainland with the coming of dawn.

In the Town Records for 1650 we read that "Tho' Munt hath liberty to mow the marsh at Bird Island this yeare." We cannot tell how many years Munt gathered hay from this island, but we do know that in 1658, "Bird Island is lett to James Euerill & Rich Woody for sixty years, paying 12 d siluer or a bushel of salt every first of March to ye town Treasurer."

We are coming now to the period in Boston Harbor history when the pirates occupy the center of the stage.

In the old colonial days, long before Dana and other vigilant social workers of the sea had made people of civilized countries realize the hardships of the common sailor, it was not unusual to hear of mutiny on the ocean. Crews would overthrow their superior officers, kill or put in irons those who would not join them, and sail the high seas as pirates. Of course they knew the dangers of the profession and were aware of the chances of ending their days on the gibbet. Because of the treatment they received on board ship, the mutineers probably believed that a quick death was infinitely better than the lingering tortures of the life they were leading.

Captain John Quelch is the first subject for discussion, and special attention should be paid to one of the members of his crew, John Lambert. The remains of John Lambert still repose in Boston's King's Chapel Burying Ground. In August 1703, Quelch sailed in command of the brigantine *Charles* from

Marblehead. The pirates locked the real captain in his room before the ship had left the harbor and, after reaching the high seas, threw him overboard. In the next few months Quelch captured nine Portuguese ships, with each pirate in the crew making a small fortune. Returning home the middle of the following May, the *Charles* dropped anchor at Marblehead and the men went ashore, apparently believing that they would not be molested. When the authorities in Boston heard of the ship's arrival, however, they sent Attorney-General Paul Dudley to capture the crew of the pirate ship. He brought Quelch, Lambert, and five other pirates back to Boston with him.

There were many buccaneers still at large, however, and late one night Samuel Sewall was notified that there were "9 or 11 Pirats, double arm'd, seen in a Lone-house" at Cape Ann. He arose immediately and alarmed the soldiers of the countryside. There was great excitement until the capture of these notorious men was effected. The twenty-fifth of June saw 25 of these pirates safely imprisoned at the Boston jail. Only seven were eventually sentenced to death, as the rest were given pardons upon the condition that they should enter the Queen's service.

June 20, 1704, the Silver Oar, the emblem of the Court of Admiralty, was carried in front of the condemned pirates as they made their way down to Scarlett's Wharf, located at the foot of Fleet Street. They were taken to the gallows erected out over the water. Cotton Mather, the well-known Boston clergyman, went in a boat to give the men their final admonitions. The surrounding shore was lined with men and women, and Broughton's Hill, overlooking the gallows, was crowded. The spectators eagerly waited to hear the last words of notorious Captain Quelch. He informed the gathering that he was on the verge of eternity merely because he had brought money into New England, money that could not be said to be dishonest. He told his listeners to be careful lest they also be hanged. "I am condemned only upon circumstances," he concluded.

When the scaffold dropped from under the seven men, there was such a screech from the women present it was heard by the wife of Samuel Sewall at her house, located a mile from the scene of the execution. This was in spite of a strong wind blowing from the opposite direction.

The bodies of all the pirates but one were taken down the harbor and either buried or hung in chains on Nix's Mate or Bird Island. Sewall gave permission for the body of John Lambert, a member of a prominent Salem family, to be smuggled up to what is now King's Chapel Burying Grounds and interred in the family lot at midnight. Although the pirate was not given a tombstone, the graves of his wife and his son in the same lot are still to be seen. Thus we have a bloodthirsty pirate buried in the peaceful haven of Boston's own King's Chapel Graveyard.

On the second day of June 1724, William White and John Archer were executed over the waters of Boston Harbor. This act ended an exciting adventure for White, who had started his unfortunate career in the seizure of the sloop *Revenge* at Newfoundland, August 23, 1723. John Phillips was elected captain of this band of ruffians. Under his leadership several small fishing boats were overtaken, and John Rose Archer joined the pirates from one of these captured vessels. Far from being a "forced" pirate, he was in a class of his own, having once served under the notorious "Black Beard" Teach.

Captain Phillips overtook the sloop *Squirrel,* under Captain Haraden April 14, 1724. The *Boston News-Letter* of May 7, 1724 tells us that this daring pirate captured 34 vessels in less than eight months! Haraden was made a forced man, but soon found the ship had many sailors who were waiting for a chance to mutiny. Edward Cheeseman was accepted as the leader of the men who were planning to mutiny, and with Haraden on board, they believed that the time had come for the surprise attack. Among the forced men was John Filmore, the great-grandfather of President Millard Fillmore. One bright day the ship was plowing along through the waves when Cheeseman gave the prearranged signal, whereupon Filmore raised his broadax and split the head of the boatswain, killing him instantly. Cheeseman grabbed the largest pirate on the ship, threw him over the side, and, when the man hung on, chopped at his hand with the broadax until the buccaneer fell into the water. Captain Phillips rushed on deck but received a broken jaw from Cheeseman, and Captain Haraden's blow with an adz ended the life of buccaneer John Phillips.

The ship, now in possession of the forced men, turned about and headed for Annisquam. The rest of the pirates were saved from death to be used as witnesses in court to prove that the forced men were not buccaneers themselves. The pirates were landed and sent to Boston with the head of Phillips preserved in a pickle barrel.

The trial of the buccaneers was held May 12, 1724, and ended in the execution of White and Archer. John Rose Archer, after his execution, was hung in chains at Bird Island, with the body of William White buried in the sand underneath the gibbet. Before the execution both men were penitent, and spoke against the evils of drink. White declared that he "was drunk when enticed aboard the Pyrate." John Rose Archer made this impressive remark on the gallows: "I could wish that masters of Vessels would not use their men with so much severity, as many of them do, which exposes us to great Temptations." Jeremiah Bumstead took a large party of friends and relatives to Bird Island a week after the execution to see the body of John Rose Archer swinging in chains at the lonely spot.

In the spring of 1726 William Fly shipped as boatswain aboard the snow *Elizabeth*, then at anchor in the harbor of Jamaica. His captain was John Green, and the dying remarks of John Rose Archer should be remembered when judging the next act of William Fly. Captain Green's cruel and abusive treatment so angered Fly that the boatswain planned to seize the ship. At one o'clock in the morning of May 27, 1726, Fly and Alexander Mitchell invaded the captain's cabin and told him they were in charge. They then rushed him up on deck and threw him over the side of the ship to his death. As there was no strenuous opposition after this bold stroke, Fly now assumed control of the snow. Renaming this vessel the *Fame's Revenge* he captured the *John and Hannah* with her commander, Captain William Atkinson a week later. William Fly later had reason to regret the capture. He was so engrossed in the seizure of ships up and down the Atlantic coast that he did not realize the plot which was being formed against him. After a thrilling capture, Fly placed most of his loyal men aboard the captured vessel. Still on the pirate ship with Captain Fly, Atkinson and three other forced men surprised the buccaneers and captured the ship. The rowdy William Fly was placed in irons. Atkinson now sailed for Boston Harbor, and June 6, 1726, William Fly saw the Island of Nix's Mate, where he was soon to be hanged in chains.

We quote from John Campbell's *News-Letter* of July 14, 1726:

"On Tuesday the 12th Instant, about 3 p.m. were executed here for Piracy, Murder, & c. Three of the Condemned Persons mentioned in our list, viz. *William Fly, Capt. Samuel Cole,* Quartermaster, and *Henry Greevill,* the other viz. *George Condick,* was Repriev'd at the Place of Execution . . . Fly behaved himself very unbecomingly even to the last; however advised Masters of Vessels not to be Severe and Barbarous to their Men, which might be a reason why so many turned Pirates . . . Their Bodies were carried in a Boat to a Small Island called Nick's Mate, about 2 Leagues from the Town, where the abovesaid Fly was hung up in Irons, as a Spectacle for the Warning of others, especially Sea faring Men; the other Two were buried there."

Two hundred years have elapsed since the last pirate was buried in the shifting sands of Nix's Mate and Bird Island. The sinister part of their careers now over forever, the two islands were assigned more pastoral duties. Nix's Mate was advertised from time to time for grazing purposes, and in 1735 the New England *Courant* carried an advertisement of sixteen lines stressing its suitability along this line.

A rather amusing incident took place on September 18, 1863, when "four gentlemen ran their boat onto Nix's Mate and found themselves in the water." They were rescued by parties from Snow's Island, or Gallop's Island, as it is known today, and according to the newspaper account, returned to their homes much wiser gentlemen.

We shall now go ashore at both islands. A good high tide submerges Bird Island, so we must pick a low tide for our journey to the forgotten ledge. Landing at the pyramid of granite stones, we climb to the top. Governor's Island lies off to the southeast of the airport. With perhaps a thought or two for Quelch and Archer, we return to the boat and push off for Nix's Mate. Passing down the ship channel we reach Long Island Head, and there lies Nix's Mate Beacon, between the Nubble and the Narrows. As it is still low tide, we land on the sand bar and walk up to the ominous and sinister pyramid. On the southwestern corner of this seawall there is a stairway and the first step up these grimy stairs is so high it recalls climbing the pyramids. Brushing aside spider webs, we reach the top of the wall.

The legend of Nix's Mate, although a story without foundation, should be remembered. Late on a summer's day in 1689 as darkness descended on the waters of Massachusetts Bay, Captain Nix was guiding his ship into Boston Harbor. He anchored off what is now Nix's Mate Island. During the night screams were heard coming from the vessel, and in the morning the captain was found murdered. Accused of the crime, the mate was convicted by a Puritan jury, and sentenced to be hanged from the nearby island. The next morning, when they took him ashore to be executed, Nix's Mate asked permission to make a final statement. He declared that as proof of his innocence the island would some day wash away.

We cannot deny that the island did wash away, leaving a small area around which the present seawall was built in 1805, but there are reasons why the legend is false. The British Admiralty laws were very strict, so that any trial would have to be recorded, and any hanging of necessity had to take place between the rise and fall of the tide in Boston proper. There is no record either of the trial or the hanging. In addition, Nix's Mate Island was so called at least forty years before the first marine execution took place in the colony.

A letter from Richard Burbeck to Nicholas Merrit in Marblehead, written around 1700, explains the mystery of the name. William Coddington, a passenger on the *Jewel,* one of Winthrop's fleet, asked the Dutch pilot about an island near which they were anchored. At the time the waves were making a great noise as they madly dashed against the island cliffs. Burbeck's story follows:

"Dirke Stone was on the deck of the *Jewell,* and Master Coddington, one of the passengers, ask'd Dirke, as Dirke did thinke, about the noise. And Dirke told him the name of the noise in Dutch. And so when Master Coddington saide, 'What do you Dutch call that?' Dirke said 'Nixie Shmalt; I do not know how to spell it, but it meaneth the Wail of the Water Spirits . . .' But Master Coddington thought it was the name of the Iland, and set it down on a map he had 'Nix his Mate Island.'

"And after that, in order to account for the name, Dirke did saie that your Massachusetts people had made up a fairy Tale about a Captain Nix and hys mate, and a Kyling and a Hanging and a Sheriff and a neckespeche which was a prophecy."

At the turn of the century the Boston Marine Society became interested in preserving Nix's Mate Island. This society, the oldest of its kind in America, started agitation for the preservation of the landmark, but not until 1805 was the seawall built around the island which at that time had dwindled to approximately 25 by 50 feet. Knox received $400 from the Commonwealth of Massachusetts for the Island. The wooden column or marker placed on what remained of the island was 32 feet high. During the World War the marker was changed and is now a cement pyramid.

The next time you sail by the low marker at Bird Island or the high cement pyramid at Nix's Mate, think back two hundred years to the days of Quelch, Archer, and Fly, whose skeletons were buried in the shifting sand bars around the two islands, and be thankful that you are living today, instead of in that far-off time when the emblem of the skull and bones sailed the Spanish Main.

ALONG THE BACK CHANNEL

THOMPSON'S ISLAND

CAPTAIN STANDISH had left the Pilgrim settlement in an open sailboat to explore the coast line of Massachusetts Bay, as well as to make trading arrangements with the Indians of this region. His party of thirteen had expected to reach Boston Harbor the same day they left Plymouth, but it was not until the following night that they anchored off Thompson's Island, where the Farm and Trades School is today. Standish and the others, including William Trevore, went ashore the next morning. Back in London, David Thompson had asked Trevore to pick out a likely island that Thompson could use for a trading post, so Trevore took possession of the island for his London friend.

Myles Standish believed, and Shurtleff contended, that the Indians never made their home at this island, but a well-stocked museum at the school proves that they were mistaken. Mortars, pestles, axes, plummets, spear-heads, and arrow-heads which were dug on the island are in the collection, and all point to long-established homes of the red men at Thompson's Island. The Indian residents were probably all killed in the pestilence which swept the Massachusetts area a few years before the white man arrived. Morton of Merrymount speaks of this terrible plague.

Shortly after Gorges' colony of 1622 had settled at Wessagusett, another party landed at Little Harbor, New Hampshire, on the west side of the Piscataqua River. Among them was David Thompson for whom Trevore had claimed Thompson's Island. Thompson is mentioned in the Council of New England Records, being linked with another early settler whose name is perpetuated by a Boston Harbor island: "Mr. Thompson is ordered to pay unto Leo. Peddock £10 towards his paynes

for his last Imployments to New England." While working for
the Council in London, Thompson had naturally become quite
interested in America, and his name disappears from the records
after December 3, 1622, when he "propoundeth" for the transportation of ten persons to New England. As Thompson was
not wealthy enough to assume the responsibility for all the expenses of the undertaking, he mortgaged one-fourth of his new
lands to three other men.

Thompson's settlement became firmly established on the
Piscataqua River, near the mouth of the westerly branch. The
ruins of the first house in what is now New Hampshire are on
the peninsula there, and were described by Samuel Maverick
when he visited the location in 1660. David Thompson, in spite
of his pleasant situation on the Piscataqua, was anxious to come
down to his island, and, after spending three years at what is
now known as Odiorne's Point, moved to Boston Harbor in
1626. Thompson built a substantial home near the eastern
shore, just south of the centre of the island bearing his name.
Part of this building was discovered in 1889 by students digging on the bank. The old cellar floor was almost intact, but the
eastern and southern walls had fallen over the cliff years before. Bowls and stems of long Dutch pipes were unearthed in
the ruins. This building was probably the first house in Boston
Harbor, for we can find no evidence of the erection of any
earlier edifice. Thompson died before 1630, as the tax paid by
the Thompson family for their share in the eviction of Morton
of Merrymount was charged to Mrs. Thompson, which would
not have been the case had her husband been alive.

Thompson's wife, at different times called Amias, Ems,
and Aimes, was the daughter of William Cole of Plymouth,
England. She married Samuel Maverick of Noddle's Island
some time before 1632. For a while they lived in a house located where the Marine Hospital now stands in Chelsea, then
moved to Noddle's Island. In 1635, she wrote to Robert Trelawny from "Nottell's Island." As soon as she and her son John

had left Thompson's Island, the Massachusetts Bay Colony took possession. In 1634 the Court granted the island to Dorchester.

John Thompson, the first white child born in what is now New Hampshire, was then a boy of nine living with his mother and step-father at Noddle's Island. For fourteen years Dorchester collected taxes from residents on Thompson's Island, and in 1639 the yearly tax was set at twenty pounds.

The ownership of the island passed to John Thompson. Mortgaged in 1650, by 1658 Simon Lynde had acquired it. A few years later Lynde presented it to his young son Benjamin, confirming the gift in his will.

Benjamin Lynde grew up to be one of the best educated lawyers in America, and was a classical scholar of note. Let us read from his poem on Thompson's Island, probably written in imitation of *Echoes from the Sabine Farm*, by Horace, the Roman poet who lived just before the birth of Christ:

> *To save these queries about our isle,*
> *Kind heaven which placed it well does on it smile;*
> *In form triangular, its gradual sides*
> *Rise from the arms of Neptune's gentle tides.*
> *Southwest of Royal William's Citadel*
> *On Castle Isle, by Romer finish'd well*

This Thompson Island poet passed away in 1745, and Benjamin Lynde, Junior, became the owner. He gave the island to his two daughters, Mary and Lydia. Mary became the wife of the Honorable Andrew Oliver, while Lydia married the Reverend William Walter, pastor of Christ Church on Salem Street.

The trying days of the American Revolution were now at hand. After the British established themselves in Boston the Colonists raided all the islands in the harbor. American troops landed on Thompson's Island and burned all the buildings, orchards, and crops, the blaze lighting up the entire section as darkness fell. When the British were finally forced to leave the Harbor in March 1776, Colonel Tupper cannonaded them from the East Head at Thompson's Island. Following the Revolution it cost two thousand pounds to replace the ruined buildings and orchards which had been destroyed to prevent their falling into British hands.

George Minot, during the Revolution, often came from Dorchester to Boston on horseback, his panniers bulging with market produce, and on selling the vegetables to British soldiers in Boston would purchase some much-needed saltpetre, loading it into the empty panniers. He then slipped back through the British lines to the American soldiers. George Minot made many dangerous trips with the valuable material, doing much to help the American forces with this vital supply. His father, John Minot, had supplied the original money for the saltpetre, and after the war he bought Walter's share of the island with the funds with which the Government reimbursed him for the saltpetre furnished during the British occupation of Boston.

Peter Oliver, the son of Andrew Oliver and Mary Lynde Oliver, sold his share of the Island in 1814. From this time on Thompson's Island is so subdivided that a discussion of the many tenants would be tedious. The family names of Baxter, Fenno, Sargent, and Beale, however, are well-represented. George W. Beale was the last individual owner of the island, selling it in 1832 to the trustees of the Boston Farm School Society for $6,000.

THE FARM AND TRADES SCHOOL

We shall now consider the original organization of the Farm and Trade Schools. The Boston Asylum for Indigent Boys had been incorporated in 1814, with William Phillips and James Lloyd among those whose names appear in the act of incorporation. The trustees bought as a home Sir William Phips' former residence, located on the corner of Salem and Charter Streets. In 1832 John D. Williams headed an organization which became "The Boston Farm School Society." After purchasing Thompson's Island, the group sent the Reverend

E. M. P. Wells down the harbor to begin construction work. He started operations Easter Monday, April 8, 1833, and the boys who accompanied him began farming the same morning. Wells, a veteran of the War of 1812, continued working at the island for the next six months. Wells was the first to make a distinction between the worthy and the delinquent boys. The Wells Memorial for Workingmen is a splendid commemorative organization in Boston honoring this far-seeing minister whom Phillips Brooks called a "remarkable man."

Captain Daniel Chandler, active in the War of 1812, assumed office on October 26, 1833, as the second superintendent of the School. In 1834 the State transferred the island from Norfolk County to Suffolk County, and it was now under the jurisdiction of Boston. In 1835 an act of the Massachusetts Legislature united the Boston Asylum for Indigent Boys with the Farm School. Chandler left the island in 1839 to become superintendent of the House of Industry in South Boston.

When Chandler left the island, a period of crisis was at hand for the school. The great panic of 1837 had left its mark on Thompson's Island; building construction was at a standstill. Edwin J. Mills was in charge for three months, Payson Williams stayed on twice that length of time, and James Locke served over a year before being asked to resign.

Now desperate, the members of the Board of Directors realized that a strong man was needed to put the school on a sound footing. At this time the Board asked Cornelius Conway Felton, a professor at Harvard College, to become superintendent. Allowed to retain his professorship at the college, Felton would lend the needed dignity to the school on Thompson's Island. Cornelius Felton accepted the offer, and from that time much progress was made. Although Felton was not long in active charge, his influence lasted for years, and he took an interest in the school even after he was elected President of Harvard College in 1860.

Theodore Lyman was made president of the Board of Di-

THE ISLANDS OF BOSTON HARBOR

rectors in 1841. His first act was to obtain Robert Morrison as superintendent, and during his term of office the main buildings were completed, and the enrollment, which had dropped off to 41, soon became normal. President Lyman, who had always been an admirer of the efforts of Eleazer Wells to distinguish between worthy and delinquent boys, asked the Massachusetts Legislature to take steps for their segregation. As a result of Lyman's hard work, the first state school for boys in the world was opened at Westboro, Massachusetts.

Gradually the islanders became accustomed to the marine aspect of their location. In 1842 the boys made their first cruise to Boston, thus inaugurating a custom which lasted for half a century. When their boat reached Boston, the boys formed in line and marched up to City Hall where they listened to an address by the Mayor. After visiting many of the historical points in the city, they assembled on Boston Common where the afternoon was spent with their relatives and friends. As the sun began to set, they started for the steamboat landing and finally crossed the bay on the school boats, the *Vision*, the *Annie*, and the *Polka*.

On April 29 of the same year, a large party of boys accompanied by their instructor was returning from the outer harbor in the *Polka* when the boat capsized and 25 of the passengers lost their lives. It was the worst tragedy in the history of the school. Only the day before, relatives and directors had visited the island and had given 27 boys permission to go on a fishing trip down the harbor as a reward for their fine work. Mr. Oakes, an experienced sailor, and Mr. Peabody, a teacher, had charge of the trip which the boys greatly enjoyed. At the close of the day the party was returning to the school against a headwind, passing so close to the eastern head of the island that they were given a cheer by their schoolmates who did not make the trip. Having stood for Spectacle Island, the boat was in the act of tacking for the purpose of making the landing dock when suddenly over she went, sinking instantly. The wooden box which held the bait floated free, and four of the boys clung to it, but the other 23 and the two men were drowned. The four boys were brought into Boston by boats which had rushed to the scene. This tragedy left only half of the students to continue at school and to work on the farm.

When Nathaniel Hawthorne was active on the Boston waterfront, he visited Thompson's Island many times, and on one of his visits he took an extensive walk around the island, examining with interest the products of the farm. He saw the "wheat in sheaves on the stubble-field; oats somewhat blighted and spoiled; great pumpkins elsewhere; pastures; mowing grounds,—all cultivated by the boys." Hawthorne comments on the residence, a "great brick building, painted green, and standing on the summit of a rising ground, exposed to the winds of the bay." Let us read a few lines from this master writer:

"Vessels flitting past; great ships with intricacy of rigging and various sails; schooners, sloops, with their one or two broad sheets of canvas; going on different tacks, so that the spectator might think that there was a different wind for each vessel, or that they scudded across the sea spontaneously, whither their own wills led them. The farm boys remain insulated looking at the passing show within sight of the city, yet having nothing to do with it; beholding their fellow creatures skimming by them in winged machines, and steamboats snorting and puffing through the waves. Methinks an island would be the most desirable of all landed property, for it seems like a little world by itself; and the water may answer for the atmosphere that surrounds the planets. The boys were swinging, two together, standing up and almost causing the ropes and their bodies to stretch out horizontally. On our departure they ranged themselves on the rails of the fence, and, being dressed in blue, looked not unlike a flock of pigeons."

Another visitor in 1845, greatly impressed by the island, was reminded of the story of Latona, who had an island created in the sea as a refuge for her children. He also tells of the excitement at the island when the relatives and friends visit the boys.

This writer, John R. Dix, noticed one little boy who had no caller. The child sat in the reception room, his blue eyes filled with tears as he realized that there was no one to greet him.

"Poor little fellow, how I pitied him! I declare that I never longed for molasses candy, or something of that kind before: and I made a mental resolution that in the future I would never visit such places without a provision for a similar contingency. . . .

"Sure am I, that with so kind a lady superintendent, the little fellows must be happy—and as for Mr. Morrison, one of the lads assured us, that 'the Master was as good as father to them.'

"To the martial music of a drum the boys assembled on the greensward and paraded for some time backward and forward, in true military style, and a friend whispered in our ear, 'Why, they are the happiest lads in the world,' and we really believed him. There they were, reclaimed from the streets and lanes of the city, far away from evil influences, and safely folded on this beautiful spot, with education provided and employment afforded."

Leaving the island in the winter has always been a difficult problem, but in 1857 the boys were able to walk over the ice, across the harbor itself, to see the East Boston Ferry frozen in the ice between Boston and Samuel Maverick's old home. In this year the ship channel was frozen over to a point half a mile below the Castle. Horses and sleighs went as far as Spectacle Island, and one of the managers of the school rode in a sleigh from City Point right up to the door of the main building!

The same year, Morrison left Thompson's Island, returning to his home in Portsmouth, New Hampshire. His place at Thompson's Island was taken by William A. Morse, who had come there in 1850 as supervisor of the farm.

Morse remained at the island during the trying days of the Civil War, when over 150 undergraduates, graduates, and teachers of the school on Thompson's Island enlisted. Morse was active in over twelve different positions in this trying period, including the following: purchasing agent, accountant, secretary, headmaster, nurse, captain of the boat, head of the graduate employment agency, blacksmith, agricultural expert, head slaughterer, minister, and organist! Under his leadership the new barn was erected, the first steamer was purchased, the first boys' band in America was organized, and printing was introduced.

After a long and happy period of office at the Farm School, William Appleton Morse resigned as superintendent in 1888 and was succeeded by Charles Henry Bradley, author of an unpublished history of the school. It was in Bradley's first year that the "Cottage Row" plan of government and recreation was started in rather an unusual way. While baseball, swimming and football came and went, the one interest which never flagged was that of Cottage Row, the miniature city which the boys have built, cared for, and governed. Its innovation should interest the reader.

In the summer of 1888 the boys were given some cast-off bedticking. This they made over into tents, which they soon arranged in rows at the northern end of the playground. When the autumn weather arrived, some of the boys reinforced their tents with boards, but the cold winter soon forced them inside. With the coming of spring, some of the boys believed that a wooden cottage could be built to take the place of the tents. With the help of Superintendent Bradley, they planned and erected a small cottage, the manual training department being utilized in this rather novel venture.

Cottage after cottage was built, until in 1891 Superintendent Bradley decided to limit the number of buildings to twelve, and to divide each cottage into twelve shares. Certificates of ownership were given for these shares, transferable through the Farm School Bank, which is another feature of this enterprising little community. The whole idea worked so well that in 1893 the superintendent of the school issued a proclamation officially naming the playground settlement "Cottage Row" and announcing the various officers to be elected. After the election, a city hall, six by ten feet, was erected, soon followed by Audubon Hall, a building used as a home for the pets of the boys. Any visitor to the school who has witnessed an election at this little island-city government never forgets the orderly example of how politics should be run.

A disaster took place a few years after the Cottage Row plan was begun, almost fifty years to the day since the 1842 tragedy. On Sunday afternoon, April 10, 1892, Instructor A. F. Nordberg had been attending church in South Boston, and ten picked boys left Thompson's Island by boat to bring him back to the school. Soon after seven p.m., with the instructor safely on board, they began the return trip. At a point between Spectacle Island and Thompson's Island, evidently quite near the spot where the *Polka* had gone down half a century before, the sailboat struck a sudden squall and capsized. The 11 people clung to the bottom of the craft and waited for help. A tug steamed by; they shouted for assistance; but the night was getting dark and they were not noticed.

Back on the island, terribly worried by the prolonged absence of the boys, Superintendent Bradley was walking along the beach with his lantern. The two boys who survived told him afterwards that they saw his figure, but he could not see them. He did notice a fire on an island far in the distance, and tried to pick up the silhouette of the boat against the background of the fire as he walked up and down, but his efforts were in vain. The water was cold, and as the night wore on the more exhausted boys, one by one, slipped into the water. By 11 o'clock there were only two boys left, O. W. Clemenson and C. A. Lind —a few minutes later the boat touched the beach at Spectacle Island. The tragic news was soon told; a boat was secured and rushed to Thompson's Island where Superintendent Bradley, already prepared for the worst, received the word that Nordberg and eight of the boys had drowned.

Another disaster of 1892 was witnessed by the boys at the school when the great balloon of Professor Rogers plunged into the water just off the island. Professor A. A. Rogers, Assistant Thomas Fenton, erstwhile employee of Austin & Stone's Museum, and Delos E. Goldsmith, a reporter, had taken off from Boston Common on the afternoon of July 4. A hundred thousand people were on the Common, and a million others were watching the event from nearby vantage points. It was Rogers' 118th ascension, and he was full of confidence as the huge balloon rose into the air and out over the harbor. As the gas bag passed over Castle Island, Rogers saw that he would soon be swept out to sea so pulled at the safety valve. The valve would not open. As he struggled with all his strength, the fabric above the valve began to rip. It widened to a foot, then a yard, and the escaping gas almost overcame the three men. The balloon dropped like a rock as the gas escaped. Boats from all over the harbor headed for the spot it must hit. Just before the ship struck the water, Goldsmith released two carrier pigeons from their cage. When the great bag crashed into the ocean he was drawn under the sea. Rogers and Goldsmith struck out for Thompson's Island from which the school boat had already started to go to the rescue. Goldsmith was saved by the Farm School boys, but Rogers had sunk beneath the waves before the boat reached him. Fenton, entangled in the meshes of the net, was picked up in an unconscious condition and died before he could be taken to the hospital. Goldsmith recovered and was able to write the story of the accident, while his brother Wallace illustrated the tale with some vivid sketches.

In the terrible storm of 1898, Thompson's Island suffered damage amounting to $10,000. Four large schooners drifted ashore against the island, smashing one another and crushing the school's trim little steam launch. The landing floats were carried away, the dike which protects the low land was severely damaged, and three of the island's smaller boats were ruined beyond repair. Because of generosity of friends, the steamer and the other boats were replaced.

Charles Henry Bradley died in office January 30, 1922. Before he became sick, he had appointed Paul Francis Swasey as supervisor of the school, and this young Massachusetts Institute of Technology graduate now became acting superintendent. The appointment became permanent February 18, 1923. He increased the number of classes from four to six, thus making it possible for the boys graduating from the Farm and Trades School to enter the second or third year of high school. Mr. Swasey resigned on November 30, 1926.

William Maxfield Meacham, his successor, was installed in office under the first formal ceremony of its kind in the history of the school. It is of interest to note that the place of his birth, Hyde Park, Vermont, is within twenty miles of the birthplaces of his predecessors, Bradley and Swasey. Mr. Meacham was graduated from Middlebury College in 1921, engaged in teaching, was principal of Barton Academy in 1924-26, and went from Barton Academy to the Farm and Trades School as superintendent. In 1921 he married Miss Rena Mack, and there are three children, William, Linwood, and Joyce.

I shall mention a few of Mr. Meacham's accomplishments. Under his supervision a modern dieting system has been introduced, and a fine herd of registered Guernsey cattle has considerably improved the farm. Mr. Meacham is also carrying out an extensive poultry and orchard improvement plan, with a four-year course in theoretical agriculture included in the curriculum.

A substantial sum of money was left to the school by John D. Williams with the proviso that each year when the building was painted, pea-green paint, mixed by special formula, should be applied. The formula has been carefully preserved and every time the building was painted some pea-green paint was mixed in, and one of the Board of Managers took oath to the fact.

The students of Thompson's Island school who have achieved notable success have been many, but naturally I can include only a few of the outstanding graduates in various lines of life.

Thomas J. Evans was the last survivor of those connected with Thompson's Island who fought in the Civil War. He entered the Farm and Trades School in 1859 and enlisted at the age of 16, five years later, serving in Virginia. After the War he became a shoe operator and later was secretary of the Brockton Shoe Manufacturers' Association. He was the first alumnus to become a member of the Board of Managers and also served as President of the Alumni Association. Thomas J. Evans died March 9, 1934, in East Weymouth, at the age of 85.

LeRoy S. Kenfield, nationally known musician, was a member of the Class of 1882. In 1899 he joined the Boston Symphony Orchestra, remaining with this organization until his death. A career of a third of a century with this great orchestra places LeRoy Kenfield on a pedestal by himself. Mr. Kenfield died October 5, 1934.

There are four distinguished graduates of the school whom I have been fortunate enough to interview.

The first is William Alcott, of the Class of 1884, who is at present the librarian of the *Boston Globe.* He was appointed city editor in 1906, holding this position for sixteen years. He has served as president of the Special Libraries Association and also of the Boston Chapter of the association, and as chairman of the Newspaper Group. He has served as historian (and also as president) of the alumni association of the school, and in 1935 was elected a member of the school's Board of Managers.

Henry A. Fox, '79, is the former chief of the Boston Fire Department, having attained this distinction in 1930. After leaving the Farm and Trades School in 1879, he worked for a time at John C. Gilbert's grocery store, then entered the Boston Fire Department in 1886. He became Chief in 1930. One of his happiest recollections is marching up State Street in uniform as a member of the school band.

Clarence DeMar is perhaps the best-known marathon runner in the world. He has won the Boston Marathon many times and has triumphed in many other parts of the country while performing his specialty.

R. Claire Emery, '12, the radio announcer, formed the Big Brother Club of New Englanders, and his programs were eagerly followed. Mr. Emery is now on another city's station, but his fine entertainment and cooperation in the early days of the radio will always be remembered.

The farm itself fills a very important place in the island's activity. The boys work on the farm half a day for about two years. Over 100 of the island's 157 acres are available for grazing or farming purposes. A herd of pure-bred Guernsey cows keeps the boys supplied with fresh milk. A flock of 600 Rhode Island Red hens provides an abundance of fresh eggs. Turkeys, pigs, hens, and cattle produce part of the meat supply. The pupils also grow all their own potatoes, beets, and other vegetables. About 100 tons of hay are harvested annually. There is a large flower garden, in which each boy has his individual plot. A fine library of 1000 volumes is in use at the school and the boys spend many hours of their free periods here.

Ever since the 1850's the Farm School Band has been in existence. The history of this band is unusual. Back in 1858 the first concert in America ever played by a school band was given by the boys of the Farm School. John Ripley Morse, brother of the superintendent, was their director, and his name goes down in history as the organizer of the first school band in America. Mr. Alonzo Draper of South Boston was engaged to assist Morse in the musical instruction, and soon all Massachusetts was proud of its island band. At the great Peace

Jubilee of 1869, Gilmore honored the band by inviting it to play in the 1,000 piece band in the Coliseum. The boys on this occasion rubbed elbows with the musicians of five countries and played side by side with some of the most famous bands of the world.

Under the superintendency of Mr. Meacham, the band has risen to great heights. New instruments were purchased during the first years of Mr. Meacham's service, and in May 1929, Director Frank L. Warren led the boys to first prize in the New England Band contest. Several first and second prizes have been won in subsequent competitions among State and New England bands.

Many of the courses offered at the school qualify the student for life work. The sloyd course is the basis of the mechanical teaching at the school, as it is the natural stepping stone to all trades and vocational training. Besides carpentry, cabinet work, and wood turning, sloyd offers instruction in mechanical drawing. Printing covers a large field, including work in type setting, headings, business cards, and display work. The *Beacon,* printed at the school, is an example of the fine workmanship the students turn out. It is published monthly and carries many stories written by the boys. The forging course gives instruction in hand forging in wrought iron and steel. Meteorology is carefully taught and learned, the ideal location of the school giving added zest to the work. Local forecasts are made each morning, and the temperature, humidity and dew point, rainfall, barometric pressure, wind velocity and direction are duly recorded. Besides these regular courses, the students have the practical experience of caring for and running the *Pilgrim III,* the school boat of which all the boys are so proud.

Without question the groves of trees on Thompson's Island are not surpassed anywhere in Boston Harbor, and everyone connected with the school is justly proud of them. In 1846 Theodore Lyman imported 4,000 larches and 2,000 English oaks which he presented to the institution. They were set out

THOMPSON'S ISLAND FARM AND TRADES SCHOOL BAND
OLDEST BOYS' BAND IN AMERICA

WILLIAM MAXFIELD MEACHAM

GOVERNOR'S ISLAND FROM THE AIR

SHOWING ZIGZAG STAIRS, SCENE OF 1902 EXPLOSION, ENTRANCE TO THE LONG TUNNEL, AND THE CASTLE

on the southeastern side of the island and formed what is now known as Lyman Grove. In 1854, Superintendent Morrison did some extensive transplanting; again in 1896, 1898, 1900, 1901, and 1903 new additions were made. It is now the custom for the boys at the school to plant a few new trees every year. An airplane view of the island gives the flyer a feeling of gratitude for the restoration of thousands of trees which have given a "sylvan covering" to at least one island in the harbor.

We have visited this island scores of times in summer and winter. Under the able leadership of Mr. Meacham wonderful work is being done there. If the proud parent who raises one son to manhood is said to have done the community and his country a worthy service, think what we owe to this society, which has supplied fatherly interest and guidance to two thousand times this number. The Farm and Trades School at Thompson's Island is a splendid example of what can be done for the needy boy of today.

The 1944 members of the board of trustees include Augustus P. Loring, Jr., Philip H. Theopold, William Alcott, Alfred C. Malm, and Governor Leverett Saltonstall. During recent years several members of the school faculty have made outstanding contributions. They include Bror Y. Kihlstrom, sloyd instructor, Dr. John B. Cook of the college preparatory department, Mrs. William M. Meacham, dietitian, with her able assistants Mrs. Henrietta Coffill and Mrs. Affie G. Plummer. Head Farmer Mark C. Baird and Poultryman Robert Kitching have done their share in making the island one of the country's leading agricultural schools. Mrs. Mary F. Mathewson is the excellent instructor in the school laundry, while Abijah Matteson is the school engineer in charge of the central heating plant. Recreational Director Clifton E. Albee is to be complimented on his fine programs and the Boy Scout troop, while Band Director Frank L. Warren has a record of achievement which includes initiating the annual Faneuil Hall concerts in 1937. Raymond Thomas, Supervisor of Boys, is in charge of life saving, swimming and first aid. The school secretary is Mrs. Wilhelmina B. Thomas, while the Alumni Secretary is Merton P. Ellis. With over 200 boys in the service who attended the island school, theirs indeed are busy positions.

Other noted graduates include the following: John F. Peterson, former superintendent of Mt. Auburn Cemetery; Clarence W. Loud, engaged in real estate and trusteeships; William Frank Davis, now a resident of New York; Rev. George W. Russell, teacher and clergyman; Harold E. Brenton, former member of the Boston Music Commission; Silas Snow, trustee and town official; Lieutenant-Colonel Franklin P. Miller, U. S. A.; Professor Robert H. Bogue, research director of the Portland Cement Association Fellowship at the National Bureau of Standards; Cyrus W. Durgin, assistant dramatic editor of the *Boston Globe*; and Leslie Jones, *Boston Herald* photographer.

The new athletic field was conceived more than ten years ago by Headmaster William M. Meacham and built under his careful supervision. It consists of a regulation football field, baseball diamond, and track, with softball field, tennis court, badminton court, and playground nearby. From 1936 to 1941 five new brick buildings and one wooden frame building were built, enabling the boys to live under modern home conditions in buildings which are better equipped than the average private family home.

The endowment funds of the school have been substantially increased through the merger of the Liversidge Institute, gifts of the Charles Hayden Foundation, and legacies and gifts from the many friends of the school.

There is no question but that the natural beauty of Thompson's Island definitely affects every boy privileged to enjoy and appreciate it. Surely over a century of this magnificent, unsurpassed environment closely associated with the natural, beautiful life at the island has influenced generation after generation of the nation's youth.

SPECTACLE ISLAND

L YING between Castle and Long Islands, the two cliffs of Spectacle Island occupy a commanding location in Boston Harbor. The earliest mention of this *pince-nez* island is in 1635, when it was included with Deer, Hog, and Long Islands for a total yearly rent of four shillings. The first known excitement took place three years later when 30 woodsmen were marooned here by the cold weather. Twelve of the men were later able to reach Governors' Island, but seven of them were carried on the ice out to the Brewster Islands where they remained for two days without food or fire. One woodcutter died, and many of the men had their arms and legs frozen.

Spectacle Island was made the quarantine station in 1717, and for twenty years was used for that purpose. When the station was moved to Rainsford's Island in 1737, Richard Bill purchased Spectacle Island from the town.

Wild animals have at various times lived on the islands in the harbor, but very few have actually come to live there while they were occupied by white people. In 1725, however, so many bears were being killed around Boston that some of the beasts took to the ocean for refuge, several of them swimming across to Spectacle Island. Two were killed as they tried to escape, but only after a desperate struggle.

Two summer hotels were established at Spectacle Island in the 19th century, one run by a Mr. Woodroffe and the other by a Mr. Reed. A thriving business was enjoyed, but the existence of certain games not allowed by the city of Boston brought police raiders in the year 1857, and from that time on the hotel business failed to prosper. The same year Nahum Ward paid $15,000 for the property, including two houses and two brick powder magazines similar to those at Governor's

Island. One of these powder magazines is still to be seen near the bridge of the nose on the low land. The history of these powder storerooms is unknown, as no one knows when they were built. The first house on the island was brought down on lighters by Mr. Ward from Boston.

Nahum Ward had a prosperous business of rendering dead horses and cattle. His son, Francis J. Ward, in 1882 said his work at Spectacle Island prevented many a plague in Boston, for if the dead animals had been allowed to stay in the city as long as three days, serious results might have followed.

In 1886 Joseph Marion moved to Spectacle from Long Island and built a cabin on the southern side of the cliff. Marion died in 1892, and his wife later married Jose Safarino, who had come to live at Spectacle Island in 1888. He had one son, Jose, aged 18, who made frequent visits over to Quarantine Rocks where he called on the jovial Grisiano Rio, otherwise known as Joe the Rock and Portuguese Joe.

The year 1898 had much excitement in store for the Safarino family. On April 24, during a severe blow, a cat-boat capsized right over Sculpin Ledge, half a mile from shore. Jose and his son rowed out in the gale and rescued the four men in the boat. One man was unconscious when picked up and died shortly afterwards. That November brought the dreadful *Portland* Storm and the great four masted steamship *Ohio* of the Wilson line went ashore close to their home. It was later pulled off.

In 1892 the garbage reclaiming plant was located at Moon Island. Twenty years later, on April 12, 1912, the establishment was moved over to Spectacle Island and became known as the Boston Development and Sanitary Company, with Mr. Cranford in charge. In 1922 the contract was given to the Coleman Disposal Company and ten years later it was again awarded to this firm. The refining business of the Ward Plant gradually dropped off, and not for many years have dead horses and cows been brought to this plant, being now sent to Billerica instead. Ward, however, still owns the northern bluff of the island, except for the acre of land occupied by the Lighthouse Department.

Just after the turn of the century four range lights were erected, but with the widening and straightening of the main channel, two of the lights were found unnecessary and demolished. Mr. Creed was keeper at this time, remaining at the lights for over twenty years. He was succeeded by Captain Lelan Hart who came from Boston Light in 1926.

We visited the island on Sunday, August 9, 1934, and spent the entire day rambling about the farm, lighthouses, and the two refineries. Walking toward Jose Safarino's cottage on the southern cliff, we reached the hut just as night was coming on. Safarino invited us in, and we sat down at his table. Lighting his lantern, he spun story after story of his childhood in the harbor, telling how he played around the guns at Long Island Head as a child. He also spoke of his service aboard the Lighthouse Tender *Mayflower*, and of the rescue in 1898 which earned him the Massachusetts Humane Society's medal.

As the evening wore on, the time came to go back to our boat, so we bade farewell to this island fisherman. He warned us against the dangers of the garbage dump, where the rats grew as large as cats. We were lucky, however, to encounter the night watchman of the island, George Lowther, who guided us along the road, keeping the great rodents away with his flashlight. We reached our boat without further incident.

Roy E. Wyatt is in charge at the plant. A fire in 1934 destroyed many of the buildings on the northern bluff. Fruit and vegetables grow on the dump in the summer time, with squash, watermelons, honeydews, and tomatoes all coming up of their own accord. Incidentally, the garbage dump has completely changed the contour of the island so that it no longer resembles a pair of spectacles.

Unfortunately for those people who live nearby, the odors wafted by the breeze are quite obnoxious. "Whichever way the wind doth blow," some section of the surrounding shore line receives a strong hint that the garbage incinerators are functioning.

Fast in the mud on the southwestern shore of Spectacle Island lies the four-masted schooner *Snetind*, where Mrs. Ann Winsor Sherwin has lived for the past few years.

THIMBLE, CAT, AND HALF-MOON ISLANDS

Between Thompson's Island and the mainland there is a small ledge the size of a house-lot which the government chart honors by calling Thimble Island. It is a very appropriate name as it is a diminutive island.

Two other islands, formerly much larger than the area the Government Chart indicates for Thimble Island, have disappeared from the waters of the harbor. Cat Island, located in Town River Bay is only mentioned twice in history. It was the home of one John Bond, a native of Boston, who gave a mortgage for it sometime before 1700. Some years later, Joseph Palmer sold it to James Brackett, and since it has now been dug up and taken away as filling material, it is quite probable there will be no occasion for further historical research.

Colonel John Quincy once lived at Wollaston where he often entertained his friends, and traditions have come down to the present time of his famous strawberry parties given at Half Moon Island before the top of "that now submerged gravel ridge" had been wholly washed away. When the Moon Island sewer was put in, much of the earth needed to construct the strandway out to the Head was taken from Half-Moon Island.

HANGMAN'S ISLAND

Hangman's Island is the next subject of our tour. It was often used in colonial days as a source of slate material, Mrs. Olive Smallpiece owning the slate rights in the last part of the seventeenth century.

For some unknown reason, the town of Quincy never claimed Hangman's Island, and the Commonwealth of Massachusetts took it over years ago. The regulations under which it may be leased prevented construction of a house or shack of any sort, but many fishermen disregarded the rules and built small service sheds in which they lived and stored their traps and seines.

On January 1, 1896, William J. Greenfield leased the island, continuing to occupy it until the World War. After the war Stewart C. Woodworth lived here for three years. G. R. Maertins leased the island for a gunning stand in 1929, but his permit expired in 1930 and was not renewed. At present there is no occupant there.

MOON ISLAND

Moon Island, now connected to the mainland by the earth and gravel brought here from Half-Moon Island, was formerly called Manning's Moone, and in 1656 was valued at 28 pounds. John Holland owned the island around 1665, and when he died the estate was sold to Henry Ashhurst. The great sewer to Moon Island was begun in 1878, and for many years has been emptying into Boston Harbor on the outgoing tides. The only recorded excitement here was during the Revolution, when a Continental soldier was killed on the Head during one of the harbor skirmishes.

NUT ISLAND

The first mention we can find of Nut Island is on August 5, 1680, when Obediah Walker sold two-thirds of the island to Richard Harris. At this time the island was also called Hoffs Thumb, because it was off the shore from Hoffs Neck, now known as Hough's Neck.

In 1793 a drift-way for cattle was constructed between Nut Island and the mainland at Hough's Neck, and it was off this same drift-way 72 years later that Marcus Cram met his death. The cattle run was covered at high tide by about seven feet of water. Cram and his family had driven over to Nut Island at low tide when the bar was bare. When they started to go back to the mainland he believed it was not too deep for his horse, but the animal, becoming confused in the current, ran the buggy off the drift-way into deep water, and the family was soon struggling in the Bay. William H. Mears saw the accident from shore and saved all the occupants except Cram, who had gone down before Mears reached the scene.

A few years later the Federal Government started a testing ground for the heavy ordnance which was built at the Alger Foundry in South Boston. A firing test might have ended disastrously had not the shell cleared Prince's Head target by several hundred feet and buried itself in the graveyard at Hull.

The road connecting Nut Island and Hough's Neck is now well above the high-water mark, permitting automobiles to drive out and around the island. At present the Southern Metropolitan District empties its sewerage into the harbor from the Pumping Station at Nut Island.

RAINSFORD'S ISLAND

Owen Rowe, writing to John Winthrop during the winter of 1636, requested that "Mr. Ransford may be accommodated with lande for a farme." Thereupon the Puritan Government gave Elder Edward Rainsford a small island of eleven acres located between Peddock's and Long Islands, about a seven miles' sail from Boston. This island has for many years been called one of the harbor's prettiest, but in its present ruinous state it is hardly attractive from the channel. West Head still contains many delightful nooks and coves, however, and the High Bluff on the eastern side is a well-known landmark. This bluff slopes away on the inside to form a flat area large enough for a baseball diamond. Between this land and West Head there is a narrow strip of beach, formerly wide enough for a road but now barely passable at high tide. When seen from the air, the island resembles an elongated animal.

In 1735 the shipowners of Boston were discussing the advisability of transferring the Quarantine Station from Spectacle Island to a more suitable location and considered Rainsford's Island with favor. The committee appointed to visit the island reported that it was a satisfactory location. At this time the property was owned jointly by at least a dozen Lorings. When the Loring family agreed to sell the island for 570 pounds, a sum which was acceptable to the committee, Selectman Jeffries duly paid them this amount.

The hospital was moved here from Spectacle Island in 1737, but before this, the island seems to have been used either by the Indians or the colonists as a burial ground. An incident which occurred many years later confirms this idea. Dr. J. V. C. Smith, on the island in the spring of 1826, watched a lad setting up posts around some young trees. The boy drove his crowbar into one of the many sunken pits and found a human skull in a fairly good state of preservation. Smith believed that the sunken pits near the old fever hospital were ancient graves, but both history and tradition are silent concerning them. Smith was able to count about five hundred graves in 1826, and believed that with careful examination perhaps seven hundred could be identified. About this time a most unusual stone grave was discovered containing a skeleton with an iron sword hilt, possibly suggesting the burial place of that ancient Norseman, Thorwald.

Diarist Ezekial Price wrote on September 2, 1778, of his visit here with many prominent dignitaries to view the French fleet then in the harbor. The men from the fleet were sent ashore at George's Island, Peddock's Island, and Nantasket to construct fortifications.

Thomas Spear, the hero of the Lovers' Rock tragedy, became keeper of Rainsford's Island in 1796, holding the position until his death in 1812. He is buried in the cemetery here, near his son George, who succeeded Thomas Spear as keeper.

A frequent visitor to Rainsford's Island in 1819 was Rev. Frederick W. A. S. Brown who lived at Deer Island during the summer and visited many of the islands around the harbor that year. Brown's impressions of Rainsford's Island follows:

> *To Rainsford's little pleasant isle,*
> *Does precedence belong;*
> *Here kindness dwells and Hobart's smile*
> *Your welcome would prolong.*
> *The sailor here when dire disease*
> *His body has oppressed*
> *May lie upon the bed of ease*
> *With kind attentions blest.*

The island in 1826 had many buildings which were torn down before the start of the present century, but we have a fairly good idea of how they looked a hundred years ago. There was a large two-story dwelling house shaped like the letter L, a licensed tavern for the accommodation of those who arrived by sea. The keeper's family lived here and enjoyed the library of the tavern, which during the summer months contained newspapers and magazines from all over the United States. To the east of the dwelling house stood the small pox hospital, while off by itself, on a rise in the ground, the fever hospital faced the west. In front of the building was a fence, ten feet high and two hundred feet long, built to keep the sight of the graveyard from the victims at the hospital.

The Quarantine Station was moved from Rainsford's Island in 1849. Dr. Smith, who later became mayor of Boston, spent much of his time engraving historical facts and pert proverbs on rocks all over the island. He was not alone, however, for there are scores of other signatures and messages in many languages dating back to 1647. Perhaps the oldest signature is that of Raynsford, presumably written by the man himself. I have spent many days on the island trying to decipher the various inscriptions on both gravestones and rocks on the shore. On the southwestern bluff, between the fever hospital of 1832 and the graveyard, we find the following epitaph cut into a rock:

> *Nearby these gray rocks*
> *Enclos'd in a box*
> *Lies Hatter Cox*
> *Who died of smallpox.*

On the southeastern shore of the West Head there is a flat, sloping rock formation, in which scores of inscriptions have been chiseled. I have listed most of them, but realizing the reader may not share my enthusiasm, I include only a few:

> *Dr. T. Welch was here 26 yrs.*
> *Dr. J. V. C. Smith was appointed June 14, 1826*
> *C. P. Tewksbury was appointed Island Keeper in July, 1841*

Tewksbury met his death some years later when a bomb exploded at a Fourth of July celebration on Boston Common. This century-old Latin advice should interest the scholar.

> *Specta mantum, non frontem hominis, nam,*
> *Verumdecus, est, positum, in virtute.*
> *Insula Rupes. A.D. 1835.*

On this ledge we also read that the island was purchased from the Indians for a pig and a pullet. Walking around toward the western part of the bluff, we find engraved the following advice to the drunkard, which, judging from what I have seen in the past few years on the island, has not been noticed by all of the visitors:

> *[He] who violates sobriety*
> *Surely [will] never prosper.*
> *Brandy is Death's first turnkey,*
> *The tomb the tipler's early prison.*

Walking up from this spot into the graveyard, we find, besides the tombstones mentioned, many of interest to the thought-ful-minded individual. An inscription which is often seen on gravestones of the period is on the stone of Nancy Smith, who died August 20, 1802:

> *Behold and see as you pass by,*
> *As you are now, so once was I;*
> *As I am now, so you must be*
> *Prepare for death and follow me.*

Then there is the stone of Lieutenant Horace Stockton White who died on board the brig *Henrico* in 1812. He was one of the two sons of Moses White of Rutland, Massachusetts, both of whom met untimely deaths. His brother Francis was killed by Lieutenant William Finch in a duel at Noddle's Island in 1817.

Richard Henry Dana, in 1836, sailed by Hospital Island in the *Alert* on his way back from California. Dana looked down from the royal yard of his ship, seeing the "island, with its hospital buildings, nice graveled walks, and green plats."

After the Quarantine Station was changed to Deer Island in 1847, the state took over Rainsford's Island and established the Massachusetts almshouse there. When the Commonwealth changed its plans in 1866, Boston bought the island for $40,000, making it the site for the city almshouse. It was during this period that the Civil War veterans lived here. In 1882 they were removed to the Soldiers Home on Powder Horn Hill, Chelsea.

The first city overseer at the island was Captain Eben Seaver, who held the position until his death in 1879. The other overseers were Colonel Whiton, Colonel Underwood, and Captain Gerrish.

When the city of Boston purchased Long Island in 1882, the male paupers were taken across to Long Island from Rainsford's Island, and the female inmates from Austin Farm took their place. In 1895 the women at Rainsford's were also transferred to Long Island.

Before 1895, boys committed for misdemeanors were sent

to Deer Island for discipline, and lived there with the men and women prisoners. The boys were transferred to Rainsford's Island in 1895 where the juvenile department was reorganized.

The first superintendent was General M. T. Donohue, who died soon after the establishment was instituted. Lorenzo D. Perkins served from June 1895 until January 1899, and Sumner D. Seavey from October 1899 until 1910. The last superintendent was John J. Ryan, who was at Rainsford's Island from 1911 until the school was moved to the mainland. In 1906 the title "House of Reformation" was changed to "Suffolk School for Boys."

At three different times boys tried to escape from the Suffolk School between 1912 and 1918. On June 15, 1912, George Kelly, age 14, and 12-year-old Michael Bongrene set out from their prison home on the island in a canoe. They landed at Moon Head but were captured a short time later by the Quincy police.

The following year, at 10:15 p.m. on July 7, Arthur Allen, Frederick McGinley, and John Scully, all 13 years old, attempted a getaway. Throwing off their nightclothes, they plunged into the water and started to swim to Joe's Rock about 400 yards away. A cry for help was heard by the night watchman, but all that he discovered were the night clothes on the beach. The next morning John Scully was found at the house on Joe's Rock, or Quarantine Ledge, but the other two boys could not be located. On the 17th of July the body of Fred McGinley was taken from the water off Winthrop by a sailor aboard the *Bumpus*, a War Department boat. Arthur Allen's body was found a week later near Graves Light.

The great escape came on February 12, 1918, when the harbor was frozen solid around the island. Seven boys ran over the ice to freedom that morning, and six more followed them later in the day. As it was the first time in a quarter century that the harbor had been frozen over as far as Rainsford's Island, the boys made the best of this opportunity. Their freedom was short-lived as one by one they were captured and brought back.

The same month the "Greek Temple" burned to the ground, and the smaller boys located there had to be crowded in with the older children. Conditions became so unfavorable at the school that the authorities agreed not to spend the $150,000 needed for the new building. Plans were made by Commissioner Thomas C. O'Brien in January 1920 to abandon the school, which at this time had 126 boys. Commissioner O'Brien said that the boys would be transferred to Westboro and Shirley, but planned a gradual change, as the schools in those towns were crowded. The boys were removed from the island one by one, and no more commitments were allowed. By the last day of 1920 every boy was on the mainland and the school closed permanently.

Although many people have desired Rainsford's Island for a summer camp no definite action has been taken. The island was in the care of a watchman for some time, but now the officials at Long Island watch the property. Various boats have landed at the island year after year, and the enthusiasm for destruction, so evident at Governor's Island, has been continued at Elder Rainsford's old home. One by one the remaining buildings were burned until by 1934 there were only two structures left, the coal shed and the old stable. The coal shed was destroyed in a spectacular fire one August night in 1934. The blaze started about 9 p.m. and illuminated the entire area of Boston Harbor. Thousands tried to locate the source of the flames, causing traffic jams and fire alarms in both Hull and Winthrop. In the spring of 1935 the stable was gutted, so that now, for the first time in almost 300 years, Rainsford's Island is without a building worthy of the name. The graveyard, perhaps the loneliest in all Massachusetts, is the outstanding landmark of the island at the present time.

HINGHAM BAY

PEDDOCK'S ISLAND AND FORT ANDREWS

A MILE south of Fort Warren and a quarter mile from Windmill Point in Hull lies Peddock's Island, which has more shore line than any other island in the harbor. East Head is the present site of Fort Andrews, while the rest of the island is occupied by the various summer and winter residents. West Head faces Hough's Neck, and is a little more than half a mile from the Nut Island Pumping Station.

The earliest incident to be connected with Peddock's Island occurred some years before the Pilgrims landed at Plymouth. A French trading vessel was riding anchor off the shores of the island when the Indians massacred all the men except five whom they saved to exhibit around to the various tribes of Massachusetts.

Stark tells us that when a Captain Dermer was cruising around Cape Cod early in the seventeenth century, he found two of the Frenchmen still alive and took them away after paying a ransom. Captain Dermer asked the Indians why they had killed the other Frenchmen. The Indians were not able to give a satisfactory answer, and the Englishman said that the Gods would be angry with them. A short time afterwards the entire section was visited by a terrible plague, probably smallpox, and the redmen died by the hundreds. A reminder of this fatal sickness is still to be found at Nantasket, where Skull Head was so named because of the great number of unburied skeletons which the English settlers found at this spot.

During the Revolution Peddock's Island, together with so many others, was raided by the Continental troops for the sheep and cattle, five hundred sheep and thirty cattle being safely carried to the mainland. August 1776 saw many hundreds of the colonial militia organizations encamped at Peddock's Island ready to meet any effort of the British fleet to return to Boston Harbor. Since the English did not return, the soldiers later withdrew to the mainland for other duties. Two years later Count D'Estaing's battered French fleet took refuge in Boston Harbor, many of the marines landing on Peddock's Island. The legend has come down that these French marines constructed fortifications on East Head.

In 1844 the whole island, with the exception of Middle Hill and Prince's Head, was owned by Thomas Jones, the grandfather of Eliza A. J. H. Andrew, who was the wife of Governor Andrew of Massachusetts. In 1860 Miss Sally Jones was the owner of the property, but on her death it passed to Mrs. Andrew. Governor Andrew died, and in 1897 his widow gave the Government a quit-claim for the 88 acres needed for fortifications. Under General Orders Number 43, April 4, 1900, the post became officially known as Fort Andrews in honor of General Leonard Andrews, a Civil War hero. For many years Bostonians believed it had been named in honor of Governor Andrew, but of course they were in error.

Colonel S. C. Vestal was commander of the first garrison at Fort Andrews in May 1904. Under him were Lieutenant James E. Wyke and Post Surgeon Luke B. Peck.

During the fall of 1908, managers of the resorts on the island, the Y. O. West End House, and the Island Inn, were under suspicion for conducting gambling houses and similar establishments. As a result, on July 29, 1909, Chief of Police Reynolds of Hull arrested John Irwin, proprietor of the Island Inn. In the case which developed it was brought out that so-called Chinese picnics were the primary factor in bringing the action. A rather amusing part of the procedure was that at the time of his arrest John Irwin was Chief of Police at Peddock's Island. Irwin was let off with a slight fine, but activities were thereafter conducted in a more orderly fashion.

During the World War there were possibly 2,000 troops quartered at one time at Peddock's Island, mostly belonging to the original 55th Regiment and its subsequent replacements.

Fort Andrews became the headquarters for the 241st Regiment during World War II, with Colonel William D. Cottam in active residence there. Well loved by his soldiers, and admired by all who knew him, the colonel established a fine record for his regiment.

BUMPKIN ISLAND

Desiring to visit Round, or Bumpkin Island today, we pass through the swift waters of Hull Gut and continue in a southeasterly direction. The island cannot be confused with any other in Hingham Bay, as its 48 acres of sloping terrain with the yellow hospital building at the summit give it a distinctive appearance. Landing at the pier on the southern side of the island, we go up to the hospital building and look out over the Bay. Just across the Bay is Sunset Point in Nantasket, and off to the south lies Ragged Island and Crow Point. Little Sheep Island is due west, with the water tower at Fort Revere, Hull, off to the north.

Samuel Ward bought the island early in the seventeenth century, and his will, executed March 6, 1682, "gave the Island leying Betwixtt hingham and hull, called Bomkin Island unto the collidge; and my mind is that it be called By the name of wards Island." A year later he wrote that he wished it always to remain the property of Harvard College. The island was then appraised, and found to be worth 80 pounds.

It was valued in 1865 at $1200 and brought Harvard $50 a year, an amount which Shurtleff cleverly suggests "is fully equal to that yielded to Boston by the famous Franklin Medal Fund." Samuel Ward's daughter married a member of the Lobdell family of Hull; for many years the Lobdells lived on the island and paid rent to Harvard College.

The island passed from family to family, the acreage being used in the early part of the nineteenth century for drying fish, in addition to the usual farming. In 1879 the ruins of the old farm house could still be seen on the western side of the island, and an old wharf with rotten planks faced the channel. At this time, a well of excellent water was located near the wharf. Several stone walls which then crossed the property showed the extent to which the acreage had been farmed in olden times. Sweetser, in 1888, said Bumpkin Island was a "conspicuous, green dome, arabesqued with daises and thistle-tops."

Perhaps it was this description which first influenced Clarence Burrage in his search for an ideal island for the children's hospital which he planned. He was so pleased with this island that he leased it for five hundred years and arranged title to erect a hospital building on the highest point of land. The first load of lumber for the structure was delivered in September 1901; working as a deck hand on the lumber barge was John A. Glawson. When the barge was unloaded, Arthur Bemis, Secretary of the Hospital Association, stepped up to Glawson and asked him if he would like to work on the island. Glawson accepted and remained the caretaker for the rest of his life.

The hospital was ready for occupancy by July 1902, the first children then being admitted. Dr. Clarence Crane was the first physician in charge; the matron was Miss Bertha Carvell. Dr. Crane served for one year, after which he was succeeded by Dr. Thomas Strong. That year the hospital closed for the season in September, but Glawson stayed on with his wife during the long winter which followed. The wonderful work done by the Burrage organization will never be fully realized or appreciated; long summers on this delightful island did much to aid children in their battle to regain health. At one time as many as 145 children were registered and the hospital continued its work until the trumpets of war were heard.

In April 1917, Dr. Edgar, head physician at the Charlestown Navy Yard, visited Bumpkin Island and arranged that it should be used by the Navy for the duration of the war. Glawson was made watchman, sleeping on the sun porch with a shotgun for protection. The rumors concerning the German spies did not make his sleep a peaceful one, but soon the sailors began to arrive and regular guards were installed. Glawson enlisted in June 1917 and remained at the island in a semi-official capacity.

At this time numerous sailors from Boston landed at Bumpkin Island, building after building being erected to house them. At the peak during the year 1918 there were over 1300 sailors stationed here, quartered in 58 buildings.

After the Armistice, the buildings were gradually torn down and either taken off the island and rebuilt, or the material was sold to the highest bidder. Fifty-seven of the 58 buildings were removed and the great hospital once more stands alone, silhouetted against the sky line of Hingham Bay. After the war the island settled back to normal times, with Glawson once again becoming its head man.

Glawson made a splendid record in rescuing people from the sometimes turbulent waters of Boston Harbor. With 28 rescues to his credit, Glawson can be said to have as fine a record as any inhabitant of the islands of Boston Harbor. There are three which he remembered most vividly. The first occurred in June 1907, when Arthur Lane chose to sail from the Quincy Yacht Club at Hough's Neck in spite of the rough weather. Coming abeam of Bumpkin Island, his craft capsized and he was thrown into the water. Glawson rushed down to his boat, started the engine, and succeeded in reaching Lane before it was too late. The second rescue which Glawson described occurred in 1921, after a sailboat from Lynn was struck by a vivid bolt of lightning. He reached the occupants before the boat sank beneath the waves.

In Glawson's opinion, his most unusual rescue took place in 1911. He and George James were towing a dead horse to Spectacle Island, where the rendering plant was located. Passing a small boat, Glawson noticed there were five boys on board, and a moment later over she went. Glawson now had what might be termed a busy half hour trying to rescue the frightened boys from the overturned sailboat, with the dead horse still towing behind. James gave valuable assistance, and soon all were safe aboard the Glawson boat.

A rather unusual addition to the captain's stories was enacted on the afternoon of Sunday, May 19, 1935, when the writer was visiting Glawson and interviewing him on his rescues. As the captain was relating some of his many experiences, he happened to look out over the water, just in time to see a small sailboat tip over with two boys. After a race to the dock, the writer, piloted by Charles DeGaust, was able to reach the boys and bring them ashore. They were Willis H. Bagley and John Pepi of Quincy.

GRAPE ISLAND

During the Revolution, the island was owned by a prominent Tory of Hingham, Elisha Leavitt. Realizing that the British officers needed hay for their horses quartered in Boston, he sent word for them to come down to Grape Island and gather the hay. When the British arrived, the alarm went around the mainland; soon the South Shore minute men were on the job, and the Red Coats were forced back to their boats. This glorified skirmish, which occurred on May 21, 1775, has gone down in history as the battle of Grape Island.

The notorious Captain Smith settled on Grape Island shortly after the close of the Civil War, and his life history is one of the fascinating subjects of Hingham Bay. Smith's real name was Amos Pendleton. He was one of the striking characters of the last century, ruling Grape Island in true piratical style. This old sailor of a forgotten day took many thrilling yarns to his grave when he passed on. At the age of 19 he shipped aboard the *Golden Star*, a slaver bound for the West Indies. The ship was heavily armed, carrying 60 men and seven hundred slaves. One day the *Golden Star* encountered a British cruiser, the *Black Joke*, and after the flashing cutlasses were sheathed, the slaver had won a distinct victory. After such a life, it is no surprise to learn that he used to send bullets over the heads of any trespassers. There is one account of a man who was wounded by a shot from his gun. Mr. Pierce Buckley of the Boston Public Library once heard the old man's voice a mile away, warning trespassers off the premises. But Amos Pendleton, alias Captain Smith, grew old and feeble, giving up his home in 1892. He died in the Hingham Poor House in 1897 at the age of 92.

The care of the island until 1901 was in the hands of a mysterious gentleman whose name we must omit, as it is understood he had committed a serious crime in Boston. Because of a murder he retreated down the harbor to avoid capture. When this gentleman moved to the mainland, Captain Billy McLeod and his wife became the caretakers of the island and lived there 34 years.

One day as Billy McLeod was strolling along the beach he found a tiny baby seal which he took into the house. The seal soon became attached to the family, and in a few weeks was performing feats of unusual agility. In the morning it flipped its way down to the shore, took a swim, and then returned to the house. It learned to knock three times with its flippers as a signal that it wished to enter the house. Once inside, it made a straight line for the stove, behind which a little box had been placed. Here the seal remained until suppertime. After supper Captain McLeod put a little rug in the box, whereupon the seal yawned in a knowing manner and curled up on the rug for the night. Whenever the captain returned from Boston, the seal swam out to meet him and climbed into the boat for the ride back. The little seal died from eating green paint, and many children who had visited the pet mourned its death. Captain Billy said that although he had owned many dogs since then, there never was an animal as affectionate as his little seal.

One of the queer tales of the island is that of the gold mine. Over twenty years ago Billy McLeod discovered a woman and two men digging a deep pit on the other side of the island. When he ordered them to stop, they told him they were digging for gold. The woman professed to be a clairvoyant who had dreamed of gold buried on Grape Island. Whether or not they were the same people who dug for the treasure at Castle Island in 1911 is an interesting conjecture. When Captain Billy first told me the story, he said, with a twinkle in his eye, that the only gold found on the island was out on the flats where hundreds and thousands of bushels of clams have been dug throughout the years. Even the Indians knew the secret of the real treasure of Grape Island, and countless tomahawks have been found in the piles of clamshells they left behind.

Billy McLeod was stone deaf due to an accident while sailing in the outer harbor; the only manner in which we could convey our thoughts to him was by writing our message. In 1934 we visited here with a friend, Thomas Johnson of Winthrop. By various notes Johnson had found out that Billy McLeod was a former member of the South Boston Yacht Club, and he wrote out a question asking McLeod if he had ever met the great fighter, John L. Sullivan. "Never heard of him," was McLeod's astonishing rejoinder, whereupon I struck the well-known attitude the boxer usually assumed while posing for a picture. "Ah," cried McLeod, "you mean John L.   I saw him many a time."

Another of Captain Billy's stories was about his wonderful Toulouse geese. These birds grew so smart that they would swim in and out around the smelt fishermen anchored in the Bay, asking for bait! McLeod did a wonderful business selling bait to the fisherman at the height of the smelting years. Around 1912 there were hundreds of fishing boats of all descriptions anchored all the way out past Boston Light.

Captain William McLeod passed away on February 28, 1935, shortly after a tragic accident which occurred while he and Mrs. McLeod were walking over the ice to the mainland. Hundreds of members of the Massachusetts Bay yacht clubs will remember this delightful old couple who were so hospitable during their 34 years at historic Grape Island.

SHEEP ISLAND

In Hingham Bay between Peddock's Island on the north and Grape Island on the south lies Sheep Island, owned by F. L. Bicknell of Weymouth. It is occupied in summer and fall as a residence and hunting lodge.

Sheep Island has been given many names. In the *Gentleman's Magazine* for 1775 it is called Sun Island. Another chart 16 years before called it Shean Island, while Dearborn's Map of 1865 locates it with the title Sheaf Island. Mr. Bicknell would perhaps be surprised to know that a very pretentious chart made about 1780 leaves out his property altogether, while including such comparatively insignificant ledges as Quarantine Rocks and Sunken Ledge. Still another name by which it was known was Ship Island.

Perhaps the most striking feature the visitor notices are the giant decoys on the beach. The gunning on the island has of late been conspicuous by its absence. But in spite of the lack of birds we can say, along with the poet Thomas Dibden:

> *"Oh, it's a snug little island!*
> *A right little, tight little, island."*

SLATE ISLAND

A mile to the southeast of Sheep Island, and just to the west of Grape Island lies Slate Island, the quarry of the Puritan fathers. The Massachusetts Bay Records for October 16, 1650 mention the grant of this island to William Torrey, but the public was allowed to use the slate. Although twelve acres here have furnished hundreds of tons of slate, the quarry is seldom used at present. Around 1840 it was the home of a mysterious hermit who lived here for many years. Very little is known of this recluse who chose the wilds of Slate Island in preference to life with his fellow men.

The only building on the island today is an old duck preserve which is now rapidly going to pieces.

RACCOON ISLAND

Three hundred yards off the eastern shore of Hough's Neck lies Raccoon Island. It was owned early in the eighteenth century by Edward Capin, but little of its history is known. Every year the Stigmatine Fathers, the present owners of the property, conduct their summer school on the island. The little chapel is very active from late June until early September. The 2600 feet of shore line are guarded by two giant dogs who are quite successful in keeping the island peaceful and quiet for the study of the Scriptures.

THE HINGHAM HARBOR ISLANDS

Sailing the route of the famous Hingham Packet of years gone by, we pass down Hingham Bay, slip by Samuel Ward's old Bumpkin Island, then past Crow Point, and find ourselves in Hingham Harbor. Four pleasant islands dot this little bay, the first to be visited being Ragged Island. This isle, together with Sarah's and Langley's, at one time belonged to the intrepid Captain Langlee. All three islands are delightful to visit. With its many coves and inlets Ragged Island is appropriately named.

In 1880 there was a fine observation platform at one end of the property. The island is seldom used today except by the occasional yachtsman. A bridge once connected it with the mainland.

Passing across the narrow channel we reach the shore of Langley's Island. The Langleys of Hingham are mentioned in the Massachusetts Bay Records for February 1685. This island contains the same geological formation as Ragged Island, and in very early times was known as Ibrook's Island. It is a beautiful spot, thanks to the excellent taste of the man who made extensive plantings here in the early nineties. Due south of Langley's Island lies Sarah's Island.

There is an interesting legend concerning these three islands situated close together in Hingham Harbor. Mrs. Sarah Derby, according to the story, lived as a ragged young girl on the islands mentioned. When she grew older, they came to be called in her honor, Ragged Island, Sarah's Island and Langley's Island. It is a pretty story, but unfortunately a chart of the Harbor made in 1700 clearly shows that the islands went by those names at the turn of the century, while Sarah Derby was not born until 1714.

About a third of a mile away lies Button Island, close to the site of the old pier where the Hingham packets used to tie up after their long trips from Boston. In spite of extensive research, the writer has been unable to find anything of importance concerning this small island. It has a few trees and shrubs but is so small that no one has considered it except for picnicking. Made of felsite diorite, it was brought to the surface due to faults in the earth's structure.

FORT DUVALL, LITTLE HOG ISLAND

Little Hog Island is the last to be discussed in this chapter. Although at the present time it is owned by the Federal Government, it was at one time the place where old ships, having outlived their usefulness, were broken up. Henry David Thoreau believed the whole island was "gently lapsing into futurity," and said that "this isle has got the very form of a ripple." When Sweetser visited the island in 1882 there were two wrecks on the beach where "myriads of spiders, large and small have carefully woven their silken webs across every corner."

Fort Duvall is a masterpiece of engineering, but military regulations forbid revealing information on the subject. Thus we complete our summary of the islands of Hingham Bay and start on our trip across the harbor.

THE OUTER HARBOR

GEORGE'S ISLAND — FORT WARREN

THE activity George's Island saw between 1861 and 1865 was varied and spectacular with soldiers, prisoners, and even ghosts figuring in the events of the period. Hundreds of soldiers who trained at Fort Warren left the island never to return; over one thousand Confederates were imprisoned in the walls of this historic old fortress. Many attempts at escape were made here, none of which, as far as is known, was completely successful. This fort was the prison of Mason and Slidell in 1861, and four years later held Alexander Stephens in captivity.

Going back to the days before the Puritans arrived in Boston Harbor, we find that James Pemberton owned George's Island, moving there in 1628.

Pemberton's Island then passed into the possession of Governor John Leverett, whose will mentions the island as being in the occupation of Benjamin Worthylake. After the death of John Leverett, his heirs wished to sell Pemberton's Island, so paid the principal and interest on the mortgage to obtain a clear title, and in 1725 received from Samuel Greenleaf the equivalent of $5,000.

Thirteen years later Greenleaf died, his wife Hannah becoming owner of what was by this time definitely known as George's Island. John George, whose father lost his life shortly after the Andros episode, was a tenant around the first part of the century and is the man for whom the island is named.

When Hannah died in 1765, Elisha Leavitt, the famous Hingham Tory, bought the island at auction. He bequeathed George's Island in 1790 to his grandson Caleb Rice. In 1825 Rice, who also owned Gallop's and Lovell's, sold Lovell's Island and George's Island for $6,000 to the city of Boston, which transferred them at once to the Federal Government.

Having covered the various changes of ownership of James Pemberton's island, let us go back to the day in 1690 when Samuel Sewall and a group of officers went down the Harbor to George's Island. This party of dignitaries from Boston watched the English flotilla maneuver in the Road and observed the muster held on the island itself. The fleet later sailed away under Sir William Phips to participate in the disastrous expedition against Canada.

Frederick W. A. S. Brown wrote the following stanzas about George's Island shortly after his visit in the spring of 1819:

> *Of George's Isle; oh muse, now speak,*
> *Whose lofty southern shore*
> *Secures a ship from whirlwinds bleak,*
> *Until the storm is o'er.*

On September 13, 1832, the Government began the survey of the island and the following April started work on a fort there. It was this year, 1833, which saw the changing of the name Fort Warren from the fortifications at Governor's Island to the present works at George's Island.

Peter Peregrine sailed by Fort Warren July 30, 1838. The workmen had already been laboring five years when he made his trip, and their results shown on the island so impressed him that he said it suggested a sort of "Ocean Thermopylae, where a small band of Boston Yankees would as triumphantly beat back the navy of Great Britain as did the 'Immortal Three Hundred' the myriads of Xerxes." In making a comparison between Fort Warren and the Rock of Gibraltar, he thought that the fortress on George's Island commanded the entrance to Boston Harbor far more effectively than the famous rock controlled the entrance to the Mediterranean Sea.

A few years later, another observer set down his impressions after a visit to Fort Warren. James Lloyd Homer, one of the early contributors to the *Boston Post,* wrote under the

pseudonym of the "Shade of Alden." He first visited the island
with a "matrimonial party" from Weymouth in August 1845.
We quote from the survey he made of the fort at that time.

"As far as the fort is finished, it is probably the most
magnificent piece of masonry in this or in any other country . . . The dry-dock at Charlestown is a splendid piece of
workmanship, but it bears no comparison to the fort at
George's Island, the foundation walls of which are twelve
feet thick, and the superstructure eight . . . The fronts are
neatly hammered and the workmanship is as even and as
perfect as it possibly can be."

Homer's story of his visit to the semi-subterranean prison
is the most interesting part of the account of his trip to Fort
Warren. Let us accompany him on his journey of 99 years
ago. Starting at the parapets:

"You descend a long flight of stone steps. Having
touched the ground, you walk about forty feet, and then
turn to the left, when you find yourself in the 'prison-
house' of the fort, which extends, through several apartments or sections, a distance of over one hundred feet,
and is capable of accommodating one thousand prisoners,
if we should ever have as many in New England, which
is at least problematical—unless the foul fiends disunion
and insurrection should raise their bloody and unsightly
crests on the soil of the Pilgrims."

These words were written over 15 years before the actual
outbreak of hostilities, but the rooms through which he travelled
that day really held hundreds of Confederate soldiers during
the Civil War. The stairway which the "Shade of Alden" used
to enter the prison dungeons has been walled up forever, and
the only entrance today is through a small carronade embrasure
reached by ladder from outside the walls of the fort. In our
discussion of the "Lady in Black" we shall again mention the
quarters visited by James Lloyd Homer so long ago.

An interested visitor to Fort Warren landed from the 42-

ton sloop *General Warren* on October 13, 1853, after a run of one hour. Thomas Kelah Wharton, who was later to assist Beauregard in the construction of the great New Orleans Custom House, was met at the pier by Sylvanus Thayer himself. A few lines from the diary of Wharton follow:

"We sallied forth to explore the fortifications—and first took the circuit of the outer parapet, rising to the height of 69 feet above tide water, enclosing an area of about 12 acres, and faced with Granite, beautifully cut, and jointed, and 8 feet in thickness. On this exposed elevation the wind tried hard to rob us of our hats and cloaks, but it was so pure and healthy I should have been sorry had there been less of it. We descended one of the exquisitely cut spiral staircases to the 'Quarters'."

We now approach the time of the break between the North and the South, the days when Fort Warren saw more action than any other fortress in all New England. With the start of the war in April 1861, the Government made a hasty examination of the harbor defenses and was not at all reassured by the condition of the armament at Fort Warren. When Governor John Albion Andrew visited George's Island, it was said the salute due him had to be postponed until the soldiers could find enough ammunition to fire it off. It was later claimed that the *Alabama* could easily have run the gauntlet of Fort Warren and Castle Island to drop a few shells on Beacon Hill.

With the war came many patriotic songs and hymns, and Fort Warren was the birthplace of the greatest of them all. The famous Yankee song, *John Brown's Body*, was the product of the 2nd Infantry, or Tiger Battalion, and came into being while the men were quartered at George's Island. The Battalion, composed of four companies under the command of Major Ralph Newton, arrived at Fort Warren April 29, 1861.

When they landed at the island, the members of the "Tigers" found great heaps of earth lying around inside the parade ground, and it was made clear to the men that their first job would be to put the fortress into proper shape for military occupancy.

Singing seemed to be the best way for the men to pass their time while working with the pick and shovel, and all the popular songs of the day echoed and reechoed across the parade ground. After the work for the day was completed, the boys and men gathered together in the casements and sang far into the night. A really fine chorus was the result. Religious hymns were just as popular as secular songs, and the favorite hymn sung at the fort grew to be *Say, Brothers, Will You Meet Us?* The music itself was very tuneful, and the effect of scores of husky voices swinging into the air of their favorite song was remarkable. From this hymn, sung time and time again, came the tune chosen by the composers of *John Brown's Body.*

The story of the manner in which the words were written and put to music is interesting. The man who led the raid on Harper's Ferry in 1859 had a Scotch namesake in the Tiger Battalion. John Brown always joined in the fun at the fort, and when it was realized that he had the same name as the abolitionist hanged near Harper's Ferry, the others lost no time in making him the object of their fun. Whenever he chanced to be a few minutes later than the rest at one of their gatherings, they told him to arrive on time if he wished to release the slaves. At another time he was told that he couldn't be John Brown, for John Brown's body was mouldering in the grave. The same line of chatter was continued week after week, and it was soon the custom to ask, "Is that so?" when answering a statement concerning John Brown. John Brown, the Scotchman, helped compose the song with Newton Pernette, J. E. Greenleaf, C. S. Hall, and C. B. Marsh all active in its preparation. Mr. Hall actually published the song in May 1861.

While the song, *John Brown's Body*, was still in its infancy, the 12th Massachusetts Regiment, commanded by Fletcher Webster, came to Fort Warren. In a short time the tune was known by the whole regiment, having spread from company to company. The Brigade Band had been coming down to the island to play for the soldiers many Sundays, and in some manner the band leader had obtained a copy of the melody. One Sunday night the regiment and the battalion were scheduled for a joint dress parade, and as the band swung into line the musicians electrified the gathering by striking up *John Brown's Body.*

This was the first time the song was ever played by a military band. Shortly afterward the government notified the Tiger Battalion that only organizations of ten companies or over could be accepted for active service at the front, and so the soldiers disbanded and returned to the city May 25, 1861. Many of the men, however, now joined the 12th and John Brown and Newton Pernette were among them. When the 11th and 14th Regiments came to the fort, they also enjoyed singing the song even after the Tigers had left the island.

July 18, 1861, the Webster Regiment, as it was called, visited Boston for a grand review and was met at the dock by the 2nd Battalion. While marching up State Street, the band struck up the tune of *John Brown's Body,* and every man in the line joined in. The effect was startling, and the crowds watching the parade were greatly impressed by the swing of the tune. The regiment caused a sensation in New York, arousing the populace with the stirring rhythm of the new song.

When the 14th Regiment left Fort Warren and went to Washington, Abraham Lincoln and Julia Ward Howe visited the camp of the Massachusetts soldiers. The stirring strains of *John Brown's Body* so moved Lincoln that he asked Julia Ward Howe to compose a hymn from the tune. *The Battle Hymn of the Republic* was her inspired answer.

The crowds went wild everywhere when they heard the magical strains of *John Brown's Body,* and the melody soon reached the far corners of the Union. The great value and inspiration it was to the Northern troops will probably never be fully realized. On June 6, 1862, John Brown, the Scotchman, then serving with the Massachusetts Volunteers, went to his death in the Shenandoah River, Virginia. Thus passed the man who was indirectly responsible for the greatest marching song of the Civil War.

Early in the autumn of 1861 Colonel Justin E. Dimmick arrived from Fortress Munroe to take charge at Fort Warren. He had saved Fortress Munroe for the North, but because of his advancing years was sent to George's Island and the quieter life of New England. A temporary garrison was detailed from the 24th Massachusetts Infantry to prepare for the hundreds of prisoners expected at the fort.

December 2, 1861, Major Francis J. Parker assumed command of the 1st Battalion with Charles K. Cobb, Adjutant, and George W. Pearson, Quartermaster. At this time, guard duty was the most important item, as there were over eight hundred prisoners on the island. The daily detail consisted of 75 men, some of whom guarded the space where the prisoners were allowed to exercise. At retreat, the sentinels went inside the casemates. A picket line entirely surrounded the outside of the fort, with guards also at the sally port, the staircases, and the postern gate.

When the Massachusetts men were going through Baltimore on their way to battle, several were killed by shots from the crowd. Scores of politicians were arrested, taken to Fort Lafayette, and later moved on the *State of Maine* to Fort Warren. Among the political prisoners taken to George's Island was Lawrence Sangston, a former member of the Maryland Legislature. He had been confined with over one hundred other Southern civilians at Fort Lafayette. Accompanied by several hundred Confederate soldiers, the political prisoners had sailed for Fort Warren, arriving late at night on October 31, 1861. In his diary Sangston shows much of the war-time bitterness evidenced by both sides during the conflict.

The next morning Sangston arose early and began to realize that the prisoners were going to be accorded better treat-

RAYMOND HANSON

GARRISON AT FORT WARREN, WINTER 1940

NIX'S MATE ISLAND

WHERE THE BODIES OF PIRATES WERE STRUNG UP IN CHAINS

CONFEDERATE PRISONERS AT FORT WARREN

A DIVE FROM
MINOT'S LIGHT

JOHN ALBION ANDREW

DESCRIBED ON PAGE 53

DONALD McKAY AND THE WORLD'S FASTEST CLIPPER, THE LIGHTNING

ment than they had received at Fort Lafayette. "The officers appear to understand their position," he tells us, and goes on to express his delight with the speed in which the supplies ordered from Boston were received. Later in the day a driving northeast snowstorm set in during which the men were forced to stay inside the casemates. At the same time, miles out in Massachusetts Bay, the luckless square-rigger *Maritana* was plunging through ever-increasing seas which were to send her to her doom on Shag Rocks before the next sunrise. Sangston's last entry for the day is significant:

> "Storm increasing, fearful night for ships on the coast; at times the wind would whistle through the case-mate windows equal to the shrill whistle of a locomotive engine, and after listening an hour to the howling of the storm, and the waves breaking over the rocks, went to sleep."

The next day was Sunday, and at ten o'clock the gale ceased. Several of the North Carolina prisoners who were allowed to walk along the ramparts returned to Sangston's quarters with the fearful news of a marine tragedy near Boston Light. It was the *Maritana* which had piled up on Shag Rocks in the blinding storm early that morning. The North Carolina soldiers reported that they had seen the nude body of a woman being recovered from the spit of sand which runs from Greater Brewster Island.

The following week, Colonel Pegram, aided by Captain De Lagnel and Charles H. Pitts, took his turn at running the mess operated by the wealthier prisoners. This was the week Sangston received a large package from home containing liquor of various assortments. Colonel Dimmick permitted him to keep the liquor, advising him to use the same in a judicious manner. His friends were all suddenly seized with anxiety about Sangston's health which could only "be relieved by per-sonal inquiry."

We are told that Colonel Bradford, who was captured at

Hatteras Inlet and taken to Fort Warren, was one of the officers under Sylvanus Thayer, the master engineer who constructed the fort at George's Island. The irony of the situation caused much comment.

In spite of the many storms at the island and regardless of the strain under which the prisoners lived, there were many enjoyable days at the fort. Sangston's diary gives us a fine account of life in the casemates:

> "At half-past four, when we leave the parade ground and retire to our rooms, and the sentinels are drawn into our door, I trim and light my lamp, and prepare my writing table for those who wish to write, or read in quiet, leaving the front room for conversation, and the backgammon players, the only game we have, as there are not enough card players among us to make up a game; at ten o'clock, I brew a pitcher of hot whiskey punch, which we sip until eleven; Colonel Pegram, the only one among us who does not partake of the punch, gives us some very fine music from his guitar, and we put out the light and go to bed."

The first rumors regarding Mason and Slidell reached Fort Warren the twenty-third of November. Later in the chapter we shall discuss with more detail the Trent affair in which they participated. The two Confederate Commissioners arrived on November 24, 1861, and were quartered in the front room of Quarters Number Seven, adjacent to the small room Sangston was then occupying. Their secretaries, McFarland and Eustis, were also quartered with the commissioners. McFarland had an excellent voice, and would sing to the accompaniment of his guitar. The last entry for November 27, 1861, reads:

> "Colonel Pegram and Mr. McFarland entertained us with some fine singing and music on the guitar, which they continued long after the lights were put out, and we went to bed."

Colonel Pegram became the famous General John Pegram after his exchange, and was killed in a battle near Petersburg.

Another Southern prisoner, John M. Brewer, was confined in the cellar apartments. Brewer kept a diary of his trials and hardships in the New England bastile and his description of a night on the jail beds in the cellar apartments is of interest. "When we arose in the morning, the flesh of those who occupied these beds presented the appearance of checker boards," he tells us in his diary. The next night Captain Tansill, a cellmate, spread several newspapers on the bare stone floor, asserting that he could sleep better on the floor than on the "damned gridiron" he occupied the night before. Sangston records the release and departure of Mr. Brewer on December 2.

A great gale lashed the island December 28 preventing the Boston boat from landing, and the day seemed long without fresh reading matter. Sangston, however, was soon to have a surprise. The very next day Colonel Dimmick informed him that he was to be given a thirty-day leave from Fort Warren. Mason and Slidell also received word of their coming release the same day. The Confederate Commissioners left the island January first, followed by Lawrence Sangston the next day. The waves were so rough when Sangston left Fort Warren that he had to jump onto the boat when she slid by the dock, and his baggage was thrown after him. His thirty-day leave was later extended, and he never saw Fort Warren again.

The whole world trembled when the Trent affair took place, as the incident could easily have thrown England and America into their third great conflict. Let us discuss the events which led to the final release from Fort Warren of the two Confederate Commissioners.

James Murray Mason and John Slidell had been appointed Confederate Commissioners to England and France, but because the Southern ports were blockaded, had to make special arrangements for reaching Europe. They slipped out of Charleston one rainy night on the blockade runner *Theodora*, bound for

Nassau. Landing at Nassau, they found arrangements could not be made for direct passage to Europe, so they continued on to Havana where passage was obtained on the British mail steamer *Trent*, bound for England. On November 8 they were stopped on the high seas by Commander Wilkes of the United States sloop-of-war *San Jacinto*. After some discussion Mason and Slidell were forcibly removed to the American vessel, accompanied by their two secretaries, James McFarland and George Eustis.

Receiving orders direct from Washington, Captain Wilkes brought the men to Fort Warren, where they were landed at the dock Sunday, November 24. Not expecting them so soon, Colonel Dimmick was in church, but quickly went out to receive the party. Nine North Carolina officers were turned out of their quarters to make room for the commissioners. The floor was carpeted, and the room furnished in a very suitable manner.

International law was a favorite topic during the stay of the four men, and Mason predicted almost exactly the date when the United States would release them. Late in December President Lincoln gave special orders for their freedom, to take effect January 1, 1862. Because of the disturbance a few weeks before when some other prisoners had been released, Colonel Dimmick took steps to insure a silent departure when the commissioners should leave the fort.

January 1, 1862 proved to be a stormy day with great seas sweeping around the island. The wharf was under water at high tide, and, when the Confederate party left the dock on a small tugboat, there was some doubt as to whether they would reach Provincetown in safety. But the tug *Starlight* transferred its cargo in Provincetown harbor to the British 16-gun man-of-war *Rinaldo* and returned to Boston. Thus Fort Warren saw the last of "lean dyspeptic" Slidell and "portly, jovial" Mason.

A sailor, Keene by name, who had enlisted in the United States Navy for the purpose of blowing up the frigate *Congress*, was taken to Fort Warren and imprisoned in a "horrible little triangular dungeon" in the casemates. He stayed at the island many months, refusing to sign the oath of allegiance, and probably was not released until after the war ended.

A terrible winter was experienced by the soldiers during the first year of the Civil War. The parade ground frequently froze over and was more suitable for a skating rink than for its original purpose. The dress parades naturally had to be omitted under such conditions, and guard mountings took place in the casemates. Parker tells us in his *32nd Regiment* that the marching of the relief over the glare ice against a high wind did not exactly convey the impression of a precise military movement. One day a soldier was whirled along across the entire area and brought up with a crash against the granite wall. These wintry scenes must have been thrilling and terrible experiences to the North Carolina prisoners, who probably remembered for the rest of their lives the winter spent in Boston Harbor.

With the coming of spring in 1862 there seemed to be a general feeling in the North that the war was practically finished. May 1 saw the battalion reviewed by Governor Andrew. Commander F. J. Parker was so sure that the war would soon be over that he resigned the day after the review, returning to private life. Captain Stephenson was now put in charge of the battalion. But the news soon came that Banks had been driven down the Shenandoah Valley and Washington was being menaced by forces under the great Stonewall Jackson.

Parker was at once recalled and put in charge of the new 32nd Regiment, formerly the 1st Battalion. He arrived at Fort Warren an hour after midnight Monday, May 26; within thirty minutes the entire fort was aroused, and the news was travelling about that the six hundred men there would soon start for the front. At noon Monday the regiment was relieved and marched out of the main sally port for the last time, anxious for the realities of battle. The men embarked on the ferryboat *Daniel Webster*, shouting their farewells to good old Colonel Dimmick as the boat pulled away from the dock. What a picture it was as the ferryboat churned its way up the channel with every man singing the *John Brown* chorus to the accompaniment of the drums corps. Thus they left Fort Warren to the Boston and Salem Cadets. But one man did come back, long after the scars of war had healed—Francis J. Parker, who revisited Fort Warren in 1874.

The entry into the service of three units of Massachusetts Volunteer Militia can be closely tied up with this Shenandoah Valley scare. They were the New England Guards, the Salem Cadets and the First Corps Cadets, all of whom saw service at Fort Warren. The New England Guards stayed at the island less than a week, but the Boston and Salem Cadets had many weeks of duty at historic Fort Warren.

On the 27th of May, 1862, the Independent Corps of Cadets, sometimes called the Boston Cadets and often designated as the First Corps Cadets, was called out for active service by Governor Andrew. Hastily assembling at their old armory opposite the Granary Burying Grounds, the cadets formed in line and marched to Long Wharf where they boarded the boat for Fort Warren.

After a sail down the harbor they landed at George's Island, meeting Colonel Dimmick at the dock. Dimmick was greatly surprised at the fine red and grey uniforms the men wore and wondered what type of military organization it was that could have a colonel, an adjutant, and two majors in a total membership of slightly over one hundred. The Boston Cadets soon discarded their showy but then unpopular grey uniforms for the blue of the army.

There was one incident which served to break the monotony of guard duty. One stormy night the commander called together the guardsmen and warned them especially to watch for attempts at escape, ordering the men to shoot if anyone did not answer their challenge. Private James H. Ellison of Waltham was patrolling the shore line during the blustering storm with his usual careful vigilance when suddenly he thought he detected a man swimming in the water. He challenged the shadow. There was no answer. The waves hid the form for a moment, but there it was again, unmistakably outlined in the water. Once more he challenged, and fired just as the head came up with the water running off the man's shoulders. The fortress stirred at the sound of the gun, and poor Ellison soon saw, with the receding tide, that the "man" was merely a rock gradually being exposed by the ebbing water. He was teased by the prisoners at the fort for some time to come, but as was later proved, other sentinels could have profited by Ellison's cautiousness.

The rats at the fort must be mentioned. They were in complete charge of the casemates at night, and their tails, according to the men, were as large as a man's little finger. They were a great nuisance, and a certain member of the Corps had occasion to remember them for many years to come. This soldier, who had been given permission to spend the day in the city, returned to the fort on the afternoon boat, his hair slicked down with barber's oil. Weary from his holiday in the city, he retired early and dreamed that night of countless mosquitoes stinging his head, but he did not awaken. The next morning when the drumbeat aroused the fort, the young cadet jumped out of bed to find his hair neatly removed. The rats, greedy for the barber's oil, had mowed his head as smoothly as could be desired, and the poor soldier was bald for the rest of his days.

The First Corps Cadets left Fort Warren in July 1862, and Colonel Dimmick went down to the pier to see the men off. This grand old army man expressed his thanks to the men for their work in putting Fort Warren in order for war. He concluded by saying he was genuinely sorry to see them go, and the boat left the pier.

There were many notable prisoners confined at Fort Warren during the war. George Proctor Kane, the Baltimore chief of police, had been sent north after the famous riots in that city. After his release, Kane became Mayor of Baltimore and died in 1878 while in office.

General Lloyd Tilghman of South Carolina was also incarcerated in the casemates at Warren. An officer in the Dragoon Regiment, he had been decorated for bravery at Palo
Alto. Tilghman was released in the summer of 1862, and met
his death before a year had elapsed while fighting on the Mississippi River.

Commodore Barron, an Annapolis graduate, had been
captured at Cape Hatteras. He also was released in the exchange
and went to England where he superintended the building of the
famous blockade runners. Another compulsory guest at Fort
Warren was General Henry R. Jackson, a Yale graduate. He
had been prominent in the diplomatic service as Minister to
Vienna. After joining the Confederate forces, he became Briga-
dier-General, and later was captured with his entire command
at Nashville. Jackson was then sent to Fort Warren as a prisoner
of war. Twenty years after peace was signed he was the Minister to Mexico.

The capture of two Confederate warships in June 1863,
was the first step in a dramatic incident which aroused all New
England two months later. The Confederate battleship *Tacony*
was taken on the 27th of June, while the *Atlanta* had been captured by the *U.S.S. Weehauken* ten days earlier. The officers
and crew of the two captured ships were taken to Fort Warren
where they were practically forgotten until a daring escape on
the night of August 19, 1863, excited New England.

Lieutenant Joseph W. Alexander of the *Atlanta* was the
first to discover the exit which was later used in the thrilling
escape from Fort Warren. One day he was standing in the
pump room under the quarters where the men lived, looking
through the loophole at the grass on the cover face. The thought
occurred to him that it might be possible to squeeze through the
seven-inch musketry loophole. He climbed up into the opening
and was pleased to find that he could push his head through the
slit. As his clothing prevented him from getting his body out,
he removed his outer garments, and tried again. This time he

was gratified to find that he could squeeze through the aperture. Being small in stature, as is shown by his picture, he realized that only men of slight build would be able to escape by this method.

After telling the others of the discovery, he found there were only three men in the quarters who were able to go through the opening. They were Captain Charles W. Reed, who had been commander of the *Tacony* at the time of its capture, Lieutenant James Thurston of the *Atlanta*, and Major Reid Saunders, a quartermaster in the Confederate army.

On Sunday night, August 16, 1863, they made an attempt to escape. A wild northeaster was blowing, and the night was very dark. After tying together the rope from their canvas bags, they lowered themselves out of the loopholes and were soon on the floor of the dry moat with their cans and demijohns safe in the grass. Less than seventy feet away at the main sally port stood the sentry, unaware that four prisoners were escaping. The quartet cautiously made their way up the inner surface of the coverface and quietly slipped down the outer slope. At the foot of their descent was a small thicket, where they hid to plan the escape from the island itself.

After carefully surveying the situation, they made their way across the open space in the direction of a wooden target which stood on the beach a few rods from the thicket. Although the sentries were carefully patrolling the section, Alexander had a plan for passing the lines. He noticed that the soldiers walked toward each other until they met, then, turning abruptly, would walk in the opposite direction. Alexander believed they could slip by the sentries, one by one, while the soldiers were walking away from each other. This scheme worked successfully, and the four men reached the beach where the wooden target was located. They planned to tie the bottles, planks, and cans to the target, push it off into the water, and swim their way across the Narrows until they reached Lovell's Island. Alexander knew of a fine sailboat belonging to Mr. Barber pulled up on the beach

at Lovell's Island, a half mile away. Placing the oddly decorated target into the water, the four men jumped in and bravely
started kicking their way across what was then the main ship
channel.

The four men became so benumbed and confused by the
combination of water, wind, and huge waves, that they gave up
the unequal struggle after a half-hour's battle and let the ocean
push them back on the beach. Putting the target back into place,
they were successful in returning to their quarters without discovery. Some of the other prisoners, hearing rumors of the four
men's escapade, were inclined to doubt the story, but when one
smart midshipman noticed their wet clothing and tasted the
salty cloth, the others were convinced.

The next day the four men formulated plans for a release
which they hoped would be successful. If two strong swimmers
could be found in some of the other quarters, they reasoned, the
pair could swim across to Lovell's Island, get the sailboat, and
sail it back to the fort where the four officers would board it.
Two prisoners were found who claimed to be good swimmers:
N. B. Pryde of the *Tacony*, and Thomas Sherman, formerly a
sailor in the United States navy. They were given full instructions, and everything was in readiness for the next try for freedom. When the night of August 19 began dark and threatening,
every prisoner knew the break would be attempted. At about
9:15 the four men started to climb out of the casemates. All
was quiet until Alexander inadvertently knocked over a bottle,
which crashed onto the granite floor with a noise that he feared
must have been heard by the guard at the main sally port. There
was a challenge from the sentry; the prisoners shivered. Alexander looked over at the bridge and found it was merely an
officer passing into the sally port. Because of the rising west
wind, the crash of the bottle had not been heard. With great
relief the four men now climbed down into the moat and made
for the meeting-place at the top of the demilune. Pryde and
Sherman were waiting for them, having successfully escaped

from their part of the bastion.

It was then agreed that Reed and Saunders should wait in the shelter of the demilune while the four others would make their way down to the shore. Evading the sentries by the same method as before, the four men reached the beach. The two swimmers stripped off their clothing, and after a word of farewell, plunged into the dark waters. That farewell, as far as can be discovered, comprised the last words ever spoken by the men, as no trace of them has been found to this day.

When the two men failed to return, Reed and Saunders joined Thurston and Alexander. These men, desperate in their disappointment, agreed to take the target out again while Reed and Saunders were to stay behind to wait for the other two to return in the sailboat. Placing the target in the water, the two men were soon kicking their way in the general direction of Lovell's Island. Perhaps the wind had changed, possibly the tide had turned—no matter—they were successful in reaching their goal. Walking along the beach at Lovell's Island, they finally located Mr. Barber's boat and got it into the water. Jumping into the boat, they hoisted sail. By this time the first streaks of dawn were showing over Boston Light, and the men realized it was too late to go back for Reed and Saunders.

Reed and Saunders had crouched in the shadow of the seawall near the hole where the target had been. A sentinel came along and fell into the hole. His shouts caused the other sentry to walk over to find out what was wrong. The two men debated about where the target had gone, finally concluding that it had been blown away. They peered over the edge of the seawall and saw a dark mass, actually the two prisoners, below them. Believing that it might be the target, one of the men pricked at the mass with his bayonet, but as it yielded under the prods, he concluded it was seaweed and not the lost target. He ceased his effort, saying that he didn't wish to have rust from the salty seaweed on his bayonet. To the relief of the men crouching under the seawall, the sentries now returned to their posts. But dawn was rapidly approaching, and they realized that they must go back to their prison. The two men ran across the open ground on their way to the moat, but the guard caught sight of them and aroused the entire post. Reed and Saunders were captured and soon placed in solitary confinement.

Thurston and Alexander in the meantime had laid a course straight up the coast and when morning came were in the vicinity of Cape Ann. They went ashore but were not able to obtain help. The next morning they landed at Rye Beach and were successful in purchasing overalls and hats. Setting their course for St. John, they were far out off Portland when chased and captured by a U. S. revenue cutter, the *Dobbin*. After a brief stay in the jail, where the people came to see the "rebels from Fort Warren" as they would animals in a zoo, they were returned to George's Island on September 7, 1863, not quite three weeks from the time of their escape. Colonel Dimmick now had iron bars set into the stone work of each musketry loophole in the casemates occupied by the naval prisoners. This precaution did not prevent two other escapes from the island before the war ended, and we shall now discuss the first of these two tries for freedom.

The first escape occurred in October 1863, and was from the demilune outside the fort. Ever since 1875 the soldier-guides have pointed out the block of granite set into the casemate openings of the *caponniere*, or demilune, located outside of the main sally port. The original granite work had been chipped away, and a block was set into the opening. I have found definite proof of the manner in which the granite window sill was chipped away.

A deserter from a Maine regiment had been sentenced to two years' confinement at Fort Warren. This man, Private Sawyer, worked for three weeks chiseling away the edges of the granite loophole. As soon as the opening was large enough for his body, his comrades lowered him by a small rope out of the loophole twenty feet above the mud in the ditch. The rope, frayed by the sharp edge of the granite, suddenly broke, dropping him the remaining distance to the moat. He picked himself up and walked to the beach where he saw the lights of a schooner lying at anchor in George's Island Road as it was then called. After a swim out to the vessel, he secreted himself on board. The ship sailed away at about two in the morning, and Sawyer gave himself up shortly before ten a.m. The schooner was the *C. W. Dyer* under Captain Pierce, and as soon as the captain learned all the particulars of Sawyer's escape, he sailed into New Bedford Harbor and turned Sawyer over to the police. What the fate of Sawyer was when returned to Fort Warren is unknown, but there are two known cases of the execution of deserters at Fort Warren.

We now come to the unusual story of the cabin boy of the unfortunate *Atlanta's* crew, McBlair by name. This fifteen year old lad used to sit in the casemates, dreaming of almost forgotten days in the south, when one day a kind soldier brought him a book to read. It was Alexander Dumas' famous *Count of Monte Cristo*. No more suitable place to read this epic can be imagined. The book had a startling effect on the young cabin boy, who suddenly developed the spirit of a lion and determined to escape from the island. One day he hid away behind a Parrott gun on the parapet, but the guards discovered him in time. On another occasion he dressed himself in some old rags which the laborers had discarded and joined them as they walked out of the fort to take the boat to Boston. He had actually stepped on the gangplank when detected by one of the guards because of his youthful appearance. Later the commander, Major Cabot, asked him if he had been trying to escape. "I was doing my best, sir," was the plucky reply.

His third attempt at leaving the island was made in the middle of July 1864, about eleven months after the six men had escaped through the musketry loopholes. Feigning sickness, he had been transferred to the hospital where there were no bars in the loopholes. Late one night he crawled through the narrow window and let himself down by a small rope which parted and dropped him into the moat. Severely injured, he crawled to the water's edge, pulling a life preserver along with him.

At the shore's edge, the little fellow crawled into the water and started to swim away from the island. The water was so cold and his injuries pained him so greatly that he finally had to call for help. A boat was launched from the fort, and the injured boy was brought back to the prison in an unconscious condition. Major Cabot later interviewed him in his cot, promising to overlook the escapade if McBlair would in turn agree to give up his efforts to emulate the hero of *Monte Cristo*. The boy was firm, however, and answered the commander by saying he would try to escape until he succeeded; so there was no alternative but solitary confinement when he left the hospital.

Scores of prominent Southerners arrived at Fort Warren in the last years of the struggle between North and South. General Richard S. Ewell, West Point 1840, of whom Stephens speaks in 1865, General Eppa Hunton of Virginia, General Adam R. Johnson and General T. B. Smith were some of the noted prisoners at the island. Harry Gilmour, who became a writer and, later, police commissioner of Baltimore, was a prominent prisooner at Warren. Commodore Tucker was also at the famous northern bastile.

General I. R. Trimble was brought here after the battle of Gettysburg, where he lost a leg. He remained at Fort Warren until early in 1865 when he was exchanged. Trimble had graduated from West Point in 1822, a splendid soldier, and achieved a remarkable string of victories for the Confederacy until the Gettysburg conflict. When exchanged, he hastened to join Lee but reached Lynchburg the day after Appomattox, April 10.

Alexander Hamilton Stephens, Vice President of the Confederacy, is the last actor in our Civil War drama at Fort Warren. Arrested after he had returned to his home in Crawfordville, Georgia, Stephens was sent to Fort Warren along with Judge Reagan. They reached Boston Harbor at eleven o'clock on the night of May twenty-fourth, going ashore the next morning where they were met by Lieutenant William H. Woodman. The group walked around to the old entrance, through the sally port, and descended the stone stairs outside of Quarters Number Seven to the cellar casemates. Stephens was placed in the front room; his door was shut and locked. We read from his journal:

"I was alone, a coal fire was burning; a table and chair were in the centre; a narrow, iron, bunk-like bedstead with mattress and covering was in a corner. The floor was stone—large square blocks. The door was locked. For the first time in my life I had the full realization of being a prisoner."

Judge Reagan was placed in the next room. We continue with excerpts from Stephens' lengthy journal:

"Sunday—[May 28, 1865]. The horrors of imprisonment, close confinement, no one to see or talk to, with the reflection of being cut off I know not how long—perhaps forever—from communication with dear ones at home, are beyond description. Words utterly fail to express the soul's anguish. This day I wept bitterly. Nerves and spirit utterly forsook me. Yet Thy will be done.

"June 11. 7 p.m. From the parapet on the eastern bastion had a magnificent view of the ocean; as far as the eye could reach, its wide green plain stretched out, placid as the bosom of a lake. Where I stood this evening is a favorable point for a sea-view; 70 feet above high-water mark, enabling one to look much further out than from any place I have ever been before. On the N.W. bastion got a full, clear outline of Boston, Bunker Hill Monument, etc. Saw General Ewell on his crutches. He was walking on parapet. I remarked that I thought Ewell had an artificial leg; wondered he did not use it. Lieut. W. replied that Ewell said he was waiting before getting an artificial leg to see if the

authorities were going to hang him; if he was going to be
hung, he did not care to go to the expense; intended to wait
and make out on his crutches until that matter was settled.

"We heard a cannon. Turning toward the point from
which the sound came, we saw smoke near a small craft
lying at the wharf of a little town, called Hull, nearby.
Lieut. W. said, 'Oh, it's Dexter Follet's yacht.' 'Who is
he?' asked I. 'A young man of Boston, son of a rich father.
He keeps this yacht to sail about as he likes. Carries a gun
on board, and always fires it off upon landing or leaving,
upon heaving or hoisting anchor.' We saw the yacht on its
way to Boston.

"June 1. We went on the terreplein, but it was too
wet; went up on parapet; but the grass was too wet. We
saw Confederate prisoners on the bastion nearest that on
which we stood. While on the bastion, I saw a row of men,
walking two together. They were moving from the entrance
to the inside of the fort toward some underground apartments formed by a sort of mound near the water's edge. I
asked if these were soldiers going to their quarters for the
night. They looked dejected as they walked along. 'No,'
said the Lieutenant. 'They are the chain-gang, the crim-
inals, deserters, etc. They are made to work on the fort.' "

The underground quarters mentioned by Stephens were, of
course, in the demilune from which Sawyer escaped in October
1863.

"July 5. 3 p.m. The firing of a salute indicates some
notable visitor. Two officers stopped opposite my window
and looked down upon me. 6.15. Took usual walk. Lieut.
W. informed me that salute was in honour of General
Robert Anderson and Rear-Admiral Farragut who visited
the fort with a party.

"July 25. If I remain here much longer I shall be
bedridden. A little girl brought me some flowers: she got

the guard to hold her up, and gave them to me between the bars.

"July 29. Dr. Seaverns entered my room, and announced that he had just got an order authorizing my release from close confinement. The boat had come while I was writing, bringing the mail and with it the order. By it I am allowed to go in and out at pleasure, and walk the grounds when I choose, between sunrise and sunset. In other words I am simply put on parole in the fort. Lieut. Newton immediately took the lock off my door. No language can express the relief that sound gave me—the sound of the clanking iron. Jean Valjean could not have felt greater relief when the lid of the coffin was lifted and he was saved from being buried alive.

"August 8. A real prison sketch.

Prisoner: What pretty flowers! Let me see them.

Child (*handing them*): They are for you.

Prisoner: Ah! What is your name?

Child: Mabel Appleton.

Prisoner: Oh! It was you who brought me the flowers the other day! Those in the window—wasn't it you?

Mabel: Yes; and they are not faded yet.

August 12. 4.20. Major Appleton called to bid me goodbye. His name is J. M. Appleton."

F. Lauriston Bullard corresponded with this little girl Mabel sixty years later, in 1925. She was then about sixty-three years of age but still remembered vividly the scene which Stephens set down on the eighth of August, 1865. After many months of tireless effort, Mr. Bullard had located her through her brother, who was then living in Cincinnati. She wrote Mr. Bullard that she would never forget the occasion when it was her happy privilege to give flowers to the Confederate Vice President.

"Friday, Sept. 1. 7 p.m. Alone in the twilight. What

emotions have I experienced since my last entry! Linton [his brother] came by the morning boat.

"October 12. Dr. Seaverns appeared and stated that orders had come for my release. It embraced Judge Reagan and myself.

"October 13. I rose early and now make this last entry. I expect to start by this evening's boat for my dear home. It is a long and hazardous trip for me, beset with many dangers. But, O God deliver me from all evil."

Mr. William Risk of Winthrop, son of Corporal Thomas H. Risk who served almost the entire war at Fort Warren, has in his possession two gold cuff links given Corporal Risk by Mr. Stephens at Fort Warren. Corporal Risk was present at Fort Warren while a deserter was shot, and also participated in the engagement which might have become known as the battle of Bug Light.

One stormy night during the war, when the rain was falling in torrents and running down into the moat like a waterfall, the report of gunfire was heard in the distance. Rumors of Confederate ships near Boston had been travelling through the companies so that soon the entire fort was aroused and every man called to his station. They waited and waited in the pouring rain, but nothing happened. Then, suddenly, the distant booming continued. Each man stood ready. Again there was no result; orders were given to launch a small boat and try to locate the cause of the disturbance. A dory was put out from the island and, manned by sturdy oarsmen, made its way out across the Narrows in the heavy rain while the entire garrison watched it out of sight. Half an hour later the boat returned, and the oarsmen brought news of the battle. The volleys had been from the trusty shotgun of the keeper of Bug Light while he was engaged in the ignominious but necessary task of killing rats.

Major Appleton was succeeded as commander at Fort Warren by Major Charles F. Livermore, who in turn was replaced by Major A. A. Gibson. Major Gibson remained at the fort for four years. In the year 1869 Major Truman Seymour, a former divisional leader in the South, was in charge at Fort Warren. Major George P. Andrews of the Fifth Artillery was commander from 1872 until 1875. During the second year of Andrews' service at Fort Warren, the former commander of the 32nd Regiment visited George's Island. Francis J. Parker had not seen the fort since he had sailed in command of the 32nd Regiment at the time of the Civil War, and he walked about the quarters thinking of the pleasant days spent with the regiment. He roamed all over the fortress where his men had trained, and the realization that many who had learned their soldiering here would never return saddened him. We shall join him in his walk about the island.

"There were no sentinels to challenge or salute, no familiar faces in the well-remembered quarters. Even the uniforms were changed; officers seemed to be wearing sergeants' stripes on their trousers, and unknown ornaments on their shoulders. There were women about the landing, newspapers in the guardhouse(!), and a peaceful fishing pole and tackle leaned quietly against the sole survivor of all our sentry boxes. Again was paced the line of our outposts. Every step awakened old memories—every pebble seemed a friend; but there was no ice upon the glacis or the shelf at post eighteen. It would have been a sad walk but for the beauty of the summer scenes, it would have been a joyous one but for clinging memories."

The 1st Corps Cadets who had trained at Fort Warren during the Civil War met at Boston May 26, 1887, the twenty-fifth anniversary of their first trip to Fort Warren, and took the *Rose Standish* to George's Island. The men revisited the old haunts, recalling many joyful occasions of a quarter century before. After having explored through all the passages of the old fort, the members returned to the dock where they took the steamship *Nantasket* for a trip to Boston Light. At the dinner held that night an ode to the Fort Warren Cadets was read. **Part** of it is quoted here:

> *Back within the grim old fortress,*
> *Marching as in days of yore,*
> *Youthful hearts and high ambition*
> *Vigorous with hope once more,—*
> *Hopes, ambitions, born to grow*
> *Twenty-five long years ago.*

When the war with Spain began in 1898, Major C. A. Woodruff was in command and Fort Warren again assumed an important role. Thousands still remember the dreadful feeling experienced when it was learned the Spanish fleet was hourly expected near Boston. Massachusetts was again caught unprepared, as far as coast defenses were concerned.

There were but three batteries on duty guarding the entire Massachusetts coastline, and they were all in Boston Harbor. Two were at Fort Warren and one was at Long Island Head. In 1896, when $10,910,250 had been recommended for the defenses of the harbor, it was agreed that 175 breech-loading rifles and mortars were to be set up within ten years. Not only was this plan not carried out, but two years later when the war came only twenty-four pieces were actually mounted. In addition there were less than 250 officers and men stationed at the Boston Harbor batteries.

To help the defense, the 1st Regiment of Massachusetts Artillery was ordered out on April 25, 1898, and in less than twenty-four hours was marching to Rowe's Wharf where the men embarked on the *General Lincoln* for Fort Warren. Plans had been made to quarter the men in portable barracks sent down to the island, but when the regiment arrived it was found that the Deer Island prisoners engaged in setting up the barracks were not very far along in their work. The entire regiment took over the task, and before dark the combined efforts of soldiers and prisoners, who were soon christened the 3rd Corps

Cadets, succeeded in erecting enough barracks for the night. The soldiers then had a new rhyme to put to an old song:

"They broke our backs
A-lugging shacks
In the regular army-O!"

A huge mess-tent was erected, which was very pretty to look at in good weather but sagged miserably in the rainy season which soon came. One day it collapsed into the mud, and the men were forced to seek the "Dark Arch" or the casemated gymnasium facing Bug and Boston Lights.

Now began the period of rumors. Not only did the reports of the Spanish fleet persist in New England but on the night of April 26 there was a public banquet in Havana to celebrate the bombardment of Boston. It was known that the Spanish flotilla had left the Cape de Verde Islands on the 29th of April for an unknown destination. A careful record of all the rumors was kept by an officer at the fort and it is a weird collection. On one occasion, an observer watching in the gathering dusk sighted four ships in single file and believed them to be the Spanish fleet coming to destroy Boston. It turned out to be merely an innocent tug with three barges in tow!

The greatest excitement of all came shortly after midnight, May 13, when the *Tourist*, the craft employed by the United States Engineers in their mine-laying operations, rushed down to the fort with her whistle blowing continually all the way from Boston. When she was tied up at the Fort Warren dock a messenger from the Navy Department reported that the Spanish fleet had been sighted off Nantucket and was at that minute steaming for Boston. The fleet, however, never arrived.

The regiment was soon divided and scattered along the coast at strategic points; Major Frye's 3rd Battalion alone remained with the regulars at Fort Warren. The war was practically decided after the naval victories, and Spain soon sued for terms. The peace protocol was signed August 12, and eight days later the new guns were given a practice test. This had been impossible until the signing of the protocol, as the ammunition had to be saved for the possible defense of Boston.

After the Spanish War, affairs at Fort Warren settled down to routine assignments until 1900, when barracks were constructed on the northwestern shore. Battery G of the 7th Artillery, U. S. A., moved out of the gloomy casements into the new quarters. The barracks were erected under the supervision of Capt. Edward T. Brown, the commanding officer of that time.

The last prisoner to be incarcerated in the demilune from which Sawyer escaped in 1863 was a buck private who was confined in 1901. This soldier set fire to his bunk when he was in a rage. After the blaze was put out he was taken to another section of the fort.

During the World War the old quarters were again crowded with troops, and scores of tents were placed all over the island. About 1600 men were quartered at Fort Warren during the winter of 1917, mostly from the 55th Artillery. The 55th Artillery Regiment was made up of eight companies from Boston and vicinity and came into being December 1917. Many Coast Artillery units in and around Boston aided in building the 55th up to the needed regimental strength. The Boston Fusiliers, the Famous Tiger Battalion of *John Brown* fame, and the Washington Light Guards were some of the well-known units which were assimilated in filling out the 55th.

On March 8, 1918, came the first news that the men were soon to leave for the front. The notification was in the form of a scarlet fever quarantine, but the troops guessed the real significance of the quarantine—to keep them at the island until called for the trip to France. The expected orders came March 15, and the 55th Regiment of Coast Artillery left Fort Warren for New York and the *Mauretania*.

The soldiers who later came to Fort Warren as replacements for the 55th tell the story of the attempted murder of a captain while he was stationed at Fort Warren. As far as can be ascertained the incident occurred in the spring of 1918 when replacements for the 55th were training at the island. A private who had grown to hate his captain planned a terrible death for the officer. Every day he watched the captain come up the walk, go through the postern gate, and walk out on the parade ground. He gradually evolved the plan of dropping a one hundred-pound cannon ball, a relic of the war of 1861, on the head of the officer just as the captain stepped onto the slate walk of the parade ground.

The time for the attempt at murder came, and the captain started up the walk. The private hidden on the terreplein high above the doorway had the cannon ball in readiness. The officer went through the postern gate and was about to come out into the parade ground when the cannon ball crashed onto the slate walk at his feet. Fortunately the private miscalculated, having dropped the 100-pound ball too soon, and instead of crushing the captain's head, cracked the slate walk into several pieces. When apprehended, the private claimed innocence; he had so timed his movements that no serious charge could ever be proved against him. The cracks in the walk can be seen today.

On the 26th of July, 1922, headquarters for the harbor defenses were moved to Fort Banks, in Winthrop. September 2, 1924, Colonel Charles E. Kilbourne became the Commanding Officer in charge of Fort Warren. He had already won great honor for his bravery in the Spanish-American War. Colonel Kilbourne climbed a telegraph pole in the Philippines under heavy rifle fire to repair a broken wire, and for this act was given the Congressional Medal of Honor. In France his gallantry in action won him the Distinguished Service Cross and the Distinguished Service Medal.

Modern warfare was so changed by 1928 that it was decided to reduce grand old Fort Warren to a caretaking status, and the fort was decommissioned late in the summer of that year. The 13th Infantry, then at the island, was sent to Fort Ethan Allen. Sergeant James F. Ward, James Moriarty of the

Quartermaster Corps, with Privates Barrito and Green made up the lonely foursome which remained at Fort Warren. A short time later Ward met his death in a tragic accident.

On the ninth of June, 1935, many patriotic and historical societies met at Fort Warren to dedicate a tablet honoring three of the Southern notables who had been imprisoned at George's Island during the era of the Civil War. The men so honored were James Murray Mason, John Slidell, and Alexander Hamilton Stephens. President-General Mrs. W. E. Massie of Hot Springs, Arkansas, spoke for the United Daughters of the Confederacy and the South. Confederate Veteran William B. Newell took the long journey from Richmond, Virginia, to represent the survivors of Lee's armies. Commander Charles L. Robinson, 93, represented the Grand Army of the Republic. Francis De-Celles, representing the Governor of Massachusetts and the North, spoke very effectively. President Mrs. Albert L. Rider of the Boston Chapter, U. D. C., added much to the ceremony with her words of welcome, while Mrs. Roscoe H. Chesley, President of the Woodrow Wilson Chapter, U. D. C., gave a fine reading of *The Blue and the Gray*. The most impressive part of the ceremony, however, was when the two men, the Blue and the Gray, met and shook hands beneath the tablet. It was a very touching scene as they stood with clasped hands in the crowded casemate of Quarters Number Seven, probably the last time two veterans of the North and South will ever meet at Fort Warren. Both veterans have since died.

Every island has its legends, but perhaps the most famous of them all concerns the Lady in Black at Fort Warren.

The legend of this famous Lady in Black has been whispered at Fort Warren for many, many years, until now there are quite a few who believe in the existence of this lady of the black robes. I herewith offer the reader the legend without the slightest guarantee that any part of it is true.

During the War between the States, hundreds of prisoners were captured by Burnside at Roanoke Island. Among the group incarcerated at Fort Warren in the corridor of dungeons was a young lieutenant who had been married only a few weeks before. He succeeded in getting a message to his young wife by the underground railroad, giving complete directions as to where he was and how she could reach him. Being very much in love, she obtained passage on a small sloop, and landed in Hull a few weeks later. She quickly located the home of a Southerner in that town and was fitted out with a pistol and dressed in men's clothing.

Choosing a dark, rainy night, the lady rowed across Nantasket Road and finally landed on the beach at George's Island. Slipping noiselessly by the sentries, she reached the ditch under the Corridor of Dungeons. After giving a prearranged signal, she was hoisted up to the carronade embrasure and pulled through the opening. As soon as husband and wife had exchanged greetings, they made plans for the future. The prisoners decided to dig their way out of the dungeon into the parade ground and immediately set to work. Unfortunately for their plans, a slight miscalculation brought their tunnel within hearing of Northern soldiers stationed on the other side of the wall. Colonel Dimmick was notified and the whole scheme was quickly exposed. The brave little woman, when cornered, attempted to fire at the Colonel, but the gun was of the old fashioned pepper box type and exploded, killing her husband.

Colonel Dimmick had no alternative but to sentence her to hang as a spy. She made one last request,—that she be hanged in women's clothing. After a search of the fort, some robes were found which had been worn by one of the soldiers during an entertainment, and the plucky girl went to her death wearing these robes.

At various times through the years the ghost of the Lady in Black has returned to haunt the men quartered at the fort. Some winters ago three of the soldiers were walking under the great arched sally port at the entrance to the fort, and there before them, in the fresh snow, were five impressions of a girl's shoe leading nowhere and coming from nowhere. Ten years ago a certain sergeant from Fort Banks was climbing to the top of the ladder which leads to the Corridor of Dungeons when he heard a voice warning him, saying: "Don't come in here!" Needless to say, he did not venture further.

There actually are on record court-martial cases of men who have shot at ghost-like figures while on sentry duty, and one poor man deserted his post, claiming he had been chased by the lady of the black robes.

For many years the traditional poker game was enjoyed in the old ordnance storeroom, and at ten o'clock one night a stone was rolled the entire length of the storeroom. As all the men on the island were playing poker, no explanation could be found. When the same thing happened the next time that the men played poker in the evening, the group at the card table decreased appreciably. By the end of the month the ordnance storeroom was deserted, and since that time, if any of the enlisted men wish to indulge in this pastime, they choose another part of the Island. The ghost of the "Lady in Black" was of course blamed for the trouble.

Warrant Officer Richard Kurth composed a group of Black Widow waltzes which were inspired by the ghost of the lady of the black robes.

* * * * *

Since Fort Warren is still an integral part of Boston's Harbor Defense system, I cannot give a description of the fortifications of the present day. But the War Department has released to me some interesting data on the defenses named after Joseph Warren. The fort has a direct fire on Broad Sound and commands both Nantasket Road and the Narrows. It bears a close resemblance to five-bastioned Fort Independence, having five fronts which vary in length from 600 to 666 feet. On the three faces exposed to a breaking fire from adjacent islands, the granite scarp is covered by a coverface and ravelin.

The coverface was formerly connected with the *enceinte*

by a wooden bridge in the center of the northern front. It had fallen into ruin before 1907 and was later torn down so the timber could be used for a mule fence. In front of the main sally port there is a demilune, technically called *caponniere*, which flanks two of the coverfaces.

This *caponniere* is semi-circular and casemated, and loop-holed for musketry. At the time the deserter Sawyer escaped, there was a deep ditch going around the base of the demilune, possibly 15 or 20 feet below the musketry loophole.

In 1885 there were platforms for 248 guns. I do not be-lieve the commanding officer at Fort Banks will object to a de-scription of some of these guns of fifty years ago now removed from the island. In the casemates there were two converted eight-inch rifles and 23 twenty-four pound howitzers. Mounted *en barbette* were five fifteen-inch Rodmans, 96 ten-inch Rod-mans, two eight-inch converted rifles, one two-hundred-pound Parrott, and one one-hundred-pound rifle.

Colonel F. J. Parker's description of the Fort Warren of two generations ago is the best ever written on the famous five bastioned fortification, and I offer you a paragraph.

"To one who thoroughly explored the island there will recur vivid reminiscences of the mysterious castles of romance and history. He will find there a sally port, a pos-tern, a draw bridge, and a portcullis. Here, too, are pas-sages under ground and in the walls; turret staircases, huge vaulted apartments, and safe and dark dungeons, the ways to and through which may be set down upon the plans of the engineer corps, but are familiar to no living man. One can be easily bewildered among the crooks and turns, the ups and downs of the corridors, and it needs only a dark and windy night to make almost real the romantic de-scriptions of the Castle of Udolfo, with its clanging sounds of chains, its sweeping gusts of air, its strange moanings and howlings, and the startling noise of some sudden clang of a shutting door reverberating through the arches."

On November 24, 1933, the Government announced that several of the islands down the harbor would be reforested, and headquarters were to be set up at Fort Warren. Park Superintendent Richard Hayden endorsed the program, and on April 16, 1934, Warren E. Stiles of the National Park Service started the work in earnest. This wonderful project was finally completed by mid-summer, and the C.C.C. workers created a living memorial to their hard work which should stand for many years. At least 3000 of the trees are flourishing, and the planting of 100,000 trees on the islands of Boston Harbor should go down in history as an important achievement.

If you ever are lucky enough to obtain a pass to Fort Warren, there are nine points of interest you should visit. The Corridor of Dungeons, the passageway under the harbor with its reverberating tunnel, the cracked sidewalk where the cannonball fell, and the great sally port with its legend *Fort Warren 1850* are four places no one should miss. The musketry embrasure where Sawyer squeezed his way to freedom, the bastion where the six naval prisoners escaped, and the dark arch are worthy of your attention. The front room of Quarters Number Seven, where Mason, Slidell, and Stephens were imprisoned can be identified by the tablet over the fireplace. This room has become a shrine for Southerners, and is used as a library by the men at the post. The ninth and final point of interest is the chapel, where beautiful murals, illustrating outstanding episodes of the fort's history, have been painted on the walls. The murals have inspired all who have seen them, and Chaplain David Harold Hickey should be very proud of them.

Units of the 9th and 241st Regiments have been active at Fort Warren during World War II, and are now fighting in all parts of the world after their training at the historic fortification down the bay. I recall meeting veterans from Fort Warren both in England and in the Mediterranean. Some are prisoners of the Japanese, while others are buried in the roadside cemeteries overlooking beautiful Oran in North Africa.

Sergeant Charles E. Black came to Fort Warren in March 1938, and is still at the island citadel, making his service the longest at the post. He and his wife Charlotte have seen many changes at old John George's island during the years of their residence there.

And so we say farewell to Fort Warren. Hardly a handful of the thousands who were at George's Island during the Civil War are now living, but their descendants, both in the North and South, should always keep fresh the thoughts of the men who were here during that war. Fort Warren itself is a splendid memorial to them, and should be preserved, after its usefulness to the Government is over, as an everlasting tribute to those who fought in the conflict of 1861.

GALLOP'S ISLAND

Possibly a quarter-mile to the eastward of Lovell's Island and exactly a mile to the northwest of Rainsford's Island lies Gallop's Island, the present location of the Maritime training school. On December 30, 1916, the Government paid $150,000 for the island which in 1649, according to the will of John Gallop, was worth the equivalent of $75. Captain Gallop was mentioned frequently in early maritime accounts of Boston Harbor.

The shape of this island has been likened by Shurtleff to that of a leg of mutton, with the shank pointing easterly across the Narrows to Bug Light. The fixed beacon which flashes its warning a few score feet from Beachy Point at Gallop's Island is known as Peggy's Point.

In 1827 $2,429.51 was appropriated to cut down the cliff so as to eliminate too commanding a view on the future Fort Warren. So much of the soil from the cliffs was washing away at this time that Dr. J. V. C. Smith believed that the island would disappear before 1860. Peter Newcomb who had a fine farm on Gallop's Island, died in 1833. His wife Margaret stayed on at the island, opening an eating establishment there a few years later. Spending a summer at Newcomb's Island soon became the custom of many Bostonians, and Mrs. Newcomb's cooking came to have a very enviable reputation around the city. When Mrs. Newcomb died, her son Charles sold the property to the city of Boston, receiving $6,500. Joe Snow purchased Mrs. Newcomb's boarding house about 1855, and Snow's Island, as it became known, again was noted as the scene of many lively chowders and clam bakes.

Boston loaned the island to the Government during the Civil War, and hundreds of soldiers were soon encamped on the slopes of Peter Newcomb's old farm.

The war ended, and happier days were in store for Gallop's Island. At nine o'clock July 6, 1865, the steamship *Fairbanks* anchored off Deer Island with the 38th Massachusetts Regiment on board. After the ship had been inspected, the men went ashore at Gallop's Island. They were paid off a week later and left the camp by ferryboat for the trip to Boston. On August 28, 1865, the famous 54th Massachusetts Regiment of colored troops reached Gallop's Island and spent a few pleasant days there until their final discharge on September 2.

With the coming of peace and the threatened infection from disease, the deserted barracks at Gallop's Island were turned over to the city. On June 1, 1866, the Quarantine Station for Boston Harbor was moved from Deer Island to Gallop's Island. The first twenty years of quarantine there saw an annual average of fifty patients, and there are 248 graves in the hillside cemetery of those who failed to recover from their sickness. In 1879, according to a sketch of that time, there were two hospital buildings, a dwelling, and several other sheds and barns on the southern side of the island. Today there are over a score of well-equipped buildings.

The United States assumed control of Boston Harbor quarantine at Gallop's Island in 1916. A year later, when America joined the great conflict, the German sailors who were on the interned ships in Boston were taken down to the island and held as prisoners. These sailors had ruined the engines of their German ships before abandoning them, and were forced to stay at Gallop's Island for the duration of the war.

Shortly before the World War II began, the quarantine station was moved from Gallop's Island to the City of Boston.

After many changes, Gallop's Island today is a radio training school, under the United States Maritime Service. Commander Sherman W. Reed, U. S. M. S., is the able superintendent of the station. The captain, as he is known on the island, has an outstanding record of twenty-five years at sea, and is well liked by all who come in contact with him.

Gallop's Island is one of the best-equipped and most efficient radio schools ever established. Those who have graduated from the training school here since its inception are recognized from coast to coast for their expert knowledge and fine work. The school did so well that only a few months after its beginning the complement of students was raised from 400 to over 1000 men.

A journey to the island today is a privilege and a real lesson. We find out the manner in which the Maritime Service handled its share of one of the greatest tasks ever confronting a nation. With hundreds of new ships commissioned month after month, the post of radio operator was one of the key positions to fill. Not only must the men here excel as radio operators, trained in the various types of sending and receiving sets, but the graduates from Gallop's Island must pass the various tests in seamanship as well, with boat drills and mastery of all the important knots prerequisites for their diplomas.

The actual training period is crowded into twenty-eight weeks of intensive study and examinations, with a close, friendly relationship existing between students and instructors. From 8 a.m. Monday morning until noon Saturday the students stay at the island, except possibly on Wednesday night, when the high-ranking platoon is given liberty ashore. At noon Saturday the old excursion steamer *Calvert*, with its penetrating whistle, leaves John Gallop's home with almost the entire school aboard. A few, of course, are left behind for fire watch and other duties, but they will get their liberty on Wednesday night.

Head Chaplain Harold W. Arthur has done fine work at the island, giving spiritual guidance, assisted by Chaplain A. E. Bernhard. Varied recreation is provided for the men. Ping pong is a popular evening game, motion pictures are shown nightly, while boxing matches, basketball, smokers, and amateur nights are enjoyed from time to time.

After the student graduates he must go ashore for his examination by the local inspector for his Federal Communications Commission license. Very few ever fail to pass this test, for they have been trained by Lieutenant T. H. Grant, himself a former F. C. C. inspector.

It is literally true that the sun never sets on Gallop's Island graduates, for their ships are sailing from Calcutta to Melbourne, from New Orleans to Cairo. It is probable that many think back from time to time of those twenty-eight active weeks at John Gallop's old residence down Boston Bay, when they were under the careful supervision of the officer they like to call captain, Commander Sherman W. Reed.

LOVELL'S ISLAND AND FORT STANDISH

Lovell's Island is probably named after William Lovell of Dorchester. In 1636 and in 1648 Charlestown was given permission to use the island. Nantasket strenuously objected to Charlestown's owning the island, but in vain. The first recorded disaster occurred in 1645, when a ketch pulled her moorings and smashed to pieces on the shores of Lovell's Island. George Worthylake, the first keeper of Boston Light, moved here about 1700 from George's Island.

Lovell's Island, separated from Gallop's Island by the Narrows, is located about a mile to the south of Deer Island and

GALLOP'S ISLAND FROM THE AIR

LAYING THE LOWEST BLOCK AT MINOT'S LIGHT

SCITUATE'S AMERICAN ARMY OF TWO

THE APPLE ISLAND ELM
CUT DOWN IN 1938

ANCIENT CANNON AT BOSTON LIGHT

THE AMERICA PASSING THE CASTLE

BRITISH MAIL STEAMER COMING UP BOSTON HARBOR THROUGH THE ICE

is approximately three-quarters of a mile long and one-third of a mile wide. About a century and a half ago there was a large tree standing on the southern point of Lovell's Island which was used as a marker by the mariners. Because of a blinding snow storm in 1767, the captain of a brig was unable to see the marker and lost his bearings. The ship crashed on the beach at Lovell's Island, the vessel luckily holding together until the next morning when the sea subsided enough to allow the passengers to reach the shore. A little girl was lowered over the side of the ship by a rope. This little girl, Susanna Haswell, grew up to become a very versatile woman, well-known as author, actress, and school-teacher; such a combination today would indeed be unusual. Later in life she married and became Mrs. Rowson. Her novel, *Rebecca*, describes the shipwreck on lonely Lovell's Island.

In 1782 the great French fleet of Admiral Vaubaird sailed into Boston Harbor. A Boston pilot, David Darling, was unfortunate enough to wreck the great *Magnifique*, a man-of-war of 74 guns, on a bar leading from the West Head of Lovell's Island. Badly damaged, she filled and sank in deep water right off the inner shore. Whether the day was stormy or the pilot alone was at fault probably will never be known, but David Darling lost his job.

It was a sad day for the new republic when Darling's piloting carried the vessel to her doom, for America felt obliged to give France as compensation her own 74-gun ship then nearing completion at Portsmouth, New Hampshire. The boat was launched on November 5, 1782, but when John Paul Jones found that he was not to command the new battlship, he resigned from the service, and America lost the man who was perhaps her greatest naval hero. Thus we have the carelessness of a young Boston pilot contributing to the final chapter in the career of a great commander. David Darling, the unfortunate pilot, obtained a position as sexton of the Old North Church, succeeding Robert Newman. Shurtleff tells us that the children of the

North End bothered the poor man by writing in chalk on the door of the church:

"Don't you run this ship ashore
As you did the seventy-four."

David Darling was buried in the Copp's Hill cemetery on September 10, 1820, and the skeleton of the *Magnifique*, buried under tons of sand, was quite forgotten by the average Bostonian. Our "Shade of Alden," James Lloyd Homer, was sailing up the Narrows a quarter of a century later, and as he looked over at Lovell's Island an old man stepped up to him and mentioned the story of the *Magnifique*. The elderly gentleman told Homer he well remembered the day the *Magnifique* went down and pointed out the exact spot of the wreck. The currents of the Narrows had created a bar over the hulk in the 63 years which had passed since the man-of-war went down, and possibly Homer's mention of the incident caused some of the treasure seekers to make an attempt for the gold which was lost with the ship.

Attempts had already been made around 1840 to recover the treasure from the *Magnifique*, but they had failed. Again in July 1859, excavations were made, but all that the searchers could find were some beautiful pieces of wood from the hull of the ship. During 1868 and 1869 more timbers were uncovered, but, since nothing of intrinsic value was found, it was decided to abandon further attempts. When Shurtleff visited the island, he found that the spot where the *Magnifique* had gone down was not covered by water even at high tide, thus showing how the contour of Lovell's Island had changed since the 1782 wreck.

Continuing with the story of the *Magnifique*, we move to the twentieth century. On a cool spring morning 15 years ago, Keeper Charles H. Jennings was industriously digging near his house on the island when suddenly his spade struck an object that resembled a coin. Jennings stooped over and picked it up. He continued his excavations until he had unearthed many of the round, flat disks. Taking them into his house, he scrubbed and dug the deposit away from one of the objects, and there was revealed a gold coin, worth by its size and weight about $29. The other coins yielded under the rubbing and scraping to reveal that they, too, were valuable silver and gold pieces of long ago.

Jennings, however, was about to leave the island on his annual vacation, and when the assistant arrived at the lighthouse station, Jennings told him the interesting news. He noticed that the assistant seemed quite attentive to his account of how he found the gold and silver, but Jennings promptly forgot all about the incident as he boarded the afternoon boat for the mainland.

When Jennings returned from his vacation on the mainland, the assistant left the island as soon as possible with all his baggage. Walking up to his house, Jennings went around to the spot where he had dug up the coins, and there was a deep, yawning hole. A few months later the assistant retired from the Lighthouse Service and lived in comfort for the rest of his life. The reader may draw his own conclusions.

Four years after the wreck of the *Magnifique* the most tragic incident in the history of Lovell's Island took place. On the fourth of December, 1786, a packet from Maine, under Captain Atkins, crashed on the beach at the eastern side of the island. A bitter snowstorm was sweeping up the coast. All of the passengers and crew were successful in reaching the shore, but they could find no shelter anywhere on the island. At the top of the hill was a large rock which gave them some protection against the fierce blizzard which was raging. There the people, 13 in number, huddled in their wet clothing as the thermometer went lower and lower. The temperature in surrounding towns that night dropped far below zero.

With the coming of dawn, a fisherman on a neighboring island, Thomas Spear by name, noticed the wreck and crossed over. He saw the group crouched together in the shelter of the rock and went up the hill to investigate, finding all of the party apparently frozen to death. Among the group were two young people, Miss Sylvia Knapp and a young man whose name has been forgotten, who had been on their way to Boston to purchase furniture for their home-to-be. The two lovers were found locked in each other's arms.

Although the usual story told for almost a century and a half has been that all were frozen to death, the *New England Courant* for that period will reveal the fact that one man survived the terrible ordeal and lived for almost a fortnight afterwards. He was Theodore Kingsley of Wrentham, Massachusetts. Thomas Spear brought him up to town as soon as possible, but he was so badly frozen that after lingering for many days, he grew worse and died. The story of the tragedy has been told by the Reverend Brown, and a few verses describing the incident follow:

> *The tempest hid the cheering Light,*
> *So thickly flew the snow;*
> *Alas, what horror fill'd the night,*
> *With bitter, piercing woe.*
>
> *At length they gained the sea-beat strand,*
> *And rescued from the waves;*
> *On Lovell's Island only land,*
> *To find more decent graves.*
>
> *Among the rest, a youthful pair,*
> *Who from their early youth;*
> *Had felt of love an equal share,*
> *Adorn'd with equal truth,*
>
> *Lay prostrate mid the dire alarms,*
> *Had calm resign'd their breath;*
> *Fast lock'd within each other's arms,*
> *Together sunk to death.*

A rabbit run on Lovell's Island supplied the markets of Boston for many years, and quite a few of the little pets of the boys and girls in the capital city came from this island down the Harbor.

In 1874 the Government established the Lighthouse Buoy Station at Lovell's Island. On the wharf were to be seen duplicates of many of the giant buoys located around the harbor, ready for instant service whenever the occasion demanded. A track formerly ran from the wharf to the northern end of the island, which is called Ram's Head.

The War Department established Fort Standish on Lovell's Island soon after 1900, notifying the Lighthouse Department to look elsewhere. In 1902 the twin range lights were erected near Ram's Head and when the foundation for the lower light was being dug the skeleton of a man was found far under the surface. Whether or not the bones guarded some pirate's treasure has not as yet been discovered.

With the coming of the second World War, Fort Standish underwent a transformation, with first a tent city and then substantial barracks placed on the sandy soil of the island. The newspaper of the fort, the *Sand-Spit Sentinel,* came into being, and various authors among the soldiers contributed to its columns. I visited at the fort frequently, and found the commanders and the men gracious hosts, interested in the history of the fort and proud of their part in it.

In many respects Lovell's Island is *the* island of Romance. Lover's Rock, the treasure, the pirate's skeleton, and the mysterious underground passageway which shoots off under the harbor make up an unusual combination for one small island of 62 acres.

If any adventurous readers care to make the trip down the tunnel, don the oldest clothes you have. The location is easily found to the left of the steps leading up to the top of the hill. Opening the old studded door, we flash our lights into the darkness of the passageway to find that the arched tunnel takes a sharp turn to the right. We again turn to the right, and continue down the passageway. Some 20 feet beyond, the corridor opens into a large, arched room having a rectangular hole in the middle of the floor. Anyone who did not bring a flashlight is surely in danger here.

Turning our light down into the opening, we see that the hole is about five feet in depth; we jump down and find another surprise. The wall of the pit farthest away from the tunnel has an opening, and when we flash our light down we find another passageway which seems to be endless. At this point in our adventure quite a few of those who had declared their bravery in the sunlight decide they have had enough excitement for the time being and, telling us they will wait outside, beat a hasty retreat.

The only way we can travel through this new opening is on our hands and knees, as it is no higher than the space under the average office table. Crawling down this tunnel, we find we are gradually getting lower and lower. After a few hundred feet the end is reached at a point where the top of the passageway has caved in. Here we join the elect by scraping our names on the damp walls before starting on the long journey back to the sunlight.

After we retrace our steps and blink our way out into the sunlight, we walk down the road to visit the commanding officer of Lovell's Island.

BUG LIGHT

Bug Light, formerly a lighthouse but now only an automatic beacon, stands at the entrance to the Narrows, guarding the Spit, a bar that runs from Greater Brewster Island. It is less than a third of a mile across Black Rock Channel from Lovell's Island and almost a half-mile from Fort Warren. Built back in 1856, the original Bug Light stood until 1929 to warn the mariner of the dreaded Harding's Ledge, four miles to the southeast. The lantern was about 35 feet above sea level, and when a sea captain brought Bug Light in range with Long Island

Light, he knew he was clear of Harding's Ledge and could safely enter the harbor.

Although the romance of this lighthouse is now a thing of the past, we can recall a small group that once occupied Bug Light, so named "because of its many legs." In the year 1893 Gershom C. Freeman was given the position of keeper at Bug Light, succeeding the bearded Captain Turner. Three years later Mrs. Frank Tenney became his housekeeper, moving to the lighthouse with her six-year-old son Francis. In 1908 her son attended English High School, each day making the long row around to the lee side of George's Island from which he took the boat to the city. If a bad storm came up, he would stay on George's Island till the weather abated; otherwise he returned in the dory.

Mrs. Tenney well remembered the *Portland* storm. She had been digging clams on the bar that afternoon, and there was no sign of the blizzard then on the way. The light successfully withstood the terrible gale which came up that evening. The stones striking against the iron legs of Bug Light played weird tunes for the occupants above in the lighthouse, as every upright was keyed to a slightly different pitch.

Tom Small was the last keeper of Bug Light. On June 7, 1929, he was painting the woodwork of the house when his blowtorch tipped over; the blaze which followed destroyed the light. The lighthouse board voted against rebuilding the structure, erecting an automatic bell and light in its place, and for the last fifteen years no one has lived at the end of Great Brewster Spit.

In the summer of 1934, Ralph Keller of Point Shirley was cruising by Bug Light and noticed that the automatic machinery of the station was ringing the bell as usual every twenty seconds, but in a tone pitched two or three degrees higher than usual. He went ashore where he found that a seagull had built its home inside the bell, and that the nest had actually changed the tone of the bell. The mother seagull chose a rather startling place to bring up her young, with the monotonous bell sounding more than four thousand times every day.

THE BREWSTERS

The Brewsters were named for the children of Elder William Brewster of Plymouth. Let us discuss a little of the topography of this group of islands.

Greater Brewster is the highest island in the outer harbor, its northern bluff rising 104 feet above high water. The southern bluff has been almost washed away and is not quite 50 feet high. Some 600 yards to the north lies Calf Island, its seventeen acres rocky and fairly low in the water. Away to the eastward in a straight line stretch Middle Brewster and Outer Brewster, both very rocky and surrounded by stony ledges. Outer Brewster is perhaps a few feet higher than Middle Brewster, and is a larger island, containing seventeen acres as compared with twelve for Middle Brewster. Green Island's single acre, with its rocky slopes, has a fairly steep cliff on the northern side and is separated from Little Calf Island by Hypocrite Channel. It is almost due north of Calf Island.

The pirates were very active in early days. One incident of 1665 makes us realize just how strong and bold they had become by that time. Captain John Prentice of Boston reported on July 8, 1665, that two days earlier he had been chased all the way across the bay and right up to the Brewster Islands by these seventeenth century buccaneers. The pirates gave up the chase as soon as Captain Prentice's ship passed Outer Brewster Island, and the captain duly reported the incident when his ship's cargo was discharged.

GREATER BREWSTER

In 1681, on the highest part of Greater Brewster Island, the town of Hull placed a beacon and received £8 from the Council for the land so used. In 1726 a well was dug two hundred yards away, by Captain Hayes, the keeper of Boston Light. The well is still giving fine water.

John Jenkins bought a large part of the property on April 26, 1774, and the following October made the unusual gift of his share to the Second Baptist Church of Boston. The Reverend Isaac Skillman, who was the preacher at the time, valued the property at £18. In 1792, the church, owning 29/32 of the island, voted to lease it for any term of time. When James Brackett of Quincy desired to buy the island, he was informed an outright purchase was not to be considered, but he could lease it indefinitely. He chose to take full advantage of this offer, and leased it from February 8, 1817 until February 8, 2816, or for a period of 999 years, paying £150.

Honorable Benjamin Dean rented Greater Brewster for many years and around 1875 moved a large house there from Long Island. It is still standing.

Very few ships have been wrecked on the shores of Greater Brewster Island. The wreck which can still be remembered by some of the older residents was that of the *Clara Jane*, February 1, 1898. In command of Captain Maloney, the *Clara Jane* pounded on the beach for two days but did not go to pieces and was finally pulled off and repaired. There was no loss of life.

MIDDLE BREWSTER ISLAND

Around 1840, fishermen moved to Middle Brewster. Augustus Russ, visiting here shortly afterwards, became interested in the island which he finally bought in 1871. Russ was known all over New England as the principal founder of the Boston Yacht Club. A few years later his friends called him the King of Middle Brewster Island.

In 1890 Benjamin P. Cheney and his wife, the former Julia Arthur, moved to a little house on Middle Brewster Island. In the summer of 1891 Cheney desired an ice-house, but, as he had only bought a house lot on the island, Russ did not wish

him to put up an additional building. Cheney therefore moved
off the island and purchased Calf Island outright.

When Russ died in 1892, the island was sold to Charles
Adams who soon sold it to his brother Melvin. Melvin O.
Adams thought so much of Augustus Russ that he had a tablet
sunk into the rock on the side of the residence on the property.

IN LOVING MEMORY OF AUGUSTUS RUSS

Born February 6, 1827   Died June 7, 1892
>Lord of this isle for twenty years
>Generous, brave, and true in the hearts
>Of his friends he reigns still supreme.

MELVIN O. ADAMS   POSUIT 1905

An interesting log book, begun by Augustus Russ and containing names of many notables who visited the island is now
in the possession of the Adams family.

The flag staff at the Calf Island end of Middle Brewster
bears an inscription which tells us Richard S. Whitney erected
it here in 1902.

CALF ISLANDS

Many important people have owned property on Calf
Island. Lieutenant Gould of Hull was a prominent owner of
Calf Island, and had a peculiar arrangement whereby he could
keep one and a half sheep on his part of the island. Although
he was absent for many years from the harbor, his rights were
carefully observed.

It was some years after this time that a ship, driven far off
her course, crashed on the rocks near here, the crew of seven
losing their lives. The men were buried on the island, but nothing can be found as to who they were, or what ship it was that
foundered there.

The *Mollie Trim* hit the ledges January 9, 1886. This
vessel, under Captain Christian Olsen, was heavily loaded with

coal and bound for Rockland, Maine. When the gale blew up, he tried to make Boston Harbor and slid in between Outer Brewster and Green Island, finally going ashore at Calf Island. Olsen, when the ship hit, ordered the crew into the rigging, and climbed to the masthead himself. When the masts fell he was thrown clear onto the beach, and, after a few moments of unconsciousness, was able to get up and survey the position of the ship. To his horror the bodies of the four men of his crew came floating in on the shore. After pulling them above the raging sea, he walked up to the home of a fisherman. When the waves finally went down the fisherman rowed him over to Boston Light where a signal was set for aid. The tug *Emily* soon came to his rescue.

Shortly after the Civil War, John S. Weeks purchased Calf Island. Arriving in Boston from the Provinces, he was said to have had little money, but at the time of his death was worth $900,000. After many happy years spent at his island home, Weeks leased Calf Island for ten years to Harold Gurney's uncle, Franklin P. Gurney. Harold P. Gurney of Brookline made his first trip to the island at the age of six months.

Many happy days were enjoyed at Calf Island in Boston's Outer Harbor. Franklin Gurney often entertained a Catholic priest at the island. It was said that Gurney's skeptical outlook on life was in great conflict with the teachings of the priest, but the two men struck up a deep friendship and were constantly seen in each other's company, carrying on friendly discussions. Three lobstermen are remembered as living at Calf Island during this period, Fred Zanetsky, James Turner, and a Mr. Finlay. In 1902, when the lease terminated, Benjamin P. Cheney bought the island from the Weeks estate.

Julia Arthur then moved to the Island where she lived in the residence which her husband built for her at great expense. The building still stands, facing Greater Brewster, but has been unoccupied for many years.

Wanting Calf Island and Little Calf Island during the World War, the Government paid Julia Arthur's husband, Benjamin P. Cheney, $46,500 and took possession.

We called at Calf Island many times in the summer and fall of 1934, Mrs. Grace Reekast entertaining us while we were ashore. We visited the lonely graveyard at the top of the island where the sailors were buried so many years ago in unmarked graves. The driftwood on the shore was piled up ten feet high.

Walking about Julia Arthur's former mansion, we saw the large stage which she had in the great hall. One little tragedy we noticed was that of two little swallows which had evidently flown into the house through the chimney and had not been able to find their way out again. They were lying on the floor of the hall with their beaks just touching each other—dead.

Little Calf Island, barely an acre in area, is a rough, rocky ledge, and as far as can be ascertained, never had any history worthy of mention. Hundreds of sea-gulls have their nests here, unmolested except for the casual visit of some adventuresome soul from the mainland.

GREEN ISLAND

We know very little about Green Island. On the older maps it is called North Brewster Island. The fact that it is referred to in 1788 as Greene's Island, makes me believe that Joseph Green, a well-known merchant of this period, either lived here or owned the property. There is not much to the island, however, as its single acre of rocks and soil does not permit development of the site.

Samuel Choate was rescued from this ledge in the Minot's Light storm of 1851. The lonely old man had been living there as a hermit, existing on lobsters, fish, and clams. He returned to the property after the storm, and it was not until 1862 that he was in trouble again. At this time his boat went to pieces, and he was taken up to Boston. Returning with a new boat, he was able to remain three years more, but in 1865 he was removed for the last time as he was practically starving to death. Since he had no relatives, he was taken to the Bridgewater Almshouse where he died a few weeks later.

About the year 1905 two fishermen named McFee and Johnson moved to Green Island. Every four or five days they would go to Boston with a great load of lobsters. After these fishermen left, a Mr. Young lived there for many years. The last and only house on the island was destroyed in 1932 when the crew of a boat wrecked on the shore built a fire to keep warm. The wind shifted and the house burned down. Andrew and Freeman DeGaust were the last fishermen to have the island, for the late Charles W. Harper purchased it soon after.

The wreckage of many ships is still to be seen around the island.

OUTER BREWSTER ISLAND

Outer Brewster Island is, perhaps, the prettiest of all the islands of Boston Harbor. A day spent at this site of chasms and caves will never be forgotten by the visitor. It belonged with the other Brewster Islands in the early days and was not considered as an separate entity until after 1750. At that time it was known as the Outward Island. Some charts call it the Little Brewster.

On August 21, 1799, Nathaniel Austin bought the property. After Austin's death in 1817 his son Nathaniel eventually acquired the whole island. In 1843 his brother Arthur W. Austin purchased the property and began his plans for macadamizing roads in Boston from material cut at Outer Brewster. At the same time he was cutting a canal through the outer part of the island as a possible anchorage for ships in rough weather. The demand for the stone material dwindled and the work stopped. It is believed that Elliot Street in Boston is still surfaced with material from this island, and a building in City Square, Charlestown, is known to have been partly built with material from Outer Brewster.

During the Civil War a fisherman by the name of Jeffers moved to the island with his wife and children. He built a shack on the shore near what was known as Rocky Beach and began his practice of trapping lobsters. All went well until one stormy November night when Jeffers and two companions were trying to land on the rocky shore after rowing from Middle Brewster. As anyone knows who has landed at Outer Brewster, there is no real beach, and the sailor who must reach the shore on a stormy night is in a serious plight.

The dory went down; two of the three men, including Jeffers, were drowned. When the survivor reached the rocky shore and told Jeffers' wife what had happened, she made the best of the situation, continuing to live at the island with her children. Finally she was forced to give up the unequal struggle and moved to the mainland. Hoodlums from the city soon destroyed their home on Rocky Beach.

The Honorable Benjamin Franklin Dean purchased Outer Brewster in 1871 for $1,000, and twenty years later Augustus Reekast, Senior, moved there. Mr. Reekast brought up eight children on this lonely place. Mr. Reekast built a shack ten feet square at a cost of $600; for his lease of the island he paid $25 a year. In 1894 Mr. Reekast kept three cows belonging to Mr. Richenbach at Outer Brewster. Mr. Richenbach ran a boarding house at Fort Warren, then the center of activity down the harbor.

With the turn of the century Josiah Stevens Dean took charge of the property, and Mr. Reekast moved to Middle Brewster Island. The island was leased in 1909 by Mr. Freeman DeGaust, a lobster fisherman, who now paid a yearly rent of $80. He had come to the United States from Canada at the age of 16.

One of the first steps Mr. DeGaust took was to erect on the island a sign reading: *This is private property; 10 cents a head for landing.* When engineers were measuring the channel, they had occasion to land at Outer Brewster to take their bearings, so one of them went ashore to negotiate with Mr. DeGaust. The outcome was that the latter agreed, for $17, to let the engineers land whenever they wished. Mr. DeGaust has seen a hundred ships anchored off the shores of his island; he told me that the masts made the ocean look almost like a forest.

Leading down to the water, Mr. DeGaust had a wharf three feet wide and 60 feet long, with a ladder at the end of the pier. A mooring about 200 yards from the wharf accommodated his ship except in the worst blows from the west, when Mr. DeGaust would have to use another mooring on the other side of the island. During the years spent at Outer Brewster Island, Freeman DeGaust lost five boats from various causes.

When the Government desired to purchase the island in 1913 the sole objection which the Army representatives raised was the insufficiency of fresh water to supply the number of men needed to man the proposed armament properly. Mr. De-Gaust always had plenty of water for the use of his family from his sixteen-foot well. Arrangements were completed on June 4, 1913, when Outer Brewster Island became the property of the Government which paid Benjamin Franklin Dean, 2nd, $2500 for the property.

The island is crowded with enchantment and beauty, and down through the years, various writers have extolled its virtues. Shurtleff tells us that its cliffs far surpass those of Nahant in attractiveness.

With our boat safely moored one hundred yards from the northern cliffs we shall row ashore in the tender. It is high tide, and although it is a relatively calm day, the breakers are still dashing against the outer ledges. If we are careful, we can row in between the rocky cliffs to the entrance of the canal which extends across the eastern end of the island. We locate the opening after a few troubled minutes and finally pass between the high cliffs, the noise of the breakers to the east diminishing at every stroke of the oars.

At last our craft gently slides up on the pebbly beach, which is covered with driftwood sufficient for many roaring bonfires. It is very quiet compared with the noise of the sea we have just left. We climb up the sides of the cliff and over to the southern side. Here the cliffs and chasms are of such grandeur and magnificence that they far surpass anything else in or around Boston Harbor. Back in the western cove there is a peculiar rock which resembles a pulpit, and Pulpit Rock has been pointed out for many years to visitors at the Brewsters. It is possible to explore many attractive little caves and inlets here at dead low tide.

A day could easily be spent here exploring the crags and cliffs. I like to think that an island similar to Outer Brewster, the prettiest in the outside harbor, was in the mind of Thomas Haynes Bayley when he wrote:

*"Absence makes the heart grow fonder:
Isle of beauty, fare thee well."*

PART III

North, East, and South of Boston

THE GLORY OF SALEM

During the middle of the Eighteenth Century the port of Salem, Massachusetts, was the principal sea terminal of ocean transportation between the East Indies and America. Boston itself, in this period, occupied second place in New England trade with Asia. By 1790 growing Salem was the sixth largest city of the United States, with enormous quantities of merchandise passing through Salem's custom house to their destination elsewhere in America. By 1800 eight million pounds of sugar annually came into this port, with many other commodities and supplies increasing proportionally. Salem was the maritime capital of the New World.

Evidence of this early activity can be seen at Salem today. The Peirce-Nichols House, and the Pingree House on Essex Street are still standing. Famous Derby Street, although greatly altered from its former grandeur, retains much of interest to the visitor. Countless millions of dollars' worth of almost every known commodity were stored here during the height of Salem's maritime greatness. The warehouses of Derby Street bulged with tea from China, silks from India, pepper from Sumatra, coffee from Arabia, gum copal from Zanzibar, and spices from Batavia.

Why did all this great commerce begin at this time? Where is all this trade today? These are two important matters for discussion.

The substantial increase in Salem commerce, shipping and mercantile business came directly as a result of the Revolution, when many Salem privateering captains found themselves with swift vessels capable of making long voyages into distant lands. Hundreds of young Salem lads, fresh from encounters with the British under the great West and the resourceful Harraden, were ready to man these converted privateers, for after the excitement of the Revolution, these lads were temperamentally suited for further voyages of adventure.

Adventures they had, but at the same time their exploits and daring in foreign lands brought wealth and glory to their home port of Salem, which soon rose to great prosperity. Salem's ships and crews were seen in every port of the world from 1783 to 1812, and in many cases the captains who had these splendid vessels in their command were actually too young to vote!

The value of organization quickly asserted itself in Salem, for two important societies were brought to full effectiveness during this period. The Salem Marine Society, formed in 1766, soon became a leading influence, while the Salem East India Marine Society was founded in 1799. This latter group was restricted in membership to those who had navigated their vessels in waters around Cape Horn or the Cape of Good Hope.

We shall now mention some of the masters and ships which were representative of this epoch in Salem history. Ships conspicuous in Salem annals, in addition to vessels mentioned elsewhere, include the following: The *Restless,* the *St. Paul,* the *Formosa,* the *Margaret,* two ships named *Hazard,* the *Brooklyn,* the *George,* and the *Marmion.*

The first New England ship to visit the Isle of France, China, and India was the *Grand Turk,* which cleared from Salem Harbor in the month of November 1785. Another famous voyage that signalled to the rest of America of Salem's approaching maritime maturity was that of the brig *William and Henry,* which landed one of the first cargoes of tea imported in an American vessel at Salem. The year was 1790.

Captain Jacob Crowninshield of the important Salem family of Crowninshields sailed from Salem on the *Henry* in 1791, bound for Mauritius. Her cargo, much of which he picked up along the American coast, eventually included iron, soap, gin, salt fish, tobacco, chocolate, flour, and hardware of various descriptions. Stopping to load freight whenever the occasion offered, the shrewd Crowninshield bartered with the natives in far off corners of the world, sailing in and out of various ports until his original cargo had either been sold or exchanged. Many months later he returned to Salem Harbor, and when the cargo had been disposed of, the coffers of the Crowninshield family were much the richer because of the voyage of the *Henry.* The financial success of this voyage was repeated scores of times in the following years by countless Salem vessels.

Salem merchants, as a result, became fabulously wealthy, and Salem ships were soon known in every port of the world. Israel Thorndyke of Beverly was worth more than a million dollars when he died, as was Simon Forrester. William Gray, worth $3,000,000 at one period of his career, was usually known as one of the three most prominent citizens in Salem during this remarkable period. The other two were Elias Hasket Derby and Joseph Peabody. Shipowner Derby was reputedly the richest man in America when he passed away in 1799, while William Gray six years later was identified as the owner of the greatest number of sailing ships in the United States. Joseph Peabody's vessels visited every known port of the world, including 47 trips to Saint Petersburg and 38 which his captains made to India's Calcutta.

The port of Calcutta became such a magnet for Salem vessels at this time that one of the important native merchants there had a large map of this country suspended on the walls of his Indian office. There were only two American locations identified on the chart, Salem and Boston. The word Salem stretched across the chart, while Boston was located with a small dot.

Salem's introduction to the valuable pepper trade came as the result of a secret sea voyage in 1795. In that year Captain Jonathan Carnes sailed from Salem Harbor on the *Rajah,* bound for a mysterious destination which turned out to be the pepper fields of Sumatra. Eighteen months went by, during which time there was much speculation on the wharves of Salem as to what had happened to the *Rajah*, but one day she was sighted passing Halfway Rock, homeward bound. Extreme curiosity was evidenced by every Salem merchant, but when she was warped into the pier the secret was revealed. The *Rajah's* entire cargo was pepper! The precious shipment was quickly sold at such a price that after paying off his crew and taking care of all other expenses Captain Carnes returned a net profit of 700 percent on the trip. This was the voyage which began Salem's great pepper business.

Flourishing for many years, the pepper trade brought great wealth to many Salem citizens, but the inevitable slump developed about the year 1804. Disastrous prices resulted, and those whose pepper ships came into port at that time found themselves ruined in many cases. One of the unreported vessels was the *America*, captained by Benjamin Crowninshield. He had sailed from Salem with explicit orders to purchase pepper and the market had broken during his absence. The owners of the ship were greatly worried for fear that he had followed orders, so when the sails of the *America* were reported off Baker's Island, they rushed down to the pier, unable to restrain their anxiety. As the ship came slowly up the harbor, two of the Crowninshield brothers jumped into a small boat and rowed out to the vessel, where Captain Benjamin Crowninshield, knowing what they wanted to find out, stood smiling at the taffrail.

Drawing near, Benjamin W. Crowninshield, later Secretary of the Navy, shouted through his trumpet, asking the captain what his cargo was. His cousin, enjoying the suspense to the utmost, shouted back, "Pepper." Actually, Captain Crowninshield, who had discovered the slump in the pepper market months before, had loaded the *America* with marketable coffee instead, but decided to fool the other Crowninshields as long as possible. Rowing closer, cousin Benjamin W. Crowninshield obtained a whiff of the rich coffee aroma, and the hoax was ended. Captain Ben Crowninshield then admitted his disobedience to orders, but in buying coffee he had saved the Crowninshields thousands of dollars. So all ended happily.

Salem anecdotes and stories of this era are many. The first mate on one of the China vessels from Salem became gloriously drunk one day while the ship lay at a Chinese port, and the captain, a strict teetotaler, was shocked when the mate appeared in front of the entire crew in his depraved condition. Noticing the state of the first officer, the captain assumed his subordinate's duties in writing up the ship's log, but after inscribing the remarks of the day, the captain entered, as a word of explanation:

"The mate drunk all day."

The next morning the ship sailed away, and the mate came up on deck that afternoon, thoroughly sober. The time came for him to open the log, where he was amazed and chagrined to find the captain's entry. Appealing to his superior, all he could get the captain to say was "It was true, wasn't it?" The mate worried for several days about this comment in the records which would be read in Salem when the ship returned. Finally he hit on a solution. A few days later, when the captain was making his weekly examination of the log, he found one small item, spelled out carefully in the handwriting of the first mate:

"The captain sober all day."

The Sacred Cod of Boston is well known, but Benjamin Pickman of Salem thought so much of the fish that he caused it to be carved in half model on the stairs of his Salem residence, built in 1750. When the building was torn down in 1942, a number of the cod models were distributed to several families and societies connected with Salem's mercantile background.

Captain Silsbee of the *Herald* and Captain Heard of the *Caravan* were two master mariners about whom many stories have been told. During the quasi-war with France in 1798,

Captain Nathaniel Silsbee warned another Salem master that he would sink him unless the other captain joined in line of battle with several other vessels against a French privateer which was closing in on them. The other captain, able to out-sail the Frenchman, did not dare risk Silsbee's wrath.

"Damn you, Silsbee," were his words when Silsbee threatened to sink him, "I know you would." The ships then combined to overwhelm the French privateer.

Captain Augustine Heard has become one of the legendary figures in the annals of Salem shipping. During the War of 1812 his ship the *Caravan* was captured by an English cruiser, which sent a prize crew aboard. All except Captain Heard and the negro cook were placed in irons.

One day a terrific gale came up, which was just what Captain Heard was waiting for. The English crew went aloft to take in sail, while Heard slipped into the galley for the cook. Together they went below, unnoticed in the confusion of the gathering tempest. One by one they knocked the irons from the legs of their fellow crew members, and when all were free they made a rush for the arms chest, which they easily captured. Going up on deck, the Americans seized each sailor as he came down from aloft, one by one, and placed them in irons below.

Captain Heard then informed the British master that he was sailing to Boston Bay, but gave the surprised and unhappy Englishman the freedom of his cabin. It was a proud moment when Captain Heard sailed in by Baker's Island Light, with the British prize crew still below decks.

On another occasion Captain Heard was approaching a bar near the Sand Heads. Drawing more water than was on the bar, the vessel was maneuvered so that she lay over on her beam ends to allow the ship to slide safely across the bar. At still another time Heard is known to have run a pirate ship under in the China Sea. His, indeed, was a colorful career.

No survey of Boston Bay could be complete without the story of the peer of all navigators, Nathaniel Bowditch. Born in 1773 at Salem, he was the son of Habakkak Bowditch, a retired mariner. Nathaniel Bowditch went to sea in 1796 on the *Henry*, spending all his spare hours at the study of his beloved mathematics. On this voyage Nathaniel Bowditch made hundreds of observations on the ship's position as she sailed to different ports of the world.

To his surprise, young Bowditch found that the standard British navigation book contained thousands of errors. After two more voyages he decided to work out his own navigation volume, and in the year 1801 published his first edition of *New American Practical Navigator*. This book is still the greatest single step forward in navigation contributed by an American.

Entering Salem Harbor during a blinding snowstorm aboard the *Putnam*, Bowditch was given a chance to demonstrate his unusual ability. He estimated where Baker's Island should be, and surely enough, just as there was a slight lull in the storm, the welcome flash of Salem Harbor's sentinel was seen for a brief instance in the exact location Bowditch predicted. In later years the members of his crew merely had to mention that they had sailed "with Captain Bowditch" to obtain positions, for he had taught all his crew, even the cook, the intricacies of navigation.

The glory of Salem did not last forever, of course. She never recovered from the blow dealt her when the British sealed up the New England ports during the War of 1812. There were other reasons for Salem's downfall. Larger ships were built, which could not enter Salem's shallow harbor, and the other ports took her commerce away. New Orleans, Baltimore, and the Erie Canal all did their share in destroying Salem's business. No railroad ever made Salem its terminal, so Boston gradually took business away for that reason. Boston's intense rivalry with New York affected all the other Massachusetts ports, but Salem lost more than her share. The 182 vessels which in 1807 claimed Salem as their port faded away to 57 ships by 1815. William Gray transferred his interests to

Boston, while the enterprising Lows moved away to Brooklyn. By 1835 the handwriting on the wall was plain for all to read, but it was a lingering death which sea-minded Salem suffered.

In 1824 Captain Benjamin Upton brought the first rubber overshoes to this country from Para, Brazil. Between 1836 and 1842 Salem received more than 750,000 pairs of pure gum overshoes from Brazil, and Morison observes that these boots proved just the thing "for navigating the slushy streets of Salem in winter." It all ended in 1845, however, when New York stepped in and took the rubber business away from Salem. Although Salem ships and Salem captains called for many years afterwards in South America, Zanzibar, and the Philippines, her days as a leading American seaport were numbered, and by the days of the California gold rush her maritime activities could no longer be classed on a par with other Atlantic Coast cities.

The great days of Salem's commerce are over, but New England will never forget the merchants, sailors, and shipmasters whose enterprise and daring created such an unparalleled chapter in Boston Bay history.

THE MISERY ISLANDS

Great and Little Misery, off the shores of Beverly, have long occupied a place of geographical importance in Outer Salem Harbor. Roger Moulton is believed to have been wrecked here in the early days of the settlement, for it was known as Moulton's Misery before 1659. John Winthrop himself sailed between Great Misery and Baker's Island when he came to Salem for the first time. In those days one could walk out over the bar at low tide from the mainland to Great Misery Island.

In 1673 Bartholomew Gale, after whom Gales Ledge and Gales Point are named, obtained half the island from Thomas Tyler, grandson and heir of the Ipswich Sagamore Masconnomet.

The first building erected on the island was the home of Captain George Corwin, who came to America in 1638. Securing the written tenure of the island in 1678, he agreed to pay the annual sum of three pounds for a thousand years and a day. The residence stood on the island long after Corwin's death, but in 1782 the British landed on the island from a cruiser and destroyed the house, carting off the wood for badly-needed fuel.

The next we hear of the island was in 1844, when Daniel Neville, known in Boston for his ballast business, retired from this activity to take over the island, where he indulged in farming. Known at this time as "Lord of Misery Island," he would climb to a high observation point daily carrying his enormous telescope, with which he watched the great sails of the clippers and other vessels as they passed within range of his mighty glass.

One year a strange plague of grasshoppers visited Misery Island, consuming farmer Neville's crops and all the grass and the leaves from the trees. Neville left at once for the mainland, and before the week ended he arrived back on the island with a great flock of turkeys, which in a relatively short time devoured every last grasshopper, tradition relates. Finally Neville died, and the land of Misery next attracted attention in 1882, when the Common Sense Fertilizer Company prepared to build a wharf and establish a rendering plant there. But opposition quickly sprang up which interfered successfully with the fertilizer company's plans, and all efforts by the company were abandoned. Shortly after 1900 the island became a rendezvous for Harvard reunions, chowder parties, and other social events.

A great fire swept Misery Island in May 1926, destroying many residences and doing damage estimated at $100,000. The fire was seen for miles around, but by the time help reached the scene it was too late.

Because of erosion the once dry passage between Great and Little Misery Island can be traversed only at low tide. The wreck of the *City of Rockland* still lies in the passageway between the two islands, where the ancient *Monohansett* was beached years before. The bones of the *City of Rockland* seem somehow to symbolize the former glory of the coastwise passenger excursion steamer, practically a thing of the past.

In 1935 Trustees of Public Reservations purchased Great Misery, and more than 5000 persons visited the island that year. The reason for the purchase was that an oil terminal group attempted to obtain Great Misery to erect gigantic storage tanks. United opposition resulted in the oil company's losing out.

Great Misery and Little Misery Islands today seem quiet and undisturbed, and the casual visitor will find the few residents there gracious hosts.

BAKER'S ISLAND AND THE LIGHT

Five miles out to sea from Salem lies Baker's Island. Its delightful insular aloofness makes it the ideal location for a summer colony, with the lighthouse, cottages, grassy terrain, and rocky sea-cliffs. The fifty-five acre island has had an interesting history, extending from earliest times. Among the first to mention the island was John Winthrop, who records in his journal on June 12, 1630 that he sailed into Salem Harbor between Little Misery Island and "Baker's Isle."

The next event we include occurred in 1642, when Salem Harbor froze over all the way out to Baker's Island. In the same year Boston Harbor experienced a similar intense seige of cold weather.

So much lumber was taken from Baker's Island during the middle of the 17th Century that in 1670 the removal of wood was prohibited unless special permission from the town fathers had been granted. Seven years later John Turner leased the island.

In 1685 the smallpox epidemic in Barbadoes caused a load of cotton wool to be put ashore at Baker's Island until the possibility that it contained the dreaded disease seemed to be ended. Four years later the residents of Baker's Island watched pirate Thomas Hawkins capture the ketch *Mary* near Halfway Rock, located to the southeast of Baker's Island.

Early in the Eighteenth Century the rent of Baker's Island was placed at three pounds annually, the income going to the support of the grammar school. John Turner finally purchased the island outright in 1731 for 130 pounds. Turner was born in what is now called the House of Seven Gables.

The well-known Doctor Bentley went out to Baker's Island in 1791, where he visited the newly erected beacon placed there by the Salem Marine Society. Bentley tells us that a large, joyful crowd placed the first sea marker at the island on July 28, 1791. When losses continued from shipwrecks in spite of the beacon, the Salem Marine Society petitioned Congress for the erection of a lighthouse.

Congress authorized Baker's Island Light in 1796, and the foundations were laid the next summer. On January 3, 1798, the twin lights were illuminated for the first time by Keeper Chapman. In those days, the keeper lived in a building which was a combination lighthouse and residence, for at each end of the dwelling a lighthouse tower had been erected.

During the War of 1812 the famous frigate *Constitution* was saved from the British navy by Keeper Joseph Perkins of the lighthouse, who observed *Old Ironsides* as she was beating across the bay, chased by two British warships, the *Tenedos* and the *Endymion*. Seeing that the captain of the *Constitution* needed help, Perkins rowed out to the warship, where his services as pilot were eagerly accepted. In a short time the *Constitution* was safely inside Salem Harbor, her English antagonists thwarted by the vigilance of a Yankee lighthouse keeper.

Hundreds of rabbits were raised at Baker's Island shortly after the turn of the century, according to Bentley's diary. Dr. Bentley evidently made the island his favorite resort, as he mentions it often. In the late summer of 1817 he called at Keeper Perkins' home to inspect the lighthouse mechanism, and speaks of the metallic reflectors behind the lamps, and the convex plates of glass in front. When Bentley reached the island that day, Keeper Perkins was cutting hay for the coming winter.

That same winter a great ship, the *Union*, heavily loaded with pepper, crashed on the rocks at Baker's Island. This mishap was charged to the extinguishing of one of the lights on the island. Since the ship was loaded with 3600 picals of pepper and 900 picals of tin, the wreck proved a costly one. When another unfortunate vessel crashed ashore shortly afterwards, petitions were filed to reestablish the second light. Many believed that the mariners confused Baker's Island with Boston Light, as both had but one beacon, but the Government did not restore the second light at Baker's Island until 1820.

An amusing incident is told of Joseph Perkins II, son of the keeper. A pilot at the island, he started for the wharf one day to bring in a ship when he was charged by the island bull. It is said that Perkins used much more effort and skill to maneuver himself off the island without the bull catching him than he later needed to bring the vessel in by the many dangerous ledges and reefs of Salem Harbor.

In August 1834 the last pirates to be executed in New England sailed in by Baker's Island as prisoners aboard the British warship *Savage*. After capturing and burning Captain Butman's vessel, the Salem brig *Mexican*, the pirates had been apprehended. Landed at Crowninshield's Wharf, the twelve pirates were taken to Boston, where six of them were hanged later in the year.

In 1875 the man who became Admiral Dewey visited Baker's Island Light as an inspector. He signed his name in the lighthouse guest book on October 21, 1875.

James F. Lundgren was appointed keeper in 1881. Professor Sears, the geologist, and Lundgren's son journeyed out to Halfway Rock one summer to examine the geological formation there, and to their surprise found several badly tarnished copper cents. Returning to the mainland with their coins, they learned that it has been the custom for Salem sailors leaving port to toss good luck pennies ashore at lonely Halfway Rock to bring them success on their coming voyage.

During the great tornado of July 16, 1879, when over thirty persons perished around Boston Bay, the fog bell tower was hit by lightning and demolished. Great destruction was caused by this short but frightful storm in Salem Harbor.

Professor J. H. Gilmore, who wrote the hymn *He Leadeth Me*, was at Baker's Island during the summer of 1893. On

August 21 he recorded in an island journal:

"The dreaded East is all the wind that blows. Everybody has been longing for a storm and the day brought it. The message of the sea throughout the day told us of the wisdom and the power and glory of God; and at night, when the winds were hushed . . . the sea spoke to us of God's love."

The wreck of the schooner *Jefferson* occurred on December 5, 1893, when the schooner misstayed after a sudden change of wind. Keeper Perkins boarded her soon afterwards, but the captain and crew decided to abandon ship four hours later, and the vessel soon went to pieces. The martingale of the *Jefferson* is now serving as a stanchion on the Pilot's Retreat cottage.

The great disaster of Salem Bay occurred July 4, 1898. The steamer *Surf City* had left Baker's Island earlier in the afternoon, and was halfway between Salem Willows and Beverly. Up on deck, watching a gathering storm cloud, was Mrs. Nathaniel T. Very. Suddenly, a long winding finger of whirling clouds, gigantic in size, dropped itself down from the leaden sky overhead, until it resembled an inverted cone. Lower and lower it came, until it united with the ocean at a distance of about a mile from the vessel. It was a waterspout. Mrs. Very told me that it was truly a terrifying experience, to watch this gigantic column as it moved across Salem Bay. Suddenly, however, a terrific wind hit the *Surf City*. The captain now ordered everyone inside the cabin. The tempest pushed the ship up on a ledge in shallow water, and the *Surf City* went over on her beam ends. The water slowly but surely began to rise in the cabin. There were terrible scenes as the frantic passengers tried to free themselves. Mrs. Very put her hand out through the window, and she was seized and pulled through the opening by rescuers outside. Fifty-one others were saved, but the eight persons left in the cabin drowned. The storm, with

30-METER SQUARE YACHTS MAKING A PERFECT START AT THE
MARBLEHEAD YACHT RACES OF 1941

THE THOMAS W. LAWSON

WRECKED NEAR THE SCILLY ISLES ON DECEMBER 13, 1907. THE 375-FOOT SCHOONER
WAS THE LARGEST SAILING VESSEL IN THE WORLD

ANNA-MYRLE SNOW CLIMBS
BOSTON LIGHTSHIP

BAKER'S ISLAND LIGHT AND FOG HORN
MISERY ISLAND IN BACKGROUND

EDWARD ROWE SNOW

MINOT'S LIGHT OFF THE COHASSET SHORE

its spout and fatal shipwreck, was one of the worst in Salem history.

A strange accident occurred at Baker's Island on July 6, 1901, when young Fred Hutchinson attempted to rescue Mrs. Charles Upton, who had fallen from the rocks while fishing. He was bringing her ashore successfully when Mr. Upton, over-anxious in his desire to help, also lost his balance and fell into the sea, landing on rescuer and victim. Both husband and wife now grabbed for Hutchinson, who finally pulled himself away and swam for the shore, unable to help them because of their frantic struggles. The couple drowned.

The banana steamer *Ethelwold* ran on the rocks of the Middle Breakers in the summer of 1901, and the deckload was thrown overboard to lighten the ship. Thousands of bananas soon floated ashore at Baker's Island, and this welcome fruit was plentiful for the next two weeks in the lighthouse and sum-mer cottages there.

For six years Baker's Island had a baby hospital. The North Shore Babies' Hospital was located on the island from 1904 until 1910, with hundreds of infants getting the benefit of the ocean's invigorating breezes and the life-giving rays of the sun. The Winnie-Egan, the hotel at Baker's Island, burned down in 1906, and was never rebuilt. This closed an era of the island's history.

The fog horn at Baker's Island is one of the most powerful in New England. First erected in 1907, the horn went into service at 3:25 in the morning of July 12 of that year.

The great Salem fire was seen from Baker's Island on June 25, 1914. It was an event in which many islanders lost their winter homes. Two years later the first telephones were in-stalled at the island.

The smaller of the two lighthouse towers was declared in-active on June 30, 1916, and a new light was placed in the higher tower. This new light is still in use today. Thus the lighthouse has had first two lights, then one, again two, and finally the present single light which shines from Baker's Island today.

The thirteenth and last keeper of Baker's Island Light was placed in charge in July 1918. A month later he was appointed constable of the island in addition to his position as keeper, and he has served in both capacities for many years.

With the coming of World War II Keeper Arthur Payne found himself in charge of a group of young coastguardsmen. There was much activity at the station during the danger period from 1941 until 1943, but events quieted down soon afterwards. Arthur L. Payne, the last civilian keeper of Baker's Island Light, retired from the service in April 1944. Loved and respected by all who knew him, Keeper Payne will be remembered as a brave, deserving lighthouse man who faithfully performed his duty to the end.

His successor, Chief Boatswain's Mate Benjamin Stewart of the Coast Guard, has now become firmly established at the station on Baker's Island. Technically, he is not the keeper, but the commanding officer, and the main reason for his residence on the island is the care of the light station. Stewart's many years of service to his country have been filled with thrilling adventures in Europe and Africa, as well as exciting days out on lonely Saddleback Ledge Light off the Maine coast.

The present characteristic of Baker's Island Light is an alternating red and white flash every fifteen seconds. We trust that for many more years Chief Boatswain's Mate Stewart will send out its gleam to warn the mariners of Boston Bay of the dangerous reefs along the shore.

MARBLEHEAD AND RACE WEEK

We journey now to Marblehead, the center of New England yachting activity. Every year thousands of white sails dart in and out around the islands and ledges of the outer harbor as the Massachusetts Bay mariners try their sailing skill against one another.

But it was not always so. At one time scores of Indian canoes dotted the waters of Marblehead Harbor where today the amateur sailors race. Part of Marblehead Neck itself is known as Nanepashemet, named for the last great Indian chieftain of this section of the country. In 1615 this mighty leader of the strong tribe of Naumkeag Indians saw his followers go down in defeat while battling with the Tarratines, a fierce group of northern warriors. Two years later the Naumkeags were decimated by the dread smallpox, so when the Tarratines returned in 1619, Nanepashemet and his brave Indian fighters were driven from stronghold to stronghold, with the chief himself finally captured and killed at the top of a high hill overlooking the Mystic River. For many years afterwards the place of his death was regarded as sacred ground, and none of his descendants was privileged to visit there.

Marblehead also has its stories and legends. The tale of the screeching woman is known to but a few. During the 1690's a richly laden Spanish galleon was overtaken by pirates, some of whom had Marblehead antecedents. Every passenger and crew member was brutally murdered with one exception— a beautiful young girl whom several of the local Marblehead freebooters desired for themselves. Upon reaching Marblehead with their victim, they took her ashore in a small boat on a dark, rainy night, landing at Oakum Bay. Carrying the girl to a location near the beach, they forced their attentions upon her. The young Spanish beauty fought them off, however, and they decided that she must die. Drawing a dagger, one of the men approached her, but she eluded him and ran shrieking toward the beach where the tide was low. Her screams were so loud that several villagers, asleep in their beds in Marblehead, were awakened by her piercing cries of mortal anguish.

"Oh, Lord, save me," cried the unfortunate girl. "Mercy, Lord Jesus, save me," she shouted. Finding refuge on a low tide rock, the girl awaited her fate. The men soon had her surrounded, and the pirate with the dagger crept slowly toward her. Her shrieks rang out over the town of Marblehead as the pirate leader closed in, and then finally his dagger struck. Again and again the knife descended until the girl sank down on the rocks. Her dying cries were said by those who heard them to be the most pitiful to which they had ever listened. The lifeless body was quickly buried by the buccaneers, and when the tide came in, the bloodstained rocks where she was killed were mercifully covered by the advancing sea. It is said that the ghost of the screeching woman came back each year on the anniversary of her murder for over a century and a half, but no one now living claims to have heard her pitiful cries.

Then there is the legend of "Old Dimond," the alleged wizard who lived on the northwest side of Charles Island in Little Harbor. Moving there in April 1709, Dimond soon had a fleet of vessels sailing to far-flung ports all over the world. In times of unusual storms he climbed to Burial Hill, where Dimond raised his great voice to shout orders to his captains hundreds of miles at sea. The people of Marblehead could hear his voice even above the roar of the worst storm or blizzard, and would say to each other in hushed tones, "Old Dimond's out again tonight." Many of the townspeople actually believed that the wizard could, in some mysterious way, make himself heard far at sea, and thus, with his superior knowledge of the storms, save his vessels. Old Dimond had other powers as well, according to the legend. A substantial sum of money disappeared from a residence in town one day, and the wizard was consulted. Not only did he name the actual culprits, but he also predicted the exact location where the money was later found.

Other legends told in front of Marblehead fireplaces for more than two centuries include that of the mariner who was chased from the local tavern all the way home by a corpse who carried his coffin on his shoulders. An earlier patron of the same tavern had been bothered by the Devil himself. Old Beelzebub was constantly in the habit of driving by this unfortunate, and the Wicked One was always seated in a carriage drawn by four white horses.

The fisherman's vision is another unexplained Marblehead legend. Returning home one night after a three months' fishing journey, he hastened to the home of his sweetheart, a short distance away, with a freshly caught fish as a gift. As he rapped on the door, it slowly opened, and there she stood. He entered, placed the fish on a table, and then turned to greet her. As he hurried toward her, however, she faded from the room. Terribly frightened, he rushed to the home of his mother who gave him the astounding news that his sweetheart's funeral had been held the week before. What then he asked, had he seen when he entered her home? No one has ever been able to explain this strange occurrence.

Most of us know Marblehead today for its well-deserved position as the capital of American Yachting. During Marblehead Week hundreds of the nation's outstanding sailboats and yachts complete their courses daily, darting in and out around the innumerable ledges and rocks in such a delightful fashion that it would gladden the heart of the most confirmed landlubber should he witness it. The yachtsmen of New England, and especially those of Boston Bay, deserve much credit for the enterprise which has made Marblehead Week the inspiring event it is today.

The various personalities associated with this week of racing cannot all be mentioned, but we include a few. Leonard M. Fowle was an expert reporter of these annual events, and his son Leonard is continuing the good work. David D. Nickerson is a well-known yachting figure whose presence during Racing Week is a necessity. Howard Bennett deserves much praise for his efforts. The eminent Charles Francis Adams sails his own craft across the Bay from Scituate to Marblehead alone, often starting back late in the afternoon for his home.

Racing at Marblehead really became important around 1906. It was about that time that the German Sonder yachts were brought over to race in this country. William L. Carleton of the Corinthian Yacht Club and Henry Howard were instrumental in increasing the popularity of the annual races. Then Frank Monroe took over the duties of Regatta Week promotion, and John MacBeth developed a great amount of interest in the smaller craft.

This increased importance of the smaller types of racers has caused a definite change in the habits of the yachtsmen who visit Marblehead. Formerly, as in the days when Roland Nickerson's *Memmer* and Walter Lane's *Sally* sailed in Boston Bay, the racers lived aboard their large and commodious yachts, but today, with the emphasis on the smaller craft, many of the contestants go home after the day's activities have ended.

The younger racers, with the development of the Brutal Beast class, certainly take the spotlight away from the grownups, and it is a pleasure to watch these children, sometimes as young as five and six years, attired in their kapok life preservers, sailing across Marblehead Harbor.

The days of racing week are divided. The Eastern Yacht Club has charge of activities on Sunday, Monday, and Tuesday, while Sunday's Pleon ocean race is run off by the Boston Yacht Club, which also handles Wednesday's festivities. Usually the races on Thursday, Friday, and Saturday are managed by the Corinthian Club, with sailoffs and other events taking place on Sunday. The record total for the eight leading races occurred in 1937, when 3042 boats participated in the most thrilling Marblehead Week which New England yachtsmen ever experienced. A resident of Boston Bay who misses Marblehead Week is indeed letting a glorious opportunity go by to see the modern New England sailor at his best.

NAHANT AND THE FORGET-ME-NOT

About the year 1815 the rocky shores of Nahant attracted many Boston families during the summer months, and when in 1818 the steamer *Eagle* landed scores of excursionists to visit this attractive peninsula, Nahant became the Mecca of hundreds of Bostonians. Swallow's Cave, John's Folly, Pulpit Rock, and many other interesting locations became as familiar to Boston families as the Old State House and the Great Elm on Boston Common.

Samuel A. Eliot, Frederick Tudor, Cornelius Coolidge, Thomas H. Perkins, and scores of other prominent Bostonians soon became established at either Nahant or Little Nahant. Later in the century many prominent literary figures made Nahant their summer home, including Agassiz, Longfellow, and Prescott. Later still Henry Cabot Lodge was a well-known Nahant figure.

At a period shortly after the year 1815 a Medford family journeyed to Nahant for the summer, and the cottage into which they moved was next door to that occupied by a group of Italians of high birth. One of them, a young man, soon became interested in the young lady of the Medford family, whose name was Alice. Before long they were often seen together exploring the cliffs and crags of the rocky Nahant shore. When the first suggestions of fall began to show, the couple declared their engagement. In those days, however, it was necessary to obtain parental consent of both families, and the Italian's parents were still in Leghorn, Italy. Going to Boston, he made final arrangements to sail across the seas for this blessing on his coming wedding. The last afternoon before the sailing the two lovers were sitting high on the Nahant ledges overlooking Egg Rock.

As they sat gazing out over the spacious Atlantic, the thought came into the boy's mind of the legend of the forget-me-not flowers which grew at distant Egg Rock, and of the significance of these tiny blossoms. The story was that a girl who received from the hand of her lover a forget-me-not flower growing on that particular island should remain forever constant.

"Dear Alice," he cried, "give me this final opportunity to show my love. On yonder rock grows the forget-me-not flower. Let me journey out to it, and secure for you the blossom taken from its highest pinnacle." Alice tried to prevent him from making the trip to the rock, but he at once was afraid she doubted his courage. As he stood up, the faintest caress of a breeze caused his hair to blow across his brow, and Alice was seized with a premonition of danger. Again she implored him not to make the journey, but he ran down to Little Nahant Beach where his sailboat was moored. An old man cautioned him, "Do not go out in your sailboat now, my son, for the wind is rising. Wait for the next tide."

"The next tide will take me away from my loved Alice," said the boy, "so it is now or never." Waving a fond farewell to the watching Alice, he sailed for distant Egg Rock. But the winds were increasing rapidly, and the waves mounted higher and higher.

White water showed all around Egg Rock when the sailboat approached, but the boy jumped lightly out and made the painter fast. Climbing up the sides of the high rock, he reached the sheltered nook where grew the forget-me-not flowers. High in the air he held them while he waved at his sweetheart a mile away in Nahant, and then he ran down to the sailboat. By this time the surf and wind had combined to create a terrifying situation. The waves were breaking eight and ten feet high. When he finally pushed off with his sails set for shore, the wind took him far off his course, and the sailboat was soon in the breakers off the rocks where the

couple had sat less than two hours before. Closer and closer
the craft came, and Alice, high on the cliff, watched with
curious fascination this last act of her lover. Then came a
mighty wave, larger than the others, which caught the sailboat
in its merciless grasp and rushed the helpless lad with the
speed of the wind toward the rocky cliffs. The poor boy
looked up for a final moment into the eyes of his intended
bride, and then the sailboat struck the rocks, broke up, and
was gone, together with Alice's lover. He had perished beneath the waves in a vain attempt to bring her the Floure of
Souvenance.

Alice was brought back to her home in a state of collapse.
Early the next morning fishermen knocked at her door; the
body had been found, and was, even then, lying on the great
beach between Lynn and Nahant, covered with a blanket.
Alice threw a shawl over her shoulders and rushed out of the
house. A short time later she reached the beach, and as she
drew near, her sorrowing friends gathered around the lifeless
body. She stood over her dead lover as they slowly withdrew
the blanket from his form. His right hand was firmly clenched,
and as she leaned over him, she noticed something still clutched
in his grasp—a few stems of the flower for which he had given
his life—the forget-me-not.

Taking one of the flower stems from her dead lover's
hand, Alice slowly walked away. In spite of the terrible
shock she was able to reach her home, but there she became
desperately ill. Removed to her Medford residence, she never
walked again, and, as the first flowers of spring made their
appearance, Alice, mourning her lover to the end, died. She
was buried in the family lot at Medford, and was soon forgotten by most of her friends. But there were those who said
that strange moanings were always heard near her grave whenever the wind began to rise, as though she were still protesting
her lover's departure in that gathering October gale a century
ago.

THE CHESAPEAKE-SHANNON BATTLE

In the War of 1812 there were many outstanding American victories over vessels of the British navy, but the engagement between the American frigate *Chesapeake* and the British man-of-war *Shannon* ended in disaster for the American vessel.

During the last week in May 1813, Commander Philip Broke of the British warship *Shannon* cruised back and forth between Baker's Island off Salem and Boston Light, waiting for the American man-of-war *Chesapeake* to sally forth and fight. Captain James Lawrence of the *Chesapeake*, however, was busy attempting to whip his oddly-assembled crew into an effective battle group, and stayed in port.

Fresh from his triumph over the English warship *Peacock*, which he captured in the record time of thirteen minutes, Lawrence was having his troubles, for the new members of the crew were green and untried and his veterans were grumbling about their failure to receive *Peacock* prize money.

By the morning of June 1, Lawrence decided that his ship was fit, and that the challenge of the *Shannon* was no longer to be ignored. Just before noon on that fateful day the *Chesapeake* weighed anchor and proceeded slowly down the bay, accompanied by almost a score of smaller vessels, whose owners were eager to watch another British man-of-war capitulate to the gallant Lawrence. In Boston a banquet table had even been set to dine the American victors, with a place-card for the defeated Broke as well. But it was not to be.

One of the American officers had slept the night before at the Sturgis home in Point Shirley, and as he left this historic mansion, which still stands, he suggested that his friends go to the top of Great Head to watch the victory. The headlands that day were crowded with excited observers all the way from Gloucester to Scituate. Aunt Proctor, who lived to tell her story for many years, was watching from what is now Winthrop Highlands.

Sailing in majestic splendor out beyond Boston Light, with her handsome commander a striking figure in his white jacket, the *Chesapeake* made rapid progress. The *Shannon*, several miles outside, filled under jib topsails and spanker, and awaited the American's approach. When within pistol shot, the *Chesapeake* rounded to on the starboard quarter, to windward, and Commander Broke realized that Lawrence was attempting the same maneuver which had defeated the *Peacock*. Not to be outdone, Broke waited until the *Chesapeake* ranged alongside, yard-arm to yard-arm, and gave the order to fire.

With the command "Fire!", every broadside gun of the *Shannon* discharged its fatal contents directly along the deck of the *Chesapeake*. This broadside decided the battle almost before it was under way, for a great mass of shot, splinters, torn hammocks, shredded rigging, and wreckage was blown like a huge dust cloud across the deck of the *Chesapeake*. The effects were terrible to behold. Two-thirds of the deck crew were either killed outright or seriously wounded in that single death-dealing salvo. But still another equally serious blow was about to fall.

Tall, handsome Lawrence, conspicuous in his attractive white jacket, was standing on the carronade slide when he was seen by Lieutenant Law of the British Marines. Taking careful aim, Law fired at the Chesapeake's captain just as Lawrence turned and faced him. The shot caught the American squarely in the abdomen, and Lawrence fell heavily to the deck. Realizing that his wound was probably fatal, Lawrence raised himself on the deck to shout the words which have become the watchword of the American navy: *"Don't give up the ship!"*

Borne below, Lawrence soon lapsed into unconsciousness. Another volley from the *Shannon* guns crashed into the *Chesapeake,* and then the British marines boarded the American ship. Commander Broke himself plunged into the thick of the fray, and received a terrible head injury, his skull being partly severed from his head. Just then a barrel of lime was hit by a shot, leaving the *Shannon's* captain plastered with lime and blood. The gallant Broke was removed to his quarters. With both commanders put out of action, the bloody engagement went on, but a few minutes later the Americans gave up the fight, realizing that it was a hopeless contest.

The yachts and other vessels which had accompanied the *Chesapeake* down the bay now sailed sadly back to Boston, while the *Shannon* towed the American warship away from Boston Bay. Four days later, while on the way to Halifax, Captain Lawrence died. Commander Broke recovered from his wounds, but never took command again. The engagement between the two vessels was one of the shortest and bloodiest on record; 252 men were either killed or wounded in less than fifteen minutes.

The loss of Lawrence and the *Chesapeake* was revenged on the Great Lakes, when Commodore Oliver Perry, flying the banner "Don't Give Up the Ship" from the masthead of his flagship, gave the British vessels there an overwhelming defeat.

THE THOMAS W. LAWSON

While twenty thousand people cheered, the largest sailing vessel in the world became the first ship ever launched from the Bethlehem Fore River Shipyard in Quincy. The 375-foot *Thomas W. Lawson* slid down the ways on July 11, 1902, and was soon placed in active service.

From the beginning of the *Lawson's* career the names of the masts of this great ship have created friendly controversy. Douglas Lawson, son of the man for whom the schooner was named, says that the correct title for each mast in order is as follows:

FORE MAIN MIZZEN SPANKER RIDER DRIVER JIGGER

Mr. Lawson speaks of those who insist the spanker must be the stern mast, but he does not hold to this belief, as it is his opinion it was not standard even in five or six masters. A jigger, when used, was always the aftermast, is Mr. Lawson's belief.

Several years ago a contest was held in Seattle to determine the names of the masts of the *Lawson*, but just how this would decide such an unusual problem was not explained by those in charge of the contest.

Captain Ernest D. Sproul of the Old State House Marine Museum, a mariner of long standing, gives the following titles:

FORE MAIN MIZZEN MIDDLE SPANKER DRIVER PUSHER

The late Charles H. Lincoln, of the *Boston Post*, a literary associate of Thomas W. Lawson, said the great man told him on several different occasions that the masts were named for the days of the week:

SUNDAY MONDAY TUESDAY WEDNESDAY THURSDAY FRIDAY SATURDAY

I have a signed message from Captain William Holland of Bradford. "Having served as quartermaster on the *Thomas W. Lawson,* I feel I must know the names of the sticks she had in her. They are as follows: fore, main, mizzen, jigger, spanker, driver, and rudder masts. Captain William Holland."

Captain Frank H. Peterson, secretary of the Boston Marine Society, states that Captain Arthur Crowley of the *Lawson* told him the masts were originally called

FORE MAIN MIZZEN AFTER MIZZEN JIGGER DRIVER SPANKER

Later, according to Captain Peterson, they were changed to

FORE   MAIN   MIZZEN   NO. 4   NO. 5   NO. 6   SPANKER

Captain Elmer Crowley, brother of the late Captain Arthur W. Crowley of North Attleboro, agrees with Wilfred O. White of Boston in saying that the masts were always known by the names which Captain Peterson later called them. As Wilfred O. White actually handled No. 4 and No. 5 on a voyage, his words, and those of Captain Elmer Crowley should carry considerable weight. When we combine their statements with one the writer has at hand, made by Captain Arthur Crowley, master of the *Lawson* for five years before his death, all three agreeing exactly on the names, I believe we should accept this listing of the masts as accurate. Captain Arthur Crowley said, "I have always called them fore, main, mizzen, No. 4, No. 5, No. 6, spanker."

The *Lawson* sailed from this country for the last time late in 1907, with a cargo of 2,500,000 gallons of lubricating oil. Encountering heavy seas off the Scilly Isles, southwest of England, Captain George W. Dow anchored his schooner to ride out the storm, December 13, 1907. When the British pilot came aboard, the gale had come up appreciably, and the storm increased. The anchors began to drag late that night, and the world's largest sailing vessel hit the ledges off the Scilly Isles shortly before midnight, breaking in two between her No. 6 mast and the spanker. The entire crew and the British pilot were lost with the exception of Captain Dow and the engineer, Edward Rowe, of East Boston. There are those who make much of the indisputable fact that the schooner was wrecked on Friday, the thirteenth, thirteen men were lost with her, and there are thirteen letters in the vessel's name—*Thomas W. Lawson.*

AN AMERICAN ARMY OF TWO

Most of us who have been privileged to sail into beautiful Scituate Harbor have read the tablet on the old Scituate Lighthouse.

SCITUATE LIGHT HOUSE BUILT 1810 LIGHTED 1811
SIMEON BATES—REUBEN BATES—JAMES YOUNG BATES—KEEPERS
REBECCA AND ABIGAIL BATES DAUGHTERS OF SIMEON, CALLED
"THE AMERICAN ARMY OF TWO"
PLACED BY THE BATES ASSOCIATION INC. 1928

It is unfortunate that a controversy still rages about the names of the two little heroines and what they did. Some claim that the whole story is a fabrication, but evidence points otherwise.

The usually accepted version of this interesting tale is that Reuben Bates, the keeper at Scituate Light during the War of 1812, had two young daughters, Rebecca and Abigail, who were anxious and willing to help their country against the British. In the spring of 1814 the English man-of-war *Bulwark* lay at anchor off Scituate Harbor. Keeper Bates feared that his lighthouse would meet a fate similar to that experienced by Boston Light during the Revolution when the upper works of America's oldest beacon were blown to pieces, but the British did not molest Scituate Light. On June 11, 1814, however, when the citizens of Scituate refused to furnish fresh meat and vegetables to the men on the *Bulwark,* two English barges were sent into the harbor itself, where the British marines set fires which destroyed many American boats and schooners.

Later in the summer a regiment from Boston under the command of Colonel John Barstow arrived in the vicinity, and the *Bulwark* soon left Scituate Harbor. As the summer weeks passed without incident, discipline among the American soldiers was relaxed so that the guards were visiting the village and combining pleasant diversions with their daily tasks.

One day early in September the British man-of-war *La Hogue* appeared off the coast, when there were no guards at Scituate Lighthouse. Only the eldest daughter of Keeper Reuben Bates, 14-year-old Rebecca, her younger sister Abigail, and a younger brother were at the light. Rebecca, high in the tower when she sighted the *La Hogue*, sent her brother off to the village to warn the people and then went down on the beach to plan what could be done. She watched the powerful warship tack and stand off to sea, then tack again and make for the harbor itself. The tide turned and began to come into the bay. It was a fine day, and a gentle breeze slightly ruffled the water as the *La Hogue* sailed nearer and nearer.

When high water came at two that afternoon, the man-of-war let go her bowers, swung her yards around, and lay quiet in the afternoon sun less than half a mile from the First Cliff. Climbing the light so that she might have a better vantage point, the terrified girl, alone with her sister at Cedar Point, observed that the British were launching boat after boat into the sea. The town was to be burned, she thought, just as the city of Washington had been destroyed.

In the village itself there was confusion and uproar everywhere when the boy arrived with the news. Forgetting the lighthouse, the villagers and soldiers planned to defend the shore near the town against the invaders, using the fish houses for a fort.

Then began the approach. Five large whaleboats, loaded with marines and manned by British sailors, started for the beach. It was a splendid but fearful sight, the marines with their bright red coats and their guns held upright with bayonets glistening in the sun. The oars in the whaleboat moved with orderly precision as the Britishers neared the point of land where the girls were watching.

In the lighthouse residence, which is attached to the tower itself, Rebecca remembered there was a drum and fife which actually belonged to the missing guardsmen who had amused themselves during their leisure by teaching the girls to play. In an instant Rebecca flew down the steps of the tower, handed her sister the fife, and picked up the drum. The girls stole out of the building and hid behind the lighthouse. Then, as the steady, measured strokes of the British sailors could be heard nearing the spit of land where the lighthouse stands, Rebecca began to beat the drum and her sister to play the fife. Louder and louder their efforts came, until the British oarsmen passing the lighthouse stopped their labors. Could the Americans be massing to overcome them?

The officers in the whaleboats were in a quandary. As they were debating what to do, the ship's commander aboard the *La Hogue,* hearing the drum and fife, ran up a flag signifying danger and ordered a gun to be fired. This was the signal agreed upon for a return to the *La Hogue,* so the expedition was turned into a retreat. Cheers could be heard coming from the townspeople of Scituate as the girls, triumphant but exhausted from their trying and exciting efforts, sat down to rest. What a proud moment it must have been for the young girls when they realized that their ruse had saved the town of Scituate!

As darkness fell over the bay, a gun flash was seen from the British warship. A single shot, aimed at the lighthouse tower, described its parabola from the deck of the *La Hogue,* but it screamed into the water more than fifty yards short of its mark. It was merely a parting gesture, however, for the *La Hogue* then hoisted sail and was soon hull down bound northward. In a short time the townspeople had reached Cedar Point, and the girls who had comprised the American Army of Two were soon made to feel their importance.

More than half a century later Rebecca and Abigail both signed statements which we show below. It is through the courtesy of Helen Ingersol Tetlow that we publish Miss Abigail Bates' own statement:

> "Abbie the Drummer one
> of the American Army of
> two in the War of 1812
>> Miss Abbie Bates
>> aged 81
>> Mass."

Miss Rebecca Bates made the following statement:

> "Born 1793   1878
>> Rebecca Bates, aged 84 years one of the American Army of two in the war of 1812 who with her sister aged 15 saved two large vessels laden with flour from being taken by the British with fife and drum"

In 1874 the *Saint Nicholas Magazine* published an article by Charles Barnard in which he describes the incident. He claims that Abigail had not helped in the Britishers' repulse, but gives the honor to a Miss Sarah Winsor who, Barnard relates, was visiting Rebecca at the time. There is no controversy about Miss Rebecca Bates' part in the story.

Regardless of which two girls were responsible for saving Scituate from the enemy during the War of 1812, it was a heroic incident which took place at Scituate Lighthouse that summer of 1814, when two young girls, cleverly using their wits, caused five whaleboats loaded with some of the best fighters in the British navy to be frightened away from the Massachusetts shore.

In the words of Lilla A. Ham,

> *"Thus Rebecca and Abigail, loyal and true,*
> *Once composed the American Army of Two."*

PART IV

The Beacons of
Boston Bay

THE STORY OF BOSTON LIGHT

LIGHTHOUSES and beacons have always been a fascination to the traveler and sailor, as well as a very necessary part of navigation itself.

An early mention of a lighthouse in American history occurs in Clough's *New England Almanack* for 1701, where the question is asked:

"Whether or no a Light-House at Alderton's point may not be of great benefit to Mariners coming on these Coasts?"

Shurtleff tells us there is no doubt that a beacon and watch house were built there in the early settlement of the colony, and in the Massachusetts Archives at the State House we read that the Town of Hull presented a bill for work done at the beacon. Nothing was actually done to give Boston Harbor a lighted beacon until the first Saturday in January 1713, when John George, Junior, whose father was killed aboard the *Rose,* headed a petition for the erection of a lighthouse.

From a maritime point of view, Boston was the center of the most prosperous and important of all the American colonies in the early 18th century. Many of her merchants and shipowners had followed the sea when younger and were willing and anxious that the port be properly protected. Just how progressive these merchants were can easily be seen when we realize that almost half a century elapsed after Boston Light was built before the citizens of New York erected a lighthouse.

In the town meeting held May 13, 1713, it was voted that "in case the Gen'll Court shall see cause to proceed to the establishment of a Light-House for the accommodation of vessels . . . the Town of Boston may have the preference before any particular persons in being concerned in the charge of erecting & maintaining the same. . ."

On November 5, 1714, the Court passed an order to the effect that "a Light-House be Erected at the Charge of this Province at the Entrance of the Harbor of Boston on the same Place & Rates proposed in Bill." The order was accepted June 9, and after the investigation of a committee, the Boston Light Bill was passed July 23, 1715, and provided for "Building and Maintaining a Light House upon the Great Brewster." The light was to be erected on the "South-ermost part of the Great Brewster, called Beacon Island," and the sum of £1900 was granted by the Court for the construction of the light. The preamble and act included provisions for raising the money to pay for the light, and each ship was to be charged "the Duty of one penny per Tun inwards and also one penny per Tun outwards and no more for every Tun of the burthen of the said Vessel, before they load or unlade the goods therein."

On the twenty-fifth of June, 1716, the work was so far advanced that the committee, in looking for a good man to take care of the light, believed the position worth the equivalent of five dollars a week. George Worthylake, whose father had been a resident of George's Island for many years, was now appointed the first keeper of the first lighthouse in America. His yearly salary of fifty pounds was considerably augmented by his income as one of the Boston Harbor pilots. Boston Light was first illuminated September 14, 1716.

Worthylake, keeper of Boston Light, petitioned for an increase in salary in 1717. The winter of 1716-1717 had been so stormy it had prevented him from watching his sheep at Greater Brewster. Fifty-nine of them strayed down to the end of the long bar and drowned.

The keeper with his wife and daughter was sailing off Noddle's Island in November of the next year when a gale blew up. The boat was lost, the three occupants perishing beneath the waves. This unfortunate accident caused the famous lighthouse ballad of Benjamin Franklin to be written. Thirteen years of age at the time, Franklin sold this ballad on the streets of Boston, naming his effort "The Lighthouse Tragedy." As the event had made quite an impression on the people of Boston, Franklin did a fair business with his first literary offering, but he tells us in his *Autobiography* that it was "wretched stuff." Not a single copy is now in existence. The unfortunate Worthylake family was buried at Copp's Hill, where the headstone can easily be found.

Mr. Robert Saunders, who is mentioned as a sloop captain in 1711, was now ordered to go to "Beacon Island and take care of the Lighthouse." Within a few days he also perished in the ocean, and Boston Light gained the doubtful reputation of losing its first two keepers by drowning. Although Saunders was not in service long enough to be officially appointed, we should honor his sacrifice by calling him the second "Keeper of Boston Light."

The merchants of Boston now recommended Captain John Hayes, an experienced mariner, for the position of keeper of the light, and he was appointed by the Court November 18, 1718. The duties of the keeper were many and varied at this period in the history of Boston Harbor. He was health officer, pilot for the vessels coming in and going out of Boston Harbor, custodian of the fog gun, and keeper of the light.

It was about this time that the celebrated Daniel Neal wrote his description of Boston Harbor. He speaks of Castle Island, and then says:

"But to prevent any possible Surprise from an Enemy, there is a Light-House built upon a Rock, appearing above Water about two long Leagues from the Town, which in Time of War makes a Signal to the Castle, and the Castle to the Town by hoisting and lowering the Union-Flag, so many Times as there are Ships approaching, which if they exceed a certain Number, the Castle fires three Guns to alarm the Town of *Boston*, and the Governour, if Need be, orders a *Beacon* to be fired which alarms all the adjacent Country; so that unless an Enemy can be supposed to sail by so many Islands and Rocks in a Fog, the Town of *Boston* must have six or more Hours to prepare for their Reception."

On June 29, 1719, Hayes asked for a gallery to be built on the seaside of the lighthouse so that he could "come to the Glass to clear off the Ice & Snow in the Winter Time, whereby the Said Light is much obscured." He also asked, "That a great Gun may be placed on the Said Island to answer Ships in a Fogg." The Court took steps to prevent ice from forming on the glass of the light, and also sent a cannon to Little Brewster Island. The gun, Fitz-Henry Smith, Jr. suggests, was probably taken from Long Island. In the picture of Boston Light drawn by Burgess around 1729, the gun is shown in practically the same position as that in which it still stands. The date 1700 is engraved on the gun.

On January 13, 1720, a bad fire broke out at Boston Light, caused "by the Lamps dropping on ye wooden Benches & snuff falling off & setting fire." Captain Hayes tells us that "ye said fire was not occasioned by ye least neglect of ye Memorialist." Whether or not Memorialist Hayes was to blame, £ 221 s16 d1 was expended to repair the damage done by the fire. Hayes received his salary only after an interview with the Council as to the cause of the fire.

Two years later Hayes had a hard time inspecting all the ships from plague-ridden European ports, and in this manner lost many piloting jobs. The Court granted him twenty pounds to repay him for the money lost.

The "Great Storm of 1723" did considerable damage to Boston Light. This gale, perhaps the most severe in the eighteenth century, raised a tide estimated at 16 feet. Captain Hayes weathered this terrible gale, but the people of Boston feared the lighthouse had suffered. On visiting the island a committee found that Boston Light had been damaged and the wharf ruined, but authorized expenditure of only £25 for urgent repairs. Substantial renovations were delayed, but three years later £490 was spent to put the island in proper order.

A bad gale blew up on September 15, 1727, while Captain John Bangs was bringing a sloop in past Boston Light, and the storm forced the boat ashore on Greater Brewster Spit. The next morning as the wind blew harder and the storm increased, Captain Bangs sent one of his crew to Captain Hayes at the light with a request that Hayes come out in his boat to help the sloop off. Hayes went to the assistance of the stranded vessel, but, the storm growing worse, efforts had to be abandoned until the tide turned. Hayes was then successful in pulling the sloop off the Spit. Leaving two of Bangs' crew in his boat to follow, he piloted the craft safely into Boston. The two sailors in Hayes' craft ran onto the rocks near South Battery and damaged the vessel considerably. Hayes told the Court the boat was "old and crazy" and unfit for future service, but he was advised to get the craft repaired. The government paid all of the expenses except £15, which they charged up to Captain Bangs. Probably the next time John Bangs brought his sloop into Boston Harbor he steered amply clear of that stretch of sand and rocks on which Bug Light now stands.

The infirmities of age finally forced Hayes to retire from active service, and on August 22, 1733, he notified the government he would leave the service when his year was up.

The merchants of Boston now petitioned for the appointment of Robert Ball who became the next keeper of Boston Light. Once firmly established at Little Brewster, Ball made a careful survey of the piloting business in Boston Harbor, becoming quite upset upon realizing that other sailing craft in the harbor were taking his business away from him. He soon petitioned the General Court for the right to have preference, as the others never worked in the winter while his was a year-round task. The other pilots decoyed the masters of ships coming into the harbor by "wearing a wide vane such as properly belongs to the province boat, and of the same color and livery." The Court gave Ball permission to be the "established pilot" of the harbor for the next three years, and allowed him to keep two well-fitted boats, unmistakably distinguished. It further decreed that any person who painted his boat with a similar vane would be fined five pounds, the fine to be given to Ball.

Because of the war scare of 1745, a committee went down the harbor to take measurements for the sinking of hulks in the channel. They landed at Boston Light, and the hospitable keeper at Little Brewster Island entertained them in a manner which John Hayes had long ago decided was unbecoming the keeper of Boston Light. The bill for hospitality to the committee, fifty shillings, was promptly sent up to Boston.

Three years later Ball wrote up to Boston that the lighthouse needed a fresh coat of white paint, and that the building was badly in need of renovation. The paint was applied, but in 1751 a bad fire damaged the lighthouse, so only the walls remained. A temporary light was now shown from a spar some distance from the remains of the lighthouse. The light was repaired at a cost of £1170, and, as the Court believed that "the Charge of such repairs should be bourne by those who receive the immediate benefit thereof," a higher duty was instituted.

Captain Ball usually had a negro servant at the light, and a few years ago I read in the abandoned graveyard at Rainsford Island the following inscription:

Here Lies Ye Body of Samson, Late Servant of Mr. Robert Balls
Who Died June 25th, 1762, Aged 60 Years

Robert Ball, in addition to his regular duties at the light, was quite a real estate operator, owning three islands in Boston Harbor at the time of his death. Calf Island and Green Island were then given to his son John while his daughter Sarah received the Outer Brewster. Ball petitioned the Court in February 1774 for his pay to November 19, 1773, and it is probable that his nephew, William Minns, was the actual keeper of the light from that time until the British took over the island in

1774. The name of the man who kept the light while it was under English rule will, in all probability, remain a mystery.

Early in July 1775, the Provincial Congress wished to have the lamp and the oil removed, as the Harbor was then blocked up and the establishment at the island useless. On the twentieth of July, Major Vose, leading a small detachment of American troops, visited Boston Light where the men burned the wooden parts of the lighthouse. On their way back from Little Brewster Island they were met by an armed British schooner, but they outmaneuvered the English ship and reached the mainland. An eye witness, quoted by Frothingham in his *Siege of Boston*, says that he saw "the flames of the light house ascending up to Heaven, like grateful incense, and the ships wasting their powder." The Americans had already cut 1000 bushels of grain in Hull, and now returned safely through the American lines with all their spoils.

The British began at once to repair the lighthouse, and the workmen as they labored were guarded by the British marines. But the Americans were not ones to allow the rebuilding to continue, so Washington placed Major Tupper in charge of 300 men who, on July 31 started from Dorchester and Squantum for Boston Light. They were successful in landing their armed whaleboats at Little Brewster Island, and the historic Battle of Boston Light began. A writer of the period tells us that:

> *"When Tupper and his men had landed there*
> *Their enemies to fight them did prepair*
> *But all in vain they could not them withstand*
> *But fell as victims to our valient band."*

The guard defeated, Tupper destroyed the work done on the lighthouse and prepared to leave the island. The tide, however, had gone out and his whaleboats were left stranded there. In the meantime, the British had sent their own small boats to the island and as the Americans finally pushed their boats into deep water, they were attacked by the English troops.

The Americans were helped in this new skirmish by a field piece under the command of Major Crane at Nantasket Head. When the situation looked threatening to the Yankees trying to leave the island, a direct shot from the American gun crashing into one of the English boats turned the tide of battle. After the British retired to their boats, it was found that only one American had been killed, while the English losses were comparatively heavy. Major Tupper brought a badly wounded British soldier to Hull where he soon died. His gravestone is still pointed out by the older inhabitants of Hull, the more historical of whom will tell you that Susanna Rowson herself led the services at his funeral.

George Washington was so pleased with the work of Major Tupper that he commended the major and his men for their "gallant and soldier-like behavior in possessing themselves of the enemie's post at the lighthouse."

After the British left Boston March 17, 1776, they lingered down the Harbor menacing all the towns of the bay. Samuel Adams was quite indignant that nothing was done to make the British leave the harbor and suggested in a letter that the various islands be fortified. Tudor tells us in his diary that eight ships, two snows, two brigs, and a schooner still remained in the harbor. On June 13, 1776, American soldiers landed on Long Island and at Nantasket Hill; the next day they opened fire on the fleet and soon had the English ships at their mercy. The British vessels weighed anchor and sailed down the harbor, but they sent a boat ashore at Boston Light, leaving a time charge which blew up the lighthouse, thus repaying the Americans who had twice damaged the light under British rule. It has been said that Boston Light was the last spot occupied by a hostile force in Boston Harbor, but the English landed at the outer islands during the War of 1812.

John Hancock, the Governor of Massachusetts, notified the Legislature November 8, 1780 that no light existed at the entrance to Boston Harbor, but thirty months passed without action being taken. The Boston Marine Society then addressed a message to the Senate and the House of Representatives, and pointed out that Boston was without a lighthouse to guide the shipping to its wharves, and that such a serious defect would have to be remedied before the people of Boston could expect a return of the days of good shipping. This petition had more effect than Governor Hancock's message of 1780, as the very next month the Commissary-General of Massachusetts was directed to erect a lighthouse on the site of the old structure. The sum granted by the legislature, £1,000, lasted until the lighthouse was nearly completed, when an additional £450 was appropriated to finish the job. Keeper Thomas Knox was appointed November 28, 1783.

The new lighthouse measured 75 feet high, with the walls at the base seven and a half feet thick, tapering to two feet six inches at the top. The lantern, fifteen feet high, was of octagonal shape, and its diameter was approximately eight feet.

Boston Light was ceded to the United States Government on June 10, 1790, along with twelve other lighthouses in the country. Massachusetts led the other states by transferring five lighthouses to the national government.

Thomas Knox continued in the service of the Lighthouse Department until 1811, when he was succeeded by Jonathan Bruce. The new keeper brought his wife Mary to live at the lighthouse. The couple witnessed the thrilling encounter between the *Chesapeake* and the *Shannon,* June 1, 1813, the battle lasting but fifteen minutes.

Jonathan Bruce and his wife stayed on at the Light after the war ended. In 1819 the rambling rhymester of Boston Harbor, Frederick W. A. S. Brown, wrote the following verse in honor of Keeper Bruce:

> *To Bruce, who kindles, when the night*
> *Succeeds the lightsome day;*
> *The slow, revolving, brilliant light,*
> *Now muse, thy tribute pay.*

Jonathan Bruce completed twenty-two years of service at Boston Light in 1833, and then retired to live at Rainsford's Island. His wife, Mary Bruce, died at Elder Rainsford's old home in 1851, and the inscription on her gravestone, still to be seen at Rainsford's Island, is worthy of a place here:

> *Bright be the place of thy soul*
> *No lovelier spirit than thine*
> *E'er barred from its mortal control*
> *In the orbs of the blessed to shine.*

Bruce lived until 1868, dying in Boston at the age of 76.

David Tower was the next keeper at Boston Light. The great December hurricanes of 1839, occurring on December 15, 21, and 27, threw more than a score of vessels onto the shores around Boston Harbor, but Tower was helpless to aid the crews of the Schooner *Charlotte* and the Bark *Lloyd* driven ashore at Nantasket. Less than five years after the triple hurricanes of 1839, David Tower died in service at Boston Light.

Joshua Snow became keeper October 8, 1844. In that year many fine improvements inside the light were made. The lighthouse was equipped with a cast iron circular stairway, having a central iron pipe and a wrought iron railing. "A cast iron deck and scuttle were put in, with iron window frames, a large outside door of iron, and an inside door with frame and large arch piece over it." The improvements of 1844 can be seen today, except where repairs have been made.

Captain Tobias Cook of Cohasset relieved Snow in the last week of December 1844. While Cook was keeper of Boston Light, James Lloyd Homer, the man who wrote as the "Shade of Alden," paid him a visit. He tells us that the light was eighty-two feet above the sea and makes the mistake of believing the steps leading up into the light were of stone. There were two wharves on the southwestern side of the island, according to Homer, and anyone steering his boat between the two piers would be sure of a cordial reception. A rather amazing development at Boston Light was the establishment about this

BOSTON LIGHT

OLDEST IN AMERICA, FIRST LIGHTED IN 1716

GRAVES LIGHT FROM THE AIR

time of a "Spanish" cigar factory, with young girls brought from Boston to work at Little Brewster Island. This business, set up to practice a fraud on the good people up in the city, was soon broken up, and the girls were sent back to Boston to work under less romantic conditions.

Tobias Cook resigned as keeper in 1849, and Captain William Long of Charlestown became the new official in charge of the light, bringing his family, including a daughter Lucy, out to Little Brewster. Through the kindness of Mrs. Herbert L. Wilber, I have been allowed to read the diary of her grandmother, Lucy Maria Long, which was kept at Boston Light from October 19, 1849 until October 2, 1851. I will quote a few of the entries from this almost priceless relic of Boston Harbor life ninety-five years ago:

"Sunday, October 21, 1849. Pleasant weather in the morning. I went into the Light House for the first time, the rest of the day was spent in rambling among the rocks.

"Monday, October 29.—Pleasant weather, in the forenoon I went in the cutter's boat to carry Antoinette to the Pilot Boat *Hornet*. In the afternoon I went over to the island, on returning saw the body of a man on the bar, supposedly washed from the wreck of the vessel, lost on Minot's Ledge."

At low tide it is possible to walk across the bar from Boston Light to Greater Brewster Island, and from there well along Brewster Spit; this is the route Miss Long took many times. She tells us that a gentleman came out to the Lighthouse on November 10, 1849, to try to induce her to go to Fort Warren to teach the children of the workmen, but she did not accept the offer as she enjoyed the social life of Little Brewster Island too much to leave it. When her father went ashore Lucy lit the great light herself. Her record of one of these occasions follows:

"Mon. Dec. 31.—A snowstorm, in the morning, George came over to wind up the clock, and I cleaned the light, at night I light the Light."

Other interesting incidents are included in the following excerpts:

"Sunday, May 19.—Pleasant weather, in the morning Mr. Dolliver went to Boston in the Boat *June*, in the forenoon William and myself walked on the spit as far as the beacon. At noon Mr. Phillips and Mr. Perry called from the Islands. Monday, Aug. 26.—Pleasant weather, this morning Albert came down in his boat."

The above-mentioned Albert was the Albert Small of the unusual lighthouse romance which culminated in the proposal at the top of the lighthouse. This courtship between Lucy Maria Long and Pilot Albert Small went on for many months, in spite of the scores of other young pilots who made Little Brewster Island the mecca of their leisure hours. Day after day we read of as many as six pilots landing at once to enjoy a social hour or two at the light.

One afternoon, accompanied by Sarah Godbold, a six year old chaperon, Lucy Maria Long and Albert Small went up to the top of Boston Light, presumably to admire the wonderful view from that well-known vantage point. Albert, however, had an important matter which he wished to discuss with Lucy at this time, and believing the little girl would not realize the full implications of what would occur, led Lucy a few feet away and asked her to marry him. Unfortunately for us she did not enter a detailed account of the incident in her diary, but we do know that her answer given at the top of Boston Light was "Yes."

Sarah was burdened with a very large secret for such a little girl. As soon as the three returned to the lightkeeper's house she informed the family of all which had transpired, to the embarrassment of the happy young couple, but the parents and the other pilots were quick to come to the rescue of the blushing pair with hearty congratulations. The culmination of this lighthouse romance came on June 16, 1853, when Lucy Maria Long and Albert Small were married.

In 1851 Captain William Long was succeeded at Boston Light by Zebedee Small, whose pay at the light at this time was $400 a year.

A visitor to Little Brewster while Small was in charge left an account of his impressions while there:

"Boston Outer Light, with its natural standard or tiny island, seems placed by the hand of nature in the spot for the special purpose to which the hand of man appropriated it. Though greatly exposed to the storms, and facing the severe eastern gales that blow up between the capes from the oceans, it yet is perfectly safe and secure in the hardest weather. Near the base of the light there is placed a gun, which is fired at intervals in foggy weather to warn off the mariners who may have got too near the breakers. A fog bell is also at hand to be rung by the keeper of the light in thick weather. It is difficult to express in words the thrill of delight that nerves the breast of the tempest-tossed mariner of the long voyage, when Boston Light heaves into sight, and its bright steady eye beams forth over the sea."

Hugh Douglass became the next keeper of Boston Light on June 2, 1853. The only important change while Douglass was at the lighthouse was in the rapidity of the light's revolution. In 1842, I. W. P. Lewis referred to the mechanism which turned the light as the "machine of rotation," and the speed of revolution at that time was three minutes. Elaborate changes were made by 1854 when the speed was increased to one minute thirty seconds. Today the light flashes white every half minute while the twelve bull's-eyes take six minutes to make a revolution. Douglass resigned the year Bug Light was built, 1856.

Douglass was succeeded by Moses Barrett, a native of Gloucester. Boston Light was provided with the Fresnal lamp in the third year of Barrett's term and at the same time the tower was raised to its present height of 98 feet. It was now listed as a second-order station, the rating being determined by the inside diameter of the lens. When the Fresnal lamp was lighted on December 20, 1859, the pilots protested that the new light was inferior to the old one in point of brilliancy and power. On an editorial page of the *Boston Journal* in 1860 we find the following:

"No person informed on the subject would ever venture to assert that a lens apparatus of the second order was equal in quantity and power and intensity of illuminating to a reflector of the first order . . . Mr. Barrett was the efficient keeper of Ten Pound Light, Gloucester, and appointed to this light by General Peaslee. If any man could make a second order light equal to a first order, probably Mr. Barrett could do it. No light can be too good for Boston's shipping interests, and certainly the light should be as good as those of other cities."

In the treasured collection of Mrs. J. L. Moulton of Gloucester, the granddaughter of Captain Barrett, is a clipping which recalls the days when her grandfather was keeper of Boston Light.

When the Brig *Ewan Crerar* struck on a ledge near the Graves on March 9, 1860, she came off and anchored between Shag Rocks and Outer Brewster, but filled and sank quickly in forty feet of water. The members of the crew were able to row to Boston Light in the snow-storm. It was one of the strangest wrecks in the history of the harbor.

Barrett was at Boston Light until late in 1862, and his last two years spent there were full of adventures. When Fort Sumter was fired on, April 12, 1861, he knew that exciting times were ahead.

The incident which impressed Barrett more than all the events connected with the war occurred on Sunday morning November 3, 1861, and was the worst tragedy in the history of Boston Harbor. The square rigger *Maritana*, 991 tons, had sailed out of Liverpool on the twenty-fifth of September with Captain Williams in command. She ran into heavy seas coming into Massachusetts Bay and approached Boston in a howling southeaster with a blinding snow falling. About one o'clock in the morning she sighted Boston Light and headed for the beacon which she was never to pass.

Mr. Barrett had noticed the lights of the vessel earlier in the evening. At twelve midnight she was bearing E.N.E., when she suddenly changed her course and seemed to be running for the light. At 12:20 she burned her torch lights, and by seeing the *Maritana's* yards, Barrett knew that she was a square rigger. The snow now came so fast that the lights of the ship disappeared, and Barrett prayed that she had slipped by safely and was then making her way into calmer waters.

As it later developed, the *Maritana* had crashed onto Shag Rocks, a short distance away, and the crew and passengers were then fighting for their lives. The sailors had cut the masts away soon after the ship had struck; many made attempts to reach the ledge but the great waves prevented anyone's reaching the shore of the little isle. The vessel now showed signs of breaking up, and the passengers and crew were ordered into the weather chains.

With the lifting of the snow, the anxious inhabitants of Lighthouse Island were able to see the ship stuck fast on Shag Rocks, but they were helpless to launch a boat in the swirling waters. Barrett then attempted to signal across to Hull, but the wind blew with such force that the signal flag was blown to shreds.

About 8:30 the great ship broke in two, and Captain Williams, standing on the quarter-deck at the time, was crushed to death. Seven people floated to Shag Rocks on the top of the pilot house, while five others were successful in swimming to the same ledge. After the hull of the ship had broken in two, fragments of the wreckage started to come ashore on both sides of the island, and the watchers on Lighthouse Island saw a body in the surf. By afternoon the sea and the storm had quieted appreciably, and Captain Barrett's signal to Hull was acknowledged. The bodies of the unfortunates now started to wash up on the beach, and that of Captain Williams was among the first. At two o'clock Pilot Boat No. 2, the *William Starkey*, sent a dory ashore at Shag Rocks and rescued the survivors of the tragedy. The boat was manned by Captain Samuel James of Hull, a member of the famous lifesaving family.

It was not until the following March that the last member of the crew was found and buried at Little Brewster Island. In the spring of 1862 the wife of Captain Williams came down to the island to receive her husband's watch and other keepsakes which the keeper had been saving for her, and sat with her children on the rocks under the lighthouse. She spent hours looking out at Shag Rocks, the ledge which had broken her family apart forever.

Charles E. Blair became keeper of Boston Light November 20, 1862, and saw the captured crews of the Confederate ships *Tacony* and *Atlanta* on their way to Fort Warren. Six of these prisoners escaped on the night of August 19, 1863, and two of them sailed by the island on their way down to Maine where they were captured. Blair returned to the mainland July 18, 1864, and was replaced by the celebrated Thomas Bates.

Captain Bates was honored many times for his heroism while in the employ of the Lighthouse Department, and many men still living have told me of his sterling bravery. Wesley Pingree, former keeper at Deer Island Light, related to me the story of the day at Minot's Lighthouse when two men were drowning near the ledge. Bates, alone at the light, took the dangerous risk of letting himself down in his dory from the top of the light. He reached the men and saved both of them from the raging storm. Bates took charge of another rescue January 31, 1882, at the time the *Fanny Pike* went ashore on Shag Rocks. She went to pieces quickly, but Captain Bates rowed out to the little ledge and took the crew off safely. Assistant Keeper Bailey and Charles Pochaska, a young fisherman who lived on Middle Brewster Island, helped him make the rescue.

Bates spent many pleasant nights at the lighthouse, and Assistant Keeper Edward Gorham, with his accordion, helped along the musical program which they all enjoyed on Sunday evenings. Bates, admonishing the others to sing louder, would tell Gorham to "bear down" on his accordion as they sang *When the Roll is Called up Yonder* and *Crossing the Bar*, every sailor's favorite. After almost thirty years of service Thomas Bates died on the island, April 6, 1893.

Alfred William assumed charge until the official appointment was made May 3, 1893, when Albert M. Horte was made keeper of Boston Light. His young sister Josephine played about the island at this time and still remembers when she used to turn cartwheels over the old fog gun which had been brought to the island in 1719. Horte was keeper less than a year, relinquishing his post to Henry L. Pingree, whose son, Wesley, became interested in Albert M. Horte's sister Josephine. Wesley Pingree and Josephine Horte were later married, spending their honeymoon at Deer Island Light.

Early one morning in 1897, as Pingree's son Wesley was walking down to start the fire for the fog signal, he was amazed to see the boat from Portland, Maine, in between Shag Rocks and the Outer Brewster. She backed out without striking, but a glance at the map will give the reader an idea of the craft's precarious situation.

The terrible storm on November 26, 1898 will probably always be remembered as the "Portland gale," as the Steamship *Portland* then left Boston for the last time. Another ship, the *Calvin F. Baker*, pushed up on Lighthouse Island, so close to the buildings there that when the ship rolled, the people on the island felt as if they could almost reach out to save the sailors. But the crew of the ship was frozen fast to the rigging, and cried out for help all during the next night. The keeper was unable to aid the men until morning, when the survivors were landed. Three sailors were lost from the ship. The terrible screams of the helpless men freezing in the rigging so affected Keeper Pingree's wife that she died shortly afterwards.

Henry Pingree's son was made an assistant at Boston Light, and one day he and the other assistant took the lighthouse dory to Fort Warren where they boarded the *Resolute* to go to Boston to get a forty-pound reed for the fog signal. Around noon, a terrible storm blew up, and when Pingree and the other assistant returned to Fort Warren they were warned not to attempt to reach Boston Light that afternoon. Believing that the fog signal should be repaired, they started from the dock at Fort Warren in the dory. As the little boat came out from the lee of George's Island, the full force of the gale hit them, and they could not make any progress toward the light. A mud digger was anchored a few hundred yards away, and the men fought their way to her, tying the dory in the lee of the craft. The captain told them he wouldn't take them to Boston Light that night for a million dollars, so they spent the evening with him. Later that night the dory was washed away, and the reed went with it.

The next morning, during a lull in the storm, the captain of the mud digger had them landed at Bug Light, and at low tide they successfully walked along Greater Brewster Spit and Lighthouse Bar until they reached Boston Light. The soldiers at George's Island had watched and waited for the dory to pass out through the Narrows the previous afternoon, and when it failed to come in sight the men believed the keepers had drowned. When the overturned dory washed up on the beach the next morning, their fears seemingly were confirmed. The Lighthouse Department was notified, and the *Geranium* started for the outer islands. She reached Boston Light, but the storm had so increased by this time that she could do nothing but steam up and down Lighthouse Channel, unable to send a boat ashore. In order to notify the *Geranium's* captain that all were safe, every man at the light came outside and joined hands in front of the lighthouse. The captain counted the men, and with a quick whistle of farewell turned his ship around for the trip back to Boston.

Keeper Henry Pingree left Boston Light November 1, 1909. His successor, Levi B. Clark, witnessed the terrible gale on Christmas Day, 1909, when the five-masted schooner *Davis Palmer* hit on Finn's Ledge and went down with all hands.

During the week of September 3, 1910, the Squantum Air Meet took place, and Claude Graham-White made his memorable flight to Boston Light from Squantum. Assistant Keeper Jennings waved down to the flyer as the airplane roared by just below the top of the light. An eye-witness of the event, Dr. William M. Flynn of Dorchester, tells us that there was a line of motor boats and naval launches stretched all the way from Squantum out to the light, as many thought that Graham-White would surely drop into the water at some point in his trip. The Bostonian Society has a fine collection of pictures taken at the time, one of which shows Keeper Clark and his family watching the flyer approach the lighthouse.

Keeper Levi B. Clark left the island in 1911, and for a few months George Kezar was Keeper of Boston Light. Kezar, who had been at Duxbury Pier in Plymouth, finally retired from the service in June 1935. He had passed many years of activity serving at several of the well-known lights along the coast.

Mills Gunderson became the next man in charge of Little Brewster Island. It was during his regime that the Boston Light Swim gained nation-wide prominence. This gruelling endurance test from Charlestown to Boston Light has attracted hundreds of boys and men since its inauguration. Sam Richards is perhaps the best known of all the contestants who successfully negotiated the distance.

Charles H. Jennings was appointed to take charge of the beacon on Little Brewster Island, May 1, 1916, and served during the hectic war days when the U Boat scares alarmed the coast. Before the war began, the two hundredth anniversary of the lighting of the beacon on Little Brewster Island was observed, September 25, 1916.

Perhaps the most thrilling experience in which Jennings participated was the rescue of the men on the *U.S.S. Alacrity* which was wrecked on the ice-covered ledges off Lighthouse Island, February 3, 1918 at 3:45 in the morning. Captain Jennings, awakened by the sound of gunfire, aroused the assistant keepers, Lelan Hart and Charles Lyman. They saw the doomed ship and endeavored to reach it by firing the gun of the Massachusetts Humane Society. Four attempts were made, but each time the rope parted. Jennings now brought the dory down to the shore, and, assisted by sailors Hero and Harvey of the Naval Reserves, pushed the dory over the ice and into the surf.

Twenty-four men were clinging to the wreck of the *Alacrity* and their position was precarious. If they fell in between the ice cakes, they could not keep afloat and, if they stayed on the boat, she might soon slip off the ledge and sink. Jennings and his two assistants finally reached the wreck after a perilous trip, flung a line aboard, and began the rescue of the half-frozen sailors. Four times the men ran the gauntlet of ice, rocks, and raging surf until they finally succeeded in saving all twenty-four of the men. For this heroic deed Jennings later received a letter of commendation from William C. Redfield, Secretary of Commerce.

In 1919 Jennings was given the position as keeper of the range lights on Lovell's Island. J. Lelan Hart succeeded Jennings as Keeper of Boston Light. Hart's first knowledge of the islands of Boston Harbor was obtained during the shipwreck of his boat loaded with lime at Outer Brewster Island. The vessel was a lime coaster, *A. Heaton,* owned by A. C. Gay of Rockland, Maine. As the vapor whistle at Boston Light had been out of order, the ship crashed onto the rocks in the dense fog. The lime caught fire, and Captain Hart's ship burned to the water's edge. Fortunately the captain and members of the crew escaped to safety by rowing to Boston Light in the life boats.

Maurice Babcock succeeded Lelan Hart in 1926.

On the second day of December 1934, a memorial list of the twenty-five keepers of Boston Light was unveiled in the lighthouse itself by Fitz-Henry Smith, Jr. The Coastguard boat *Pueblos*, which took the party out to Lighthouse Island, had previously stopped at Spectacle Island to pick up Keeper Lelan Hart, and had put in at Lovell's Island to allow Keeper Charles Jennings to join the group. A brisk westerly gale had sprung up, and the landing at the Light was completed under difficulty, with many of the party getting a wetting.

In September, 1941, 225 years after the first illumination of Boston Light, a historical pageant was held on Little Brewster Island. George Worthylake and his wife, Lucy Maria Long and Albert Small, Keeper Bruce and his wife were all portrayed. A squad of soldiers from nearby Fort Standish represented the Americans who fought in the Revolutionary battle at the Light. In honor of Claude Graham White's flight of 1910 a naval flyer circled the tower.

Maurice Alendo Babcock, the last civilian keeper, welcomed the group, but it was with a feeling of sadness that he announced his retirement from the service. The Coast Guard took over the Lighthouse Department the same year, and after Pearl Harbor the light was extinguished.

The new officer in charge at Boston Light was Ralph Clough Norwood, boatswain's mate first class, who came to Little Brewster Island in 1928. He and his wife Josephine have nine children. One of their girls, Georgia Faith Norwood, was born at the light itself in 1932. Coastguardsman Norwood is an expert oarsman, thinking nothing of a twenty or thirty mile trip along the Massachusetts coast. A fine workman and an efficient engineer, his career as the first coastguardsman ever to command Boston Light station promises well. His two able assistants are John Attleson, seaman first class, who hails from Iowa, and Samuel Davey, a Minnesota boy, whose rating is 2nd class boatswain's mate.

THE BOSTON LIGHTSHIP

Five nautical miles to the southeast of Graves Light is the Boston Lightship, riding at anchor in the open sea, with her red hull in striking contrast to the blue ocean. Gigantic white letters on the ship's side which spell out the word BOSTON can be read miles away, while at night her flash, occurring every three seconds, can be picked up on the surface of the water eleven miles away.

Boston Lightship forms the outermost bastion of a four-cornered marine watchtower which man has created as a safeguard against the perils of the deep. Graves Light, already mentioned, Boston Light, six miles to the west, and dangerous Minot's Ledge Light, around four miles to the southward, complete the quadrilateral safeguard.

It was off Minot's Ledge back in 1851 that Boston Bay's first lightship was located when the lighthouse fell into the ocean during the Minot's Light Storm. In 1894 the Boston Lightship was placed on station, approximately where it is today. There have been minor changes of station down through the half century of service in peacetime, but its usual position has been about thirteen miles easterly from the Boston Custom House.

Two lightships have been stationed here, the old *54*, and the present *81*, which came to the post in 1940. The *54*, identified by the single hollow mast in contrast to the two single masts on the *81*, was in two serious collisions at this lonely deep sea station.

The first occurred on September 28, 1915, when the Merchants and Miners steamer *Quantico* was carried by a strong wind directly into the side of the lightship, smashing a ten-foot hole just above the water line. Hearing of the collision, Captain Sparrow of the Stony Beach Life Saving Station at Hull brought out his crew in a fast power boat, and was the first to reach the scene of the accident. The lighthouse tender *May-flower* and the navy tug *Sioux* arrived shortly afterwards. The *Quantico,* found to have superficial damages, proceeded to Philadelphia with her passengers, while the Boston Lightship was towed to the buoy station, which at that time was located at Lovell's Island. After repairs requiring several weeks, the *54* was back at her post.

A more serious accident occurred on December 20, 1935, when the British tramp steamer *Seven Seas Spray* crashed into the lightship while going at a speed of seven knots. Captain Ernest L. Snow, commander of the *54,* later gave the following statement:

"When she bore down on us I supposed she intended to draw alongside to calibrate her compass from our radio beacon. Before I actually knew what happened, she struck us amidship."

Captain Snow tried to sound the alarm bell, saw he couldn't reach it in time, and shouted below for all hands to come up on deck. The crew members reached the deck just in time to feel the terrific impact as the steamer cut into the smaller light vessel.

The captain of the *Seven Seas Spray* kept the bow of the steamer wedged into the great hole in the side of the lightship, which extended vertically from the rail to five feet below the water line, but water began to pour into the hole of the *54.* The ship's pumps were started. Frantically the crew filled bags with coal and jammed them into the breech. Several members of the pilot boat, which was cruising nearby, jumped aboard the lightship and helped fill the bags. At the end of an hour, the combined efforts of the men and the pumps gained a temporary victory over the incoming water, and it was held at a constant level. The *Seven Seas Spray* was allowed to return to Boston Harbor, while the lighthouse tender *Arbutus* towed the wounded *54* into a Quincy drydock, where she was eventually repaired.

GRAVES LIGHT

Off by itself, a mile and a half to the northeast from Green Island and slightly farther to the north of Outer Brewster, lies Graves Ledge.

This ledge was named for Thomas Graves, an early Puritan who was captain of one of Winthrop's ships. Shurtleff insists that the rocks were called Graves to honor Captain Graves of Revolutionary War fame, but the chart of Thomas Pound, drawn well before 1700, clearly shows that Shurtleff's assertion is impossible, for even then the ledge was known as the Graves. Some have claimed that the ledge was named because of the many sailors who were supposed to have drowned near by, but they are mistaken. There is no record of a shipwreck here until long after the ledge was named. The *Ewan Crerar* hit the Graves on March 9, 1860.

The ledge in the outer harbor came into prominence soon after the start of the twentieth century, when it was chosen as the site for the lighthouse which was to be built to facilitate entering the newly-opened Broad Sound Channel. After the 776 granite blocks had been safely put in place and the huge frame of the light itself had been sent out on a barge and installed, the beacon was lighted for the first time on September 1, 1905. It was a first order light, the only one of its class in Boston Harbor.

There have been seven keepers in the thirty years during which Graves Light has flashed. The first keeper, Elliot C. Hadley, who had been transferred from Plum Island, found it a lonely station, as there was no telephone or radio at that time to help pass the evening hours. The telephone cable was brought out to the Graves during the World War, and a radio was installed a few years ago.

In the six years which Elliot Hadley spent at Graves Light

there was one major disaster. On November 21, 1908, a small fishing schooner, the *Hugh G*, sank in a collision near the ledge and all six of the crew were drowned. At another time a scow in tow went down, but the tug boat saved the crew. One day in the fall of 1910 Hadley was surprised to see two men floating by the ledge on an overturned canoe. He launched his boat into the northwestern gale which was blowing, finally reached the unfortunates, and pulled them into the dory. Clad in bathing suits, the two men presented a dismal appearance when they were taken from the water. They had left Salem that morning and were on the way to Cohasset when the gale struck them. Hadley brought them back to the light, outfitted the men with some spare clothing, and sent them ashore the next day.

Another rescue which Hadley made is well remembered. The keeper was looking out to sea from the deck of the light one day when he spied a swamped sailing boat drifting out to sea. Hastily launching his dory, he rowed out to the boat and succeeded in rescuing the occupants. Back on shore the relatives of those who had been saved had given up hope, and since there was no telephone at the light, Hadley could not inform the mainland of the rescue. Great was the rejoicing the next day when the rescued party was safely brought back to the city. In the days when Hadley was keeper, he and his son spent half of every month ashore while the assistant keepers took care of the light.

Keeper Hadley was interviewed in 1910, and discussed the directions from which the storms approach the ledge.

"The Graves doesn't get pounded so hard in a Northeast as an Easterly, and Southeast is the worst. . . . I've stood on the bridge and looked up at solid water rushing in towards the ledges. I don't know how far up the solid water comes. I've been knocked down by it on the wharf beside the light, and opening a window to look out more than half-way up the tower, I've had as much as three buckets-full dashed in my face."

George Lyons, who had 21 years of experience on Egg Rock, Nahant, became the next keeper. After two years of service, he was succeeded by Captain Towle. Keeper Carter took over Graves Light July 31, 1917, and observed Armistice Day while still in charge. Seven years later he resigned in favor of Captain P. S. King, who was at the Light less than a year. Octavius Reamy, well-known photographer, took charge on May 11, 1924.

The last civilian keeper was Llewellyn Rogers. He remembers three shipwrecks during his period of service here. In one of the heaviest fogs of 1936, the steamer *New York* crashed into the *Romance*, and although no lives were lost the *Romance* went down in twenty minutes. Her wreckage later drifted ashore at Winthrop and Nahant.

In the spring of 1938 the *City of Salisbury*, a large 419-foot freighter entered Boston Bay. Her decks were crowded with wild animals, and a million dollar cargo was below. Suddenly she struck a sunken reef a short distance from the lighthouse, and a pinnacle of rock forced itself up through the bottom of the freighter. The crew and most of the cargo were removed safely, but the ship cracked in two the next day, becoming a total loss. All that summer hundreds of sightseers made the journey out to what they called the "Zoo Ship," but when the turbulent winds of an October gale swept up the coast the great ship rolled over and disappeared beneath the waves. It had been the most spectacular shipwreck in Boston Bay history.

In the early morning hours of January 21, 1941, with a bitter westerly wind lashing the outer bay, the fishing schooner *Mary E. O'Hara* passed Graves Light inward bound. Suddenly there was a crash. The schooner had struck an anchored barge. Sheering off, the *O'Hara* slowly sank in forty feet of water. The frightened men scrambled up the rigging into the crosstrees, which were still above the surface of the sea. Hour after hour passed. One by one the discouraged sailors dropped to their death in the freezing waters, until only five remained alive. With the coming of dawn the trawler *North Star* sighted the survivors and picked them up. This tragedy was the third worst shipwreck in the history of Boston Harbor.

In the winter time the rock plovers call at Graves Light and feed on barnacles attached to the rocks. Hundreds of them settle on the ledges which at low tide stretch out for a quarter mile, and the keepers find the birds an enjoyable diversion. The plovers feed by driving their long, sharp beaks into the barnacle shells and seem to keep quite happy on this menu.

Ernest Sampson, boatswain's mate first class, formerly at Baker's Island Light, is the commanding officer at Graves Light. He is assisted by Osborne Hallett, who is one of the few men still in the service with a rating of civilian keeper. Fred Armstrong, seaman first class, is the third man at Graves Light.

We shall now sail out to the ledge, hailing the keeper from our boat; if he is not too busy, he will invite us "aboard." There is a wharf built in back of the riprap, placed here when the light was erected, with a long runway going from the storage magazine to the lighthouse proper. We anchor on the lee side of the ledge and row ashore.

The keepers help us up onto the wharf. We now get a close view of the lighthouse itself; the date, 1903, which is cut in the granite, stands out in sharp relief about 50 feet up on the stone edifice. Climbing a heavy copper ladder on the western side of the lighthouse, we reach the first stage, 40 feet above the wharf. On this level we see the cover to the cistern which is 35 feet deep and holds hundreds of gallons of water. The tank is filled twice yearly with water brought out to the light by steamboat. The second stage is the engine room, where two semi-Deisel engines are ready for an emergency. The third level is the kitchen, neat and clean at all times. The fourth staging is the bunk room, with two double bunks. The fifth floor, containing the library, is also the watch room where the men spend their leisure time before retiring. The quarters are very cosy, the telephone and radio serving as connecting links with the mainland. The sixth stage, or lantern floor, holds the mechanism of the light, while the light itself occupies the two floors above. The light is of first order, and so is the reed horn. We may go outside on the highest deck, and view the wonderful picture which unfolds itself. I shall not attempt to give you a description of the scene from the top of the light but hope that some day you may journey to this far-flung ledge and see the splendid view for yourself.

MINOT'S LEDGE LIGHT

Because of the many serious shipwrecks in the vicinity of Minot's Ledge off Cohasset, the United States Government chose Captain William H. Swift of the Department of Engineers to erect an economical iron frame tower at this dangerous surf-swept rock off the South Shore of Massachusetts.

Located a distance of eighteen miles from Boston, Minot's Ledge was dry at low tide during the limited period of three hours a day, and work there was possible only in the calmest weather. To begin operations, the engineers anchored a schooner off the ledge, the workmen going on the rock whenever the tide and weather allowed. Engineer Swift made his plans carefully, drilling nine large holes, eight of them in a circle, with the ninth in the center.

It was a continual struggle with the elements. Twice that first boisterous summer of 1847 the waves swept the machinery into the sea, but drilling was finally completed the following year. By September 21, 1848, nine iron pilings had been in-serted in the holes, and the upper structure begun. Next a cast iron capping was placed on top of the nine piles sixty feet in the air, above which the keeper's quarters and the lantern were built, making the entire structure 75 feet high.

Just before the lighting of the beacon was to take place, a terrible storm swept the vicinity, throwing a brig loaded with Irish immigrants against the ledges around the tower, and drowning 143 persons. After the damage to the tower had been repaired, the lighthouse was declared finished, and on January 1, 1850, Keeper Isaac Dunham lighted Minot's Light for the first time. I have read his diary of the first winter he spent at the beacon, which trembled and rocked during the gales that swept the coast. It is a story of storm and terror seldom equalled. The following spring he notified the Government that unless the braces and pilings were reinforced the tower would fall into the sea. When the Government refused to take him seriously, Keeper Dunham resigned, October 7, 1850.

Keeper John W. Bennett took Dunham's place at the weakening tower. The iron braces and framework gradually became twisted and bent as the months went by, and the winter of 1850-1851 proved a severe test. Bennett and his two assistants, Joseph Antoine and Joseph Wilson, feared that Minot's Ledge Light would not last the winter. It was reported the tower rocked two feet each way in the gales out on the ledge. When March had passed safely, the keepers felt the worst was over. But they were mistaken.

On the afternoon of April 14 another great storm commenced. Keeper Bennett was in Boston at the time, having left the light in care of his two assistants who were preparing for the ordeal at the swaying tower. Gradually they came to realize that it might be the end, for the gale increased rapidly, until the tower rocked back and forth on its iron spindles.

The northeast hurricane reached its height on the night of April 16, 1851, hitting the battered iron lighthouse with a fury which had never been equalled. The two assistant keepers prepared for their last hours of existence, placing their final message in a bottle and tossing it into the ocean. Picked up on the shore later, the note read, "The light will not last the night." And they were right, for, as the tide turned later that evening, gigantic waves began to surge through the braces of the tower, waves which smashed against the keeper's platform sixty-five feet above sea level with ever increasing force. An hour after midnight a violent ringing of the lighthouse bell was heard from shore, and then nothing but the roar of the storm came to the anxious watchers on the Scituate and Cohasset beaches. Minot's Ledge Light had fallen into the sea, and both keepers were lost. The Government had made a costly mistake.

The Boston Board of Underwriters now ordered the steam towboat, the *R. B. Forbes*, to anchor off the Rock and serve as a lightship. A temporary lighting apparatus was installed on the *Forbes*, and plans were made for a new lantern on the ship later in the year. But the storms were not yet over for the season. On April 20 the lightboat was in such danger that she had to leave her station off the ledge and return to Boston Harbor until the gale went down.

After a short period the *R. B. Forbes* was replaced by the old Brandywine Shoal Lightship, which had been anchored since 1823 inside the entrance to Delaware Bay. As a lighthouse had been built in the vicinity, the Treasury Department sent the ship up the coast to Minot's Ledge, where the vessel was moored outside the Rock. Captain John W. Bennett, the former lighthouse keeper, was retained in charge of the 110-ton lightship. During an official inspection aboard the vessel July 8, 1851, it was found that the ship was in bad condition, and unfit for further duty. Nevertheless, it was not until several years later that a new ship was placed off the ledge.

Although not many anecdotes have come down to us about the lightship there is an interesting account of the black Newfoundland dog which lived on the vessel with the men. The route of the various merchant ships and steamers up and down the coast carried the vessels within a few score yards of the lightship, and one day a bundle of newspapers was thrown over in the general direction of the ship. While the men made preparations to launch their dory from the lightship the Newfoundland dog leaped into the ocean and swam for the package.

A few minutes later he reached the bundle and seized the papers in his teeth. Swimming back to the lightship, he was met by the surprised men, who took the newspapers from him and helped him up into the boat. The passengers on the merchant vessel had noticed the entire episode, and soon the whole Boston waterfront knew of the Minot's Lightship dog which swam for papers. It became a common occurrence for the dog to swim to the ships as they passed and to retrieve the daily papers for the men on the lonely lightship.

But the elements were still to be considered. The next ship-wreck while the lightship was in position off Minot's Ledge was that of the brig *Marriel*, which hailed from Belfast, Maine, and was in charge of Captain Staples. Heavily loaded with hides and turpentine from Georgia, the vessel crashed against East Hogshead Ledge, April 8, 1852. All on board were drowned.

On January 29, 1853, the crew of the lightship experienced a heavy gale that later developed into a wild hurricane. Farther out to sea was the bark *Maryland*, bound from Baltimore to Boston with an assorted cargo. Since they were not able to reef topsails fast enough when the gale hit, the crew watched the sails blow to shreds. Driven in alongside the lightship, Captain Davis tried to anchor, but in vain. The cables dragged, and the helpless lightship crew watched the vessel disappear in the direction of Cohasset. A short time later the *Maryland* piled up against the north side of Gull Ledge, slid off, and drifted toward the shore. She was driven by the gale into Briggs Harbor, where she ran aground after a weird trip, with the ship and crew narrowly escaping disaster. The bark *Maryland* was later floated off, and her cargo sent up to Boston on lighters.

As wreck after wreck continued to come in on the Cohasset Ledges the United States Government realized that action on the new lighthouse would have to be speeded up. Although the lightship was properly equipped, it could only in a minor sense substitute for a tower high enough to be seen from a safe distance. Plans were rushed, and by the year 1854 many engineers had drawn their ideas for a new lighthouse.

After conferences, discussions, and visits to the ledge, all of which took several years, Captain Barton S. Alexander was chosen as the engineer to superintend the building of a new tower on the site of the old one. This time, instead of the economical iron tower, the Government authorized a stone lighthouse, built of granite from Quincy, Massachusetts.

Work out on the ledge began again in 1855. An almost hopeless task confronted the workmen at the sea-swept ledge,

but the men kept at their efforts until the lighthouse was completed. First the iron stumps of the old tower were removed,
then the ledge was prepared to receive the stone blocks. The
first block of Quincy granite was lowered into the cavity prepared for it on July 9, 1857. Incidentally, the entire stone
tower was planned and put in place on the Cohasset shore at
first in tiers, and then sent out to the ledge. The lowest stone
was set in place on July 11, 1858, four feet below the low tide
mark. Work progressed rapidly from that time on, and on
June 29, 1860 the final stone, the 1079th, was placed. The
lantern and lens were installed by fall.

On November 15, 1860, more than nine years after the
spindle lighthouse had fallen into the sea, Minot's Ledge Light
was again illuminated. In 1894 a new flashing beacon was
installed, with the count of 1-4-3 being interpreted by lovers
along the shore as spelling out I-LOVE-YOU. The last civilian
keeper of this light was George H. Fitzpatrick, and the tower
and light are now under the supervision of the Coast Guard.

Every important location up and down this romantic coastline has its legends and ghost stories, and Minot's Ledge Light
is no exception. Some of the stories which are included here
may be more than mere legends, but because of the difficulty
of placing time and persons they cannot receive the stamp of
absolute fact.

The first story is about the work at the tower. Since cleaning the lens and the lamps is an integral part of the job at a
lighthouse, anything out of the ordinary about this duty is
likely to attract attention. One morning, a short time after the
Civil War, the head keeper at Minot's Light suddenly realized
that something strange had happened. The lamp and the
lens had been brightly polished that morning, although the assistant keeper, whose task it was to shine them, was still asleep.
When it was time to awaken his helper, the head keeper asked
him about the cleaning of the lamp and lens. The assistant was
as surprised as his superior to learn that the work had already

been done. The following week it was the assistant's turn to notice the same procedure had been repeated, although neither man had performed the task. Whether or not there is another explanation, the ghosts of the two keepers lost when the old lighthouse crashed into the sea received full credit for the polishing of the lens and the lamp of Minot's Ledge Light.

For many years mariners sailing past the lighthouse have been insisting that they hear strange voices and see ghost-like figures clinging to the lower section of the ladder. It is said that the Portuguese fishermen, who had usually taken their compatriot, Joseph Antoine, out to the Light to serve his turn, in later years saw the ghost of their friend many times while passing the Rock. This belief became so strong that, according to Keeper Fitzpatrick, many Portuguese fishermen do not dare to venture close to the new stone tower today. It is said that the ghost of young Antoine has usually been heard and seen just prior to northeast storms when the spectre puts in an appearance apparently to warn his countrymen from the dangers of the ledge. Many sailors of a former generation are said to have seen him grasping the lower rungs of the lighthouse ladder, with the gathering surf sweeping over him, as he cried out, "Keep away, keep away."

There are those who tell of the lighthouse keeper at the Rock who was a good workman and who enjoyed his position, until one day an obsession seized him. It is an absurd thought, but he was dissatisfied that there were no normal square corners in the lighthouse. The idea dwelt in his mind till at last he could stand it no longer. This individual, who until then had been perfectly content at the tower, gradually went from bad to worse. Finally, he was compelled to resign his post at this great American beacon, simply because he became obsessed with the ridiculous idea that there were no square corners at the lighthouse.

Another story concerns the strange tapping at the tower. In the former lighthouse it was the custom of the head keeper to signal to his assistant by rapping on the stovepipe which went up through the various floors, in order to inform him that the watch was over. The assistant would rap to reply that he was coming. But in the new lighthouse an electric bell was installed to call the assistant. One night, however, something happened that has never been satisfactorily explained.

As the midnight watch was drawing to a close, the head keeper was sitting in the watchroom, thinking of the destruction of the old tower. When he was about to get up, he leaned forward and tapped his pipe against the table. A few moments later he was amazed to hear an answering tap from below, although the only other living person at the Light was fast asleep. Nonplussed as what to do, he decided to wait for a few minutes. Then he tapped again, and once more from the depths of the granite structure came the answering tap. He hazarded the guess that the assistant was awake, and perhaps getting dressed, so he waited, in fact he waited for some time, yet nobody appeared. Finally he rang the bell, the usual signal, and after a short wait received the usual reply from below. The steps of the keeper's helper were soon heard on the iron stairs, and when the assistant finally appeared his superior recounted the weird incident. Needless to say, both men were quite startled, especially when they recalled that a tapping from below had been the signal in the old tower where the two men had perished in the great gale.

The story has persisted through the years that the reason for the removal of the famous Longfellow's Chair from its position of active service in front of the tower to a place of honor it later occupied near the bell on the lower parapet, was the death of a lady who fell into the sea. She was being hoisted up to the landing in the chair when suddenly a great wave startled those in the boat below, causing them to release the guide rope. The chair banged against the tower half way up, and the lady fell out and was killed. I mention this story only because it has been told and is still being told, although the episode does not seem to have any foundation in fact.

A head keeper of Minot's Light once remarked, "The trouble with our life here is that we have too much time to think." Rumor has it that around fifty years ago a new assistant keeper thought too much and decided to cut his throat with a razor. Unfortunately he bled to death before the head keeper discovered him. When the writer interrogated a former keeper concerning the tragedy, the keeper said that he preferred not to be quoted.

Some of the world's highest waves have crashed against the sides of Minot's Ledge Light. In the Christmas storm of 1909 Keeper Reamy watched a wave 170 feet high soar far above the 114-foot tower. Countless times each year gigantic surges sweep over the top of the light. I have flown above the lighthouse during many storms, making pictures from the airplane of these great awe-inspiring waves, and have included some of the reproductions in this volume.

We sometimes wonder what the thoughts of the men stationed at the tower are during the long, wintry nights, when the violent gales sweep in from the North Atlantic, sending seething whitecapped waves surging up around the sides of America's most dangerous beacon. Perhaps as the granite tower shakes with the impact of tremendous billows pounding against the outside of the 114-foot structure and the lighthouse is engulfed with foam, the men think of those two keepers of the old tower, who on that far-distant night stood side by side in the face of almost certain death to keep their last faithful watch that ended in eternity.

ABRIDGED BIBLIOGRAPHY

UNPUBLISHED SOURCES

Boston Marine Society Records
Boston Town Records
Bostonian Society Scrap Books
Bradley, "The Boston Farm and Trades School"

Castle Island Records

Diary of Joel Willcutt

Gillespie, "Fort Warren"

Massachusetts Archives
Massachusetts Council Records

Nill, "The George Family"

Sparks — Manuscript Collection
Suffolk Court Files
Suffolk Deeds

NEWSPAPERS

Boston Advertiser

Boston Globe

Boston Herald

Boston Journal

Boston News-Letter

Boston Post

Boston Transcript

Boston Traveler

New Bedford Mercury

PUBLISHED SOURCES

Appleton's Monthly
Avery — *Alexander Stephens*

Ballou's Pictorial
Boston Town Records
Bostonian
Bostonian Society — *Publications*
Bouve — *History of Hingham*

Century Magazine
Chevalier — *Histoire Marine Francaise*
Clark — *Clipper Ship Era*
Clark — *North Carolina Regiments*
Coburn — *Battle of April 19, 1775*
Colonial Society — *Publications*
Cutler — *Fifty-Fifth Regiment*
Cutler — *Greyhounds of the Sea*

Davenport — *Genealogies of Cohasset*
Dix — *Local Loiterings*
Dow and Edmonds — *Pirates of the New England Coast*
Drake — *Old Landmarks of Boston*

Farm and Trades School — *The Beacon*
Forbes — *Personal Reminiscences*
Frye — *First Regiment Mass. Heavy Artillery*

Gore — *The Cadets at Fort Warren*
Gould — *Sea Serpents*

Hall — *Winthrop*
Hawthorne — *Lady Eleanor's Mantle*
Homer — *Notes on the Sea Shore*
Howard and Crocker — *History of New England*
Howe — *Wrecking and Life Saving*
Howe — *Massachusetts Humane Society*

Jones — *Loyalists of Massachusetts*
Journal of the House of Representatives of Massachusetts

Kneeland — *Journal of the House of Representatives*

Longfellow — *Ballad of the French Fleet*

MacNamara — *History of the Ninth Regiment*
Massachusetts Magazine
Maine Historical Society — *Collections*
Massachusetts Historical Society — *Collections*
Massachusetts Historical Society — *Proceedings*
Morison — *Maritime History of Massachusetts*

Morton — *New England Canaan*
Memoirs of Roger Clap

New York Colonial Manuscripts
New England Hist. Gen. Register
Neal — *History of New England*
New England Magazine
North Scituate Beach Annual

Parker — *The 32nd Regiment*
Pearson — *Life of John A. Andrew*
Perley — *Historic Storms of New England*
Pollard — *Observations in the North*
Porter — *Rambles in Old Boston*

Records of Massachusetts Bay
Rich — *The Fight at Boston Light*
Roads — *Marblehead*

Sangston — *Personal Journal*
Savage — *Boston Events*
Shurtleff — *Description of Boston*
Smith — *Description of New England*
Smith — *Storms and Shipwrecks of Boston Bay*
Smith — *The Story of Boston Light*
Snow — *Minot's Light*
Snow — *Sailing Down Boston Bay*
Snow — *Storms and Shipwrecks of New England*
Sons of the American Revolution — *Register of Old Suffolk Chapter*
Spears — *The Story of the American Merchant Marine*
Stark — *Boston Harbor*
Sumner — *History of East Boston*
Sweetser — *King's Handbook of Boston Harbor*

Talbot — *Lightships and Lighthouses*
Thoreau — *Cape Cod*
Transactions of American Engineers

United States Government Charts

Vicars — *England's Worthies*

Wheildon — *Seige and Evacuation of Boston*
Willoughby — *Lighthouses of New England*
Wilson — *Nahant*
Wines — *A Trip to Boston*
Winsor — *Memorial History of Boston*
Winthrop — *New England*
Wise — *Baker's Island*
Wood — *New England Prospect*

INDEX

A. *Heaton*, 292
Adams bastion, 67
Adams, Charles, 222
Adams, Charles Francis, 70, 254
Adams, James. 93
Adams, President John. 67
Adams, Samuel, 48. 278
Adams, Melvin O., 222
Africa, 54, 250
Agassiz, 256
Ahston. 102
Alabama, 169
Albee, Clifton E., 141
Alcott, William, 136, 141
Alderton's Point, 271
Aldrich, 77
Algeria. North Africa, 34
Alert, 152
Alexander, Captain Barton S., 304
Alexander, Lt. Joseph W., 184–188
Alger Foundry, 148
Alice, 256–258
Allen, Arthur, 153
Alumni Association, 136
America, 31, 32, 35, 36, 39, 41, 43, 46, 51, 53, 54, 63, 64. 68, 77. 80, 97, 100, 122, 125–127, 132, 137, 179, 180, 213, 231–239, 259–261, 265 267, 271, 272, 277, 2 8, 293, 306, 308
American Army of Two, 265–268
American Navy, 260
American Revolution. 46, 126
American Yachting, 253
Anderson G n Robert, 192
Andrew, Eliza J. A. H., 156
Andrew. Gov. John A., 156, 169, 181, 182
Andrews, Major George P., 195
Andrews, Gen. Leonard, 156
Andros, Sir Edmund, 40, 41, 60, 66, 78, 103. 111, 166
Annapolis. 184
Annie, 129
Annisquam, 119
Apple Island, 25, 41, 88–92
Apple Island Flats, 91
Apple Island Road, 89
Antoine, Joseph, 302, 306
Antoinette, 283
Appleton, Major J. M., 193, 194
Appleton, Mabel, 193
Appomattox, 190
Arabia, 231
Arbutus, 295
Archer, John Rose, 118, 119, 121, 123
Arkansas, 200
Armistice, 159
Armistice Day, 298
Armstrong, Fred, 299
Arthur, Chaplain Harold W., 208
Arthur, Julia, 221, 223, 224
Artillery, Fifth, 195
Artillery, 7th, 198
Artillery, 55th, 114, 198, 199
Ashurst, Henry, 147
Asia, 54, 231
Athens of America, 51
Atkins, Captain, 215
Atkinson, Captain William, 120
Atlanta, 184, 185, 288
Atlanta's Crew, 189

Atlantic Avenue, 47
Atlantic Coast, 97, 238, 257
Attleson, John, 293
Audubon Fall, 133
Austin, Arthur W., 225
Austin Farm, 152
Austin, Nathaniel. 225
Austin & Stone's Museum, 134
Australia, 53
Autobiography, 70, 273

Babcock, Maurice Alendo, 293
Back Bay, 81
Back Channel, 69
Bagley, Willis H., 160
Bailey, Assist. Keeper, 288
Baines, James, 53
Baird, Mark C., 141
Baker's Island, 234, 237, 239, 241–250, 259
Baker's Island Light, 236, 241–250, 299
Baldwin, Loammi, 98
Ball, John, 276
Ball, Robert, 275, 276
Ball, Sarah, 276
Baltic, 91
Baltimore, 103, 172, 183, 190, 237, 304
Bangs, Captain John, 275
Banks, 181
Banks, Commodore, 35
Barbadoes, 241
Barber, Mr., 185, 187
Barnacle, John, 85
Barnard, Charles, 268
Barrett, Captain Moses, 285–287
Barrito, Private, 200
Barron, Commodore, 184
Barstow, Col. John, 265
Bartlett, William Francis, 70, 73, 78
Barton Academy, 135
Bastile, 112
Batchelder, 114
Batavia. 231
Bates, Abigail, 256–268
Bates Association Inc., 265
Bates, James Young, 265
Bates, Rebecca. 265–268
Bates, Keeper Reuben, 265, 266
Bates, Simeon, 265
Bates, Thomas, 288, 289
Battalion, 1st, 172, 181
Battalion, 2nd, 171
Battalion, 3rd, 197
Battalion, 4th Mass, 70, 73
Battery G, 198
Battery H, 68
Battle of Boston Light, 277
Battle of Dorchester Heights, 64
Battle of the Nile, 96
Battle of Shirley Gut, 35–39, 103
Battle Hymn of the Republic, 171
Baxter, 127
Bayley, Thomas Haynes, 228
Beachy Point, 205
Beacon, 138
Beacon Hill, 81, 169
Beacon Island, 272, 273
Beale, George W., 127
Beauregard, 169
Beaver, 47, 48

Beck, Captain Charles, 112
Beelzebub. 253
Belcher, 93
Belfast, Me.. 304
Belle Isle, 100
Belle Isle Inlet, 100
Bellingham, Governor, 60
Belmont Square, 96, 98
Bemis, Arthur, 158
Ben de Ford, 113
Bennett, Howard. 254
Bennett, Keeper John W., 302, 303
Bentley. Dr., 241, 242
Bernard, Governor Francis, 62, 63
Bernhard, Chaplain A. E., 208
Berry, Boat-Keeper, 29
Bethlehem Fore River Shipyard, 262
Beverly, 233, 239, 244
Bicknell, F. L., 163
Big Prother Club, 137
Bill, James, 102
Bill. Richard, 143
Billerica, 144
Bird, Goodman, 115
Bird Island, 115, 116, 118, 119, 120. 121, 123
Bird Island Passage, 116
Black, Serg. Charles E., 205
Black, Charlotte, 205
Black Joke, 160
Black Rock Channel, 218
Black Widow, 202
Blair, Charles E., 288
Blue Hills, 69
Blue Jacket, 52
Board of Directors, 128, 129
Board of Managers, 136
Board of Street Commissioners, 91
Bogue, Prof. Robert H., 142
Bohm, Fred, 111
Bond, John, 146
Bongrene, Michael, 153
Border Street, 98
Boscobel Wood, 95
Boston, 25–28, 30, 32, 33, 35, 36, 40, 42, 44, 46–54, 58, 59, 61–64, 66, 68, 69, 73, 75, 78, 80–82, 85, 87, 88, 90–92, 95–99, 101–103, 111–113, 117, 119. 122, 126–131, 143, 144, 146, 148–150, 152, 157, 159, 161, 165–167, 171, 177, 179, 180, 182, 189, 191, 192, 194, 196–198, 206, 213, 214, 216, 220, 224, 225, 231, 233. 235, 237–239, 243. 256. 259, 261, 263, 265, 271, 273–280, 283, 284, 286, 287, 289–291, 301, 302, 304.
Boston Asylum for Indigent Boys, 127, 128
Boston Board of Underwriters, 302
Boston Cadets, 182
Boston Central, 23
Boston Chapter, U.D.C., 200
Boston Common, 49, 129, 134, 151, 256
Boston Custom House, 88, 294
Boston Development and Sanitary Co., 144
Boston Farm School Society, 127
Boston Fire Department, 136

Boston Fusiliers, 198
Boston Globe, 136, 142
Boston Harbor, 20, 26–29, 31, 33, 40, 52, 57, 58, 61, 63, 69, 70, 76, 77, 94, 99, 107, 111, 113, 116, 118, 120, 121, 124–126, 138, 143, 147, 154, 156, 159, 166, 167, 181, 190, 196, 202, 204–206, 213, 217, 223, 225, 228, 241, 271–273, 275–280, 283, 286, 292, 295, 296, 299, 303
Boston Herald, 142
Boston Journal, 29, 286
Boston Light, 25, 28, 32, 47, 50, 54, 64, 84, 88, 145, 162, 177, 187, 195, 197, 208, 221, 223, 242, 259, 260, 265, 271–294
Boston Light Bill, 272
Boston Light Infantry, 98
Boston Light Swim, 291
Boston Lightship, 294–295
Boston Marathon, 137
Boston Marine Society, 122, 263, 279
Boston Massacre, 63
Boston Music Commission, 142
Boston News Letter, 118
Boston Outer Light, 285
Boston Park Department, 78
Boston pilot, 34
Boston Post, 167, 262
Boston Public Library, 28, 161
Boston Symphony Orchestra, 136
Boston Tea Party, 46–49
Boston Town, 44
Boston Weather Bureau, 33
Boston Yacht Club, 221, 254
Bostonian, 22, 29, 44, 46, 156, 206
Bostonian Society, 49, 81, 291
Bostontown, 43
Bowditch, Habakkak, 237
Bowditch, Nathaniel, 236, 237
Boy Scouts, 141
Brackett, James, 146, 221
Bradford, Mass., 263
Bradford, Colonel, 177
Bradley, Charles Henry, 132–135
Bradshaw, John, 32
Brandywine Shoal Lightship, 303
Brazil, 238
Breed, John, 89, 100, 101
Breed, Richard, 100
Breed's Hill, 101
Breed's Island, 100, 101
Brennan, Peter, 75
Brenton, Harold E. 142
Brereton's Island, 94
Brereton, Sir William, 94
Brewer, John M., 179
Brewster Islands, 143, 220–228
Brewster Spit, 283
Brewster, Elder William, 220
Bridgewater Almshouse, 225
Brigade Band, 171
Briggs, Edward, 52
Briggs Harbor, 304
Briggs, Henry, 52
Brimmer, Mayor, 29
Bristol, 35
Britannia, 29, 30
British, 35, 36, 39, 61–64, 77, 80, 81, 84, 97, 103, 126, 127, 155, 160, 180, 231, 236, 237, 239, 242, 243, 259, 261, 263–267, 276–278, 295
British Admiralty, 122
British Marines, 260
British Navy, 48

Broad Sound, 202
Broad Sound Channel, 296
Brockton Shoe Manufacturers Assoc., 136
Broke, Commander Philip, 259–261
Brooklyn, 232, 238
Brooks, Phillips, 128
Broughton's Hill, 117
Brown, Captain Edward T., 198
Brown, Rev. F. W. A. S., 104, 107, 150, 167. 216, 279
Brown, John, 170, 171
Bruce, Jonathan, 279, 280, 293
Bruce, Mary, 279, 280
Brown, Sala, 85
Brutal Beast, 254
Buckley, Mr. Pierce, 161
Bug Light, 25, 110, 194, 197, 205, 218, 219, 275, 285, 290
Bullard, F. Lauriston, 193
Bulwark, 265
Bumpkin Island, 157–159, 164
Bumpus, 153
Bumstead, Jeremiah, 119
Bunker Hill, 88
Bunker Hill Monument, 191
Burbeck, Richard, 122
Burgess, 274
Burial Hill, 252
Burnside, 200
Burrage, Clarence, 158
Burrage Organization, 158
Burroughs, Stephens, 66
Butman, Captain, 243

C. C. C., 204
C. W. Dyer, 189
Cabot, Major, 189, 190
Cabot, Samuel, 22
Cairo, 208
Calcutta, 208, 233
Calf Island, 220, 222–224, 276
California, 152, 238
Calvert, 207
Calvin F. Baker, 289
Cambria, 50
Cambridge, 113
Camp Hill, 96, 98
Camp Wightman, 112, 114
Campbell, John, 120
Campello, 76
Canada, 61, 96, 167, 226
Canopic, 33
Cape of Good Hope, 232
Cape Ann, 117, 188
Cape Cod, 155
Cape Hatteras, 184
Cape Horn, 51, 52, 232
Cape Verde Islands, 197
Capin, Edward 164
Caprill, Christopher, 96
Caravan, 235, 236
Carey, Bill, 93
Carleton, William L., 254
Carnes, Captain Jonathan, 233, 234
Carter, Keeper, 298
Carvell, Miss Bertha, 158
Cask of Amontillado, 68
Cass, Col. Thomas, 112, 113
Castine Bay, 97
Castle of Udolpho, 203
Castle Island, 20–27, 30, 47, 48, 53, 57–78, 82, 85, 88, 111, 126, 131, 134, 143, 162, 169, 273
Castle William, 61–65
Cat Island, 146
Catholic, 223
Cedar Point, 266, 267
Central Wharf, 28
Cervantes, 28

Chaddock, Captain, 86
Chandler, Captain Daniel, 128
Chapman, Keeper, 242
Charles, 116, 117
Charles (King), 95
Charles Hayden Foundation, 142
Charles Island, 252
Charles River, 69
Charles Town, 64
Charlestown, 26, 40, 64, 78, 100, 168, 179, 208, 225, 283, 291
Charlestown Navy Yard, 98, 158
Charlotte, 280
Charter Street, 42, 43, 127
Chase, Nathan D., 22
Cheeseman, Edward, 118, 119
Chelsea Creek, 97
Chelsea, Mass., 40, 93, 97, 100, 125, 152
Chelsea Point, 89
Cheney, Benjamin P., 221–224
Chesapeake, 259–261, 279
Chesapeake-Shannon Battle, 259–261
Chesley, Mrs. Roscoe H., 200
Chicatawbut, 102
China, 51, 231, 232, 235, 236
Chinese, 156
Choate, Samuel, 224
Christ Church, 126
Christopher Islands, 79
Cincinnati, 193
City of Rockland, 240
City of Salisbury, 298
City Hall, 129
City Point, 32, 131
City Point Landing, 74
City Square, 225
Civil War, 22, 32, 54, 80, 86, 136, 152, 156, 160, 168, 172, 181, 190, 195, 200, 205, 206, 223, 226, 305
Clara Jane, 221
Clark, 47
Clark, Levi, 291
Clarke's Wharf, 26
Clap, Roger, 59, 60 78
Clap, Desire, Experience, Hope, still, Preserved, Supply, Thanks, Unite, Wait, Wait-still, 60
Clay, Dr. Charles L., 114
Clemenson, O. W., 133
Clement, 58
Clough, 271
Coast Artillery, 198
Coast Guard, 250, 293, 305
Cobb, Charles K., 172
Coddington, William, 122
Coffill, Mrs. Henrietta, 141
Cohasset, 280, 297, 301, 302, 304, 305
Cole, Captain Samuel, 120
Cole, William, 125
Coleman Disposal Company, 144
Coliseum, 138
Colony Records, 94
Columbian Artillery, 112
Commercial Street, 42, 44
Commercial Street Tunnel, 42
Committee of Safety, 92
Common Sense Fertilizer Company, 240
Conant, Roger, 78, 80
Conant's Island, 78
Condick, George, 120
Confederacy, 190
Confederate, 166, 172, 180, 184, 185, 192, 193, 194, 288

Confederate Commissioners, 178, 179
Congress, 241
Congress, 180
Congressional Medal of Honor, 199
Constitution, 97, 109, 242
Continental, 147, 155
Continental Army, 103
Continentals, 64
Cook, Dr. John B., 141
Cook, Captain Tobias, 280, 283
Coolidge, Cornelius, 256
Copley, 47
Copp's Hill, 214, 273
Corinthian Yacht Club, 254, 255
Cork Harbor, 50
Corridor of Dungeons, 201, 202, 204
Corwin, Captain George, 239
Cottage Park Yacht Club, 89
Cottage Row, 132
Cottam, Col. William D., 157
Cotton, Albert, 82–84
Council of New England Records, 124, 125
Count of Monte Cristo, 189, 190
Courant, 121
Court of Admiralty, 117
Coyote, 91
Cram, Marcus, 147, 148
Crane, Major, 278
Crane, Dr. Clarence, 158
Cranford, Mr., 144
Crawfordville, Georgia, 190
Creed, Mr., 145
Cressy, Josiah, 51
Crocker, Mrs. 43
Cromwell, Captain Thomas, 59
Cronin, James H., 108
Crooked Lane, 100
Crooked Lane Passage, 40
Crooker, Captain, 107
Crossing the Bar, 289
Crow Point, 157, 164
Crowley, Captain Arthur, 263
Crowley, Captain Elmer, 263
Crowninshield, Benjamin, 234, 235
Crowninshield, Benjamin W., 234
Crowninshield, Captain Jacob, 232, 233
Crowninshield brothers, 234
Crowninshield's Wharf, 243
Cunard Line, 29, 31
Cunningham, Captain, 35
Curley Building, 115
Curtis, 52
Cushing, Lt.-Gov., 65
Custom House, 88, 294

Dana, Richard Henry, 116, 152
Daniel Webster, 181
Dark Arch, 197
Darling, David, 213, 214
Dartmouth, 47–49
Davenport, Captain Richard, 58, 59. 78
Davey, Samuel, 293
Davis, Captain, 304
Dartmouth College, 66, 69, 109
Davis Palmer, 291
Davis, William Frank, 142
Dawes, William, 109
D'Aulnay, 58
D'Estaing, Count, 156
DeCelles, Francis, 200
DeGaust, Andrew, 225
DeGaust, Charles, 160
DeGaust, Freeman, 225–227

DeLagnel, Captain, 177
DeMar, Clarence, 137
DeRuyter, 59
Dean, Benjamin Franklin, 221, 226, 227
Dean, Josiah Stevens, 226
Deane Winthrop House, 101
Dearborn Bastion, 67
Dearborn's Map, 163
Deer Island, 25, 32, 35, 41, 69, 82, 88, 101–110, 116, 143, 150, 152, 153, 196, 206, 208
Deer Island Hospital, 70
Deer Island Light, 110, 111, 288, 289
Delaware Bay, 303
Department of Engineers, 301
Derby, Elias Hasket, 233
Derby, Mrs. Sarah, 165
Derby Street, 231
Dermer, Captain, 155
Devens, Charles, 70
Dewey, Admiral, 243
Dibden, Thomas, 163
Dimmick, Col. Justin E., 172, 177, 179–183, 188, 201
Distinguished Service Cross, 199
Distinguished Service Medal, 199
Dix, John R., 131
Dobbin, 188
Dolliver, Mr., 284
Dominion of New England, 60
Donald McKay, 53
Donohue, Gen. M. T., 153
Dorchester, 33, 49, 66, 126, 127, 208, 277, 291
Dorchester Bay, 32
Dorchester Channel, 33
Dorchester Court, 32
Dorchester Heights, 64, 80
Dorchester Neck, 65
Dorchester Point, 65, 66
Douglass, Hugh, 285
Dow, Captain George W., 263, 264
Dragoon Regiment, 184
Drake, 44
Draper, Mr. Alonzo, 137
Dudley, Gov. Joseph, 99
Dudley, Attorney General Paul, 117
Dudley, Gov. Thomas, 57, 57
Dumaresq, Capt. Philip, 51
Dumas, Alexander, 189
Dummer, Jeremiah, 99
Dummer, Lt. Gov. William, 62
Dunham, Keeper Isaac, 301, 302
Dunn, James, 108
Dutch, 59, 122
Durgin, Cyrus W., 142
Duxbury Pier, 110, 291
Dwiffe, Thomas, 39
Eagle, 256
Earl of Warwick, 59
East Boston, 29, 31, 32, 51, 52, 69, 77, 78, 84, 85, 88, 94, 97, 98, 113, 264
East Boston Airport, 85
East Boston Ferry, 131
East Head, 127, 155, 156
East Hogshead Ledge, 304
East India Company, 46
East Indies, 231
East Weymouth, 136
Eastern Avenue, 101
Eastern Railroad, 100
Eastern Yacht Club, 254
Echoes from a Sabine Farm, 126
Edgar, Dr., 158
Egg Rock, 256, 257, 298

Eleanor, 47, 48
Eliot, Samuel A., 256
Elizabeth, 119
Ella, 74
Elliot Street, 225
Ellis, Merton P., 142
Ellison, Private James H., 182, 183
Emery, R. Claire, 137
Emily, 223
Endymion, 242
England, 35, 40, 46–48, 60, 61, 63, 79, 81, 90, 95, 100, 179, 184, 204, 263
English, 61, 77, 89, 96–98, 100, 103, 111, 125, 138, 155, 156, 236, 259, 265, 277, 278
English High School, 219
Enoch Train, 31
Erie Canal, 237
Essex Street, 46, 231
Ethelwold, 249
Everill, James, 116
Europe, 54, 88, 179, 180, 250, 274
Eustis, 178
Eustis, Abraham, 70
Eustis, George, 180
Eustis, Henry Lawrence, 70
Evangeline, 63
Evans, Thomas J., 136
Ewan Crerar, 285, 296
Ewell, General Richard S., 190, 191

Fairbanks, 206
Fairbanks, Jonathan, 102
Fame's Revenge, 120
Faneuil Hall, 47, 112, 141
Fanny Pike, 288
Farm and Trades School, 70, 88, 124, 127–143
Farm School Bank, 133
Farragut, Rear-Admiral, 192
Farragut Day, 74
Farrar, Prof. John, 27
Fawn Bar, 108
Federal Building, 88
Federal Communications Commission, 208
Federal Government, 114, 148
Felch, Rev. Cheever, 23
Felton, Cornelius Conway, 128
Fenno, 127
Fenton, Thomas, 134
Fighting Ninth, 112
Filmore, John, 118, 119
Filmore, President Millard, 118
Finch, Lt. William, 98, 152
Finlay, Mr., 223
Finn's Ledge, 291
First Cliff, 266
First Corps Cadets, 182, 183, 195
Fitzpatrick, George H., 305, 306
Fleet Street, 117
Floure of Souvenance, 258
Fly, Captain William, 119, 120, 123
Flying Cloud, 51, 54, 98
Flynn, Dr. William M., 291
Follet, Dexter, 192
Forbes, Robert Bennet, 50
Fore River Shipyard, 262
Forget-Me-Not Legend, 256–258
Formosa, 232
Forrester, Simon, 233
Fort Andrews, 155–157
Fort Banks, 199, 202, 203
Fort Dawes, 102, 109
Fort Devens, 69

Fort Duvall, 165
Fort Ethan Allen, 199
Fort Hill, 111
Fort Independence, 27, 67, 69, 70, 73, 75, 202
Fort Lafayette, 172, 177
Fort Revere, 157
Fort Standish, 208–218, 293
Fort Strong, 93, 113, 114
Fort Sumpter, 286
Fort Warren, 69, 73, 76, 81, 82, 86, 155, 166–205, 218, 226, 283, 288, 290
Fort Warren Cadets, 196
Fort Winthrop, 82
Fortress Munroe, 172
Fowle, Leonard M., 254
Fox, Henry A., 136
France, 69, 112, 179, 198, 199, 213, 235. 236
Franklin, 35, 36
Franklin, Benjamin, 273
Franklin Medal Fund, 157
Freeman, Gershom C., 219
Freeman, Nehemiah, 67
French, 58, 111, 149, 155, 156, 213
Fresnal, 285
Friendship, 79
Frothingham, 277
Frye, Major, 197
Fullerton, Horton D., 93
Fullerton, Judson G., 93
Fusiliers, 98

Gage, General, 97
Gage, Hittinger & Company, 29
Gale, Bartholomew, 239
Gales Ledge, 239
Gales Point, 239
Gallop, Capt. John, 205, 208
Gallop's Island, 29, 121, 166, 205–208
Garibaldi, 70
Gaul, 101
Gay, A. C., 292
Gazette, 98
General Court, 58, 78, 79, 271, 272, 274-276
General Lincoln, 196
General Warren, 169
Gentleman's Magazine, 163
George, 283
George, John, 166, 205
George, John, Jr., 271
George's Island, 69, 70, 81, 96, 149, 166–205, 208, 219, 272, 290
George's Island Road, 189
Georgia, 190, 304
Gerrish, Captain, 152
Gerrish, Master James R., 108
Geranium, 290
German, 206, 207
German Saunder yachts, 254
German spies, 159
Germantown, 89
Gettysburg, 190
Gibbons, Mrs., 58
Gibbons, Captain Edward, 25, 57
Gibraltar, 167
Gilmore, 138
Gilmore, Prof. J. H., 243
Gilmour, Harry, 190
Gloucester, 20, 22–24, 260, 285, 286
Glawson, John, 158–160
Glen, 65
Godbold, Sarah, 284
Godfrey, Mr., 98
Godiva, Lady, 102

Golden Star, 160
Goldsmith, Delos E., 134
Goldsmith, Wallace, 134
Gorges, John, 94. 124
Gorham, Arthur J., 75, 76
Gorham, Keeper Edward, 289
Gorham, Serg. John, 75
Gossum, 100
Government, 303
Governor's Island, 25, 54, 58, 64, 68, 69, 78–89, 121, 143, 154, 167
Gould, Lieutenant, 222
Graham-White, Claude, 291, 293
Granary Burying Grounds, 182
Grand Army of the Republic, 200
Grand Turk, 232
Grant, Lt. T. H., 208
Grant, Ulysses S., 70
Grape Island, 160–163
Graves, Captain, 296
Graves Light, 88, 153, 286, 294, 296–300
Graves, Thomas, 296
Gray, William, 233, 237
Great Britain, 167
Great Elm, 256
Great Head, 259
Great Misery, 239, 240
Great Republic, 52, 53
Great Storm of 1723, 274
Greater Brewster Island, 177, 218, 220, 221, 223. 272, 283, 290
Greater Brewster Spit, 219, 275, 290
Greaton, Major, 103
Greek Temple, 154
Green, Private. 200
Green Island, 220, 223, 224, 276, 296
Green, John, 93. 119
Green, Joseph, 224
Greenfield, William J., 147
Greenleaf, Sheriff, 47
Greenleaf, Hannah, 166
Greenleaf, Samuel, 166
Greevill, Henry, 120
Gridley, Richard. 65
Griffin's Wharf, 47, 48
Grover Cleveland, 34
Grouchy, Captain Thomas, 42, 43, 45
Gull Ledge, 304
Gunderson, Mills, 291
Gurney, Franklin P., 223
Gurney, Harold P., 223

Hadley, Elliot C., 296, 297
Haley, John, 74
Half-Moon Island, 146, 147
Halfway Rock, 234, 241, 243
Halifax, 260
Hall, Captain, 47, 48
Hall, C. S., 170
Hall, Samuel, 51
Hallett, Osborne, 299
Ham, Lilla A., 268
Hamilton, Mass., 53
Hancock Bastion, 67
Hancock, Governor John, 46, 63, 65, 278, 279
Hangman's Island, 146
Haraden, Captain, 118, 119
Harding's Ledge, 218, 219
Harper, Charles W., 225
Harper's Ferry, 170
Harraden, 231
Harrington, Fred, 76
Harris, Richard, 147
Hart, Sergeant, 75

Hart, Captain, J. Lelan 145, 292, 293
Harvard, 27, 60, 70, 73, 95, 128, 157, 240, 292
Haswell, Susanna, 213
Hatch, Estes, 89
Hatter Cox, 151
Hatteras Inlet, 178
Havanna, 180, 197
Hawthorne, Nathaniel, 130
Hayden, Richard. 204
Hayes, Captain, 221
Hayes, Captain John, 273–276
Hazard, 232
Heard, Captain Augustine, 235, 236
He Leadeth Me, 243
Hen and Chickens Lightship, 91
Henchman's Lane, 42, 45
Henrico, 152
Henry, 232, 233, 237
Henry Gillen, 34
Herald, 235
Hero, 292
Hickey, Chaplain David Harold, 204
High Bluff, 148
Highlander, 28
Hill, John, 29, 30
Hill Prison, 108
Hingham, 160, 164, 165
Hingham Bay, 33, 155–165
Hingham Harbor, 165
Hingham Harbor Islands, 164–165
Hingham Packet, 164
Hingham Poor House, 161
Hingham Tory, 166
His Majesty's Engineers, 63
Hobart, 150
Hodgkins, Capt. Augustus L., 114
Hoffs Neck, 147
Hoffs Thumb, 147
Hog Island, 40, 89, 93, 99, 100, 143
Hog Island Hill, 100
Holland, John, 147
Holland, Captain William, 263
Holmes, Oliver Wendell, 90
Homer, James Lloyd, 93, 107, 112, 167, 268, 214, 280
Hope, 35
Horace, 126
Hornet, 283
Horte, Albert M., 289
Horte, Josephine, 110, 289
Hospital Association, 158
Hospital Island, 152
Hot Springs, Ark., 200
Hough's Neck, 147, 148, 155, 159, 164
House of Correction, 102, 108, 109
House of Industry, 108, 128
House of Reformation, 108, 153
House of Representatives, 279
House of Seven Gables, 241
Howard, John, 65
Howard, Henry, 254
Howe, Julia Ward, 171
Hugh, G., 297
Hull, 61, 148, 154–157, 91, 201, 220, 222, 271, 277, 278, 287, 288, 294
Hull Gut, 157
Hull, John, 25
Hunt, 93
Hunt, Matthew, 29
Hunton, General Eppa, 190
Hutchinson, Ann, 57
Hutchinson, Fred, 244, 245
Hutchinson, Hon. Thomas, 89

Hutchinson, historian, 47
Hutchinson, Lt.-Governor, 63
Hutchinson, Gov., 47–49
Hutchinson, Gov. Thomas, 89
Hyde, Mr., 43
Hyde Park, Vermont, 135
Hypocrite Channel, 220

Ibrook's Island, 164
Independence, 23, 98
Independent Corps Cadets, 182
India, 51, 232, 233
Indians, 48, 49, 66, 95, 100, 102, 124, 149, 151, 155, 162, 251
Infantry, 2nd, 168
Infantry, 13th, 199
Ipswich, 57, 239
Ireland, 50
Irish, 50, 107, 112
Irwin, John, 156
Irwin, Samuel G., 93
Island Inn, 156
Island Ruin, 90
Isle of France, 232
Italy, 70, 256
Iowa, 293

Jackson, Stonewall, 73
Jackson, General Henry R., 184
Jackson, Jonathan, 100
Jackson, Robert E., 52
Jackson, Stonewall, 181
Jamaica, 119
James II, 60, 111
James Adger, 91
James Baines, 53
James, George, 159
James, Captain Samuel, 288
Japanese, 204
Jeffers, 226
Jefferson, 244
Jeffries, Selectman, 149
Jeffries Point, 113
Jekyll, Dr., 43
Jenkins, John, 221
Jennings, Charles H., 214, 215, 291–293
Jewell, 122
Joe the Rock, 144
Joe's Rock, 153
John Brown's Body, 169–171, 182, 198
John and Hannah, 120
John's Folly, 256
Johnson, General Adam R., 190
Johnson, Commissioner, 109
Johnson, Fisherman, 225
Johnson, Captain Edward, 95
Johnson, Thomas, 162
Jones, John Paul, 213
Jones, Leslie, 142
Jones, Miss Sally, 156
Jones, Thomas, 156
Josias, Charles, 102
Josselyn, John, 95
Juliet, 108
June, 284

Kane, George Proctor, 183
Keene, 180
Keller, Ralph, 219
Kelly, George, 153
Kemp, Captain Joseph I., 33
Kenfield, LeRoy S., 136
Kezar, George, 291
Kihlstrom, Bror Y., 141
Kilbourne, Col. Charles E., 199
King, Joseph, 91

King, Merrill B., 110
King, Captain, P. S., 298
King Philip, 66
King Philip War, 102
King Road, 65
King's Beach, 22
King's Chapel Burying Ground, 116, 118
King's Chapel Graveyard, 118
Kingsley, Theodore, 216
Kinnear, George, 76
Kinnear, Miss May, 76
Kitching, Robert, 141
Knapp, Miss Sylvia, 216
Knox, Keeper Thomas, 123, 279
Knudson, Christian, 82, 83
Kurth, Richard, 202

La Hogue, 266, 267
La Tour, 58
Lactantius, 19
Lady in Black, 168, 200, 201
Lady Washington, 35
Lally, Mr., 33
Lambert, John, 117–118
Lane, Arthur, 159
Lane, Walter, 254
Langlee, Captain, 164
Langley's Island, 164
Lapham, 52
Larrabee, John, 62
Latona, 130
Law, Lieutenant, 260
Lawrence, Amos, 22
Lawrence, Captain James, 259–261
Lawson, Douglas, 262
Lawson, Thomas W., 262
Leach, Captain, 108
Leavitt, Elisha, 160, 166
Lee, 190, 200
Leghorn, Italy, 256
Leverett, Gov. George, 166
Leslie, Colonel, 65
Leviathan, 88
Lewis, I. W. P., 285
Lewis, O. E., 93
Lexington, 49
Liberty Tree, 46
Lighthouse Bar, 290
Lighthouse Buoy Station, 217
Lighthouse Channel, 290
Lighthouse Department, 145, 217, 279, 288, 290, 293
Lighthouse Island, 287, 289, 292, 293
Lighthouse Service, 215
Lighthouse Tragedy, 273
Lightning, 53, 54
Lightship 54, 294, 295
Lightship 81, 294
Liemann, Emil S., 91
Lincoln, President Abraham, 171, 180
Lincoln, Charles H., 262
Lind, C. A., 133
Little Brewster Island, 25, 225, 274–277, 283–285, 288, 291–293
Little Calf Island, 220, 224, 225
Little Harbor, 124, 252
Little Hog Island, 165
Little Misery Island, 239–241
Little Nahant, 256
Little Nahant Beach, 257
Livermore, Major Charles F., 194
Liverpool, 53, 286
Liversidge Institute, 142
Lloyd, 280
Lloyd, James, 127
Lobdell family, 157

Locke, James, 128
Lodge, Henry Cabot, 22, 256
London, 124
Long Beach, 22
Long Island, 25, 26, 28, 60, 91, 101, 103, 110, 111–115, 143–145, 148, 152, 154, 218, 221, 274, 278
Long Island Head, 26, 69, 112, 113, 121, 196
Long Island Hospital, 30, 88, 114, 115
Long Island Hotel, 69
Long Island Light, 69, 88, 112–114
Long, Lucy Maria, 283, 284, 293
Long Wharf, 182
Long, Captain William, 283, 285
Long, William P., 77
Longfellow, 63, 256
Longfellow's Chair, 307
Loring, Augustus P., Jr., 141
Lorings, 149
Lovell's Island, 70, 166, 185–187, 205, 208–218, 292, 293, 295
Lovell, William, 208
Lover's Rock, 149, 217
Loud, Clarence W., 142
Louisburg, 62, 65
Lowell, James Russell, 70
Lower Middle, 23
Lows, 238
Lowther, George, 145
Ludlow, Roger, 57
Lundgren, James F., 243
Lyman, Charles, 292
Lyman Grove, 141
Lyman, Theodore, 128, 129, 138
Lynchburg, 190
Lynde, Benjamin, 126
Lynde, Benjamin, Jr., 126
Lynde, Lydia, 126
Lynde, Mary, 126
Lynde, Simon, 103, 126
Lynn, 22, 101, 159, 258
Lyons, George, 298

Mabel's Room, 87
MacBeth, John, 254
Mack, Miss Rena, 135
Maertins, G. R., 147
Magnifique, 213–215
Magoun, 52
Maguire, Ordnance-Sergeant, 73
Maguire, Joseph, 73, 74
Maine, 77, 95, 188, 215, 223, 250, 288, 289, 292, 304
Malbone, William T., 23, 24
Malm, Alfred C., 141
Maloney, Captain, 221
Manning, John, 32, 33
Manning's Moone, 147
Mansfield, Colonel, 75
Marblehead, 29, 51, 117, 122, 251–255
Marblehead Harbor, 251, 254
Marblehead Neck, 251
Marblehead Week, 251–255
Margaret, 232
Marine Hospital, 125
Marine Museum, 262
Marine Park, 74
Marion, Joseph, 144
Maritana, 177, 286, 287
Maritime Service, 207
Maritime Training School, 205, 207
Marlborough, 61, 96, 112
Marliave, Edward T., 91

Marmion, 232
Marriel, 304
Marsh, C. B., 170
Marsh, William, 89, 90, 100
Marston, John, 21
Mary, 241
Mary E. O'Hara, 298
Mary and John, 60
Maryland, 304
Maryland Legislature, 172
Masconnomet, 239
Mason, James Murray, 166, 178–180, 200, 204
Massachusetts, 19, 20, 29, 53, 62–69, 80, 81, 89, 98, 101, 102, 108, 122–124, 129, 137, 146, 152, 154–156, 162, 171, 172, 196, 200, 216, 231, 237, 268, 278, 279, 287, 293, 301, 304
Mass. Archives, 271
Mass. Bay, 79, 121, 251
Mass. Bay Colony, 126
Mass. Bay Records, 163, 164
Mass. Colony, 96
Mass. Historical Society, 27, 80
Mass. Humane Society, 104, 145, 292
Mass. Infantry, 10th, 70
Mass. Infantry, 13th, 73
Mass. Infantry, 24th, 172
Mass. Institute of Technology, 135
Mass. Legislature, 128, 129, 278
Mass. Militia, 112
Mass. Regiment, 12th. 170, 171
Mass. Regiment, 38th. 206
Mass. Regiment, 54th, 206
Mass. Volunteer Militia, 182
Mass. Volunteers, 172
Massie, Robert F., 67–69, 78
Massie, Mrs. W. E., 200
Mather, Cotton, 62, 117
Mather, Increase, 40, 41
Mathewson, Mrs. Mary F., 141
Matteson, Abijah, 141
Mauretania, 198
Mauritius, 232
Maverick, Samuel, 94–96, 101, 125, 131
Mayflower, 145, 295
McBlair, 189, 190
McCabe, Keeper Joseph, 110
McCarthy, Deputy Andrew, 109
McCarthy, T. T., 91
McElroy's Seaside House, 33
McFarland, James, 178, 180
McFee, Fisherman, 225
McGinley, Frederick, 153
McGrath, Ord.-Serg. Maurice, 74, 75
McKay, Donald, 50–54, 77, 88, 98
McKay, Lauchlan, 51
McLeod, Mrs., 161, 162
McLeod, Captain Billy, 161–163
Meacham, Joyce, 135
Meacham, Linwood, 135
Meacham, William, 135
Meacham, William Maxfield, 135, 138, 141, 142
Meacham, Mrs. William M., 141
Mears, William, 148
Medford, 49, 52, 256, 258
Mediterranean Sea, 167, 204
Melbourne, 208
Melville family, 49
Memmer, 254
Merchant and Miners, 294
Meridian Street, 98
Merrit, Nicholas, 122

Merrymount, 124, 125
Methodist Church, 107
Mexican, 243
Mexico, 184
Michael J. Perkins, 101
Middle Breakers, 249
Middle Brewster, 220, 222, 226, 289
Middle Head, 156
Midlebury College, 135
Milford, 112
Military Academy, 69
Miller, Lt.-Col. Franklin P., 142
Milliken, Winnie, 108
Mills, Edwin J., 128
Milton, 48
Milton Hill, 48
Minnesota, 293
Minns, William, 276
Minot, George, 127
Mi..ot, John, 127
Minot's Ledge, 283, 294, 301, 303, 304
Minot's Ledge Light, 288, 294, 301–308
Minot's Light storm, 224, 294
Minot's Lightship, 303
Misery Islands, 239–240
Mississippi River, 184
Mitchell, Alexander, 120
Mohawk Indians, 48
Mollie Trim, 222
Money Bluff, 103, 107
Monohasett, 240
Monroe, Frank, 254
Montague, Admiral, 48
Monte Cristo 190
Montresor, Col. John, 63
Moon Head, 153
Moon Island, 144, 146, 147
Moriarty, Dr., 107
Moriarty, James, 199
Morison. 238
Morris, Richard, 57
Morrison, Supt. Robert, 129, 131, 141
Morse, John Ripley, 137
Morse, William Appleton, 131, 132
Morton, 124, 125
Moulton, Mrs. J. L., 286
Moulton's Misery, 239
Moulton, Roger, 239
Mt. Auburn Cemetery, 142
Mugford, Captain James, 35, 36, 39
Mulcahy, Major George F. A., 109
Munson, Hollis, 108
Munt, Tho', 116
Mystic River, 52, 251

Nahant, 19–23, 109, 227, 256–258, 298
Nanepashemet, 251
Narrows, 25, 52, 121, 185, 194, 202, 205, 208, 214, 218
Nantasket, 60, 65, 78, 80, 149, 155, 157, 195, 208, 280
Nantasket Head, 278
Nantasket Hill, 278
Nantasket Road, 35, 96, 201, 202
Nantucket, 19, 197
Nashville, 184
Nassau, 180
Nathan Tufts Meter Company, 44
National Bureau of Standards, 142
National Park Service, 204

Naumkeag Indians, 251
Naval Reserves, 292
Navy, 158, 234
Navy Department, 197
Navy Yard, 98
Neal, Daniel, 273
Nellie Baker, 112
Nelson, John, 60, 96, 111
Nelson's Island, 111
Neville, Daniel, 239, 240
New Bedford Harbor, 189
New American Practical Navigator, 237
New England, 19, 22–24, 50, 58, 78, 95, 97, 102, 111, 117, 125, 137, 138, 168, 169, 172, 179, 184, 197, 221, 231, 232, 237, 238, 243, 249, 251, 253, 255, *New England Almanac,* 271
New England Band Contest, 138
New England Courant, 121, 216
New England Guards, 182
New Hampshire, 124–126, 131, 213
New Jersey, 62
New Orleans, 208, 237
New Orleans Custom House, 169
New World, 231
New York, 29, 50, 51, 54, 142, 171, 198, 237, 238, 271, 298
Newbury, 62
Newcomb, Charles, 206
Newcomb, Mrs. Margaret, 205
Newcomb, Peter, 205, 206
Newcomb's Island, 206
Newell, William B., 200
Newfoundland, 59, 118
Newgate's Landing, 40
Newhouse, Albert F., 32
News-Letter, 120
Newspaper Group, 136
Newton, Lt., 193
Newton, Major Ralph, 169
Nickerson, David N., 254
Nickerson, Roland, 254
Nix, Captain, 121, 122
Nixie Shmalt, 122
Nix's Mate, 121
Nix's Mate Island, 115, 118–123
Noddle's Island, 26, 93, 94–100, 111, 113, 125, 126, 152, 272
Noddle, William, 94
Nordberg, A. F., 133, 134
Norfolk County, 128
Norseman, 149
North, 172, 181, 190, 200, 205
North Africa, 34, 204
North America, 51–64
North Atlantic, 308
North Attleboro, 263
North Brewster Island, 224
North Carolina, 177, 180, 181
North End, 42, 44, 214
North Metropolitan Sewerage District, 102
North Shore, 19, 24
North Shore Babies' Hospital, 249
North Star, 299
Northern, 201
Northern Light, 52
Northern troops, 171
Norwood, Georgia Faith, 293
Norwood, Josephine 293
Norwood, Ralph Clough, 293
Nova Scotia, 51
Nubble, 121
Nut Island, 147, 148
Nut Island Pumping Station, 155

O'Brien, Thomas C., 154
Oakes, Mr., 129
Oakum Bay, 251
Ohio, 144
Old Dimond, 252
Old Ironsides, 242
Old North Church, 42, 43, 214
Old South Meeting House, 47, 48
Old State House, 49, 50, 59, 81, 256, 262
Oliver, Andrew, 126, 127
Oliver, Mary Lynde, 127
Oliver, Peter, 127
Olson, Captain Christian, 222
Ontario, 91
Oran, North Africa, 204
Ordiorne's Point, 125
Orient Heights, 41, 94, 99, 101
Orient Heights Library, 101
Outer Brewster Island, 220, 223, 225–228, 276, 286, 289, 292, 296
Outward Island, 225

Para, Brazil, 238
Paine, Robert Treat, 66
Park Department, 86
Park Superintendent, 204
Parliament, 46
Palmer, Joseph, 146
Palo Alto, 184
Parker, Col. Francis J., 172, 181, 182, 195, 203
Patrioten, 59
Payne, Keeper Arthur L., 250
Peabody, Mr., 129
Peabody, Joseph, 233
Peace Jubilee of 1869, 137, 138
Peacock, 259, 260
Pearl, 74
Pearl Harbor, 293
Pearl Street, 47
Pearson, George W., 172
Peaslee, General, 286
Peck, Luke B., 156
Peddock, Leonard, 124
Peddock's Island, 111, 148, 149, 155–157, 163
Pegram, Colonel, 177, 178
Pegram, General John, 179
Peggy's Point, 205
Peirce Nichols House, 231
Pemberton's Island, 166
Pemberton, James, 166, 167
Pembroke, 113
Pendleton, Amos, 160, 161
Pepi, John, 160
Pepperell, William, 62
Percy, Lord, 64, 80
Peregrine, Peter, 167
Perkins Institute of the Blind, 22
Perkins, Jobe, 94
Perkins, Keeper Joseph, 242, 244
Perkins, Joseph, II, 243
Perkins, Lorenzo D., 153
Perkins, Col. Thomas H., 22, 23, 256
Pernette, Newton, 170
Perry, Mr., 284
Perry, Edgar A. 68
Perry, Commodore Oliver, 261
Petersburg, 73, 179
Peterson, Captain, Frank H., 263
Peterson, John F., 142
Phantom, 32
Philadelphia, 295

Philippines, 238
Phillips, Mr., 284
Phillips, Col., 40
Phillips, Captain John, 118, 119
Phillips, William, 127
Phips, Sir William, 42, 127, 167
Pickham, 74
Pickman, Benjamin, 235
Pierce, Captain, 189
Pilgrim III, 138
Pilgrims, 155, 168
Pilot Boat No. 2, 288
Pilot's Retreat, 244
Pingree House, 231
Pingree, Henry , 290, 291
Pingree, Henry L., 289, 290
Pingree, Keeper Wesley, 110, 288–290
Piscataqua River, 124, 125
Pittom, John, 103
Pitts, Charles H., 177
Pleon Race, 254
Plesiosaurus, 22
Plum Island, 296
Plummer, Mrs. Affie G., 141
Plymouth, 28, 124, 255, 220, 291
Plymouth, Eng., 125
Plymouth Harbor, 27, 110
Pochaska, Charles, 288
Poe, Edgar Allan, 68
Point Shirley, 32, 90, 103, 109, 219, 259
Polka, 129, 133
Port Hudson, 73
Portland, 289
Portland, Me., 188, 289
Portland Cement Assoc. Fellowship, 142
Portland Storm, 144, 219
Portsmouth, N. H., 131, 213
Portuguese, 91, 93, 114, 117, 406
Portuguese Joe, 144
Pound, Thomas, 296
Povey, Colonel, 61, 99
Powder Horn Hill, 152
Pownall, Governor, 62
Pratt, Thomas, 40
Prentice, Captain John, 220
Prescott, 256
President, 40, 41
President Road, 80, 101
Price, Diarist Ezekial, 149
Prince, 94
Prince, Marshall James, 20, 21, 24
Prince of Orange, 60
Prince's Head, 148, 156
Proctor, Aunt, 260
Provincial Congress, 277
Provincetown, 180
Pryde, N. B., 186
Public Reservations, 240
Pueblos, 293
Pullen Point, 41, 57, 58, 102, 104
Pulpit Rock, 228, 256
Pumping Station, 102, 148
Puritans, 40, 57, 78, 94, 102, 121, 166, 296
Puritan Fathers, 163
Puritan Government, 148
Puritanism, 61
Purkett, Captain, 49
Putnam, 97
Putnam, 237

Quantico, 294, 295
Quarantine Ledge, 153
Quarantine Rocks, 144, 163
Quarantine Station, 107, 149, 150, 152, 206
Quartermaster Corps, 200

Quarters Number Seven, 178, 191, 200, 204
Quebec, 111
Quelch, Captain John, 116, 117, 121, 123
Quincy, 89, 146, 160, 221, 262, 295, 304, 305
Quincy, Colonel John, 146
Quincy, Josiah, 48
Quincy Police, 153
Quincy Yacht Club, 159

R. B. Forbes, 50, 302, 303
Raccoon Island, 164
Racing Week, 254
Ragged Island, 157, 164, 165
Rainsford, Elder Edward, 148, 154, 280
Rainsford's Island, 25, 27, 28, 108, 114, 143, 148–154, 205, 276, 280
Rajah, 233, 234
Ram's Head, 217
Randolph, Edward, 40
Rangers, 98
Reagan, Judge, 190, 191, 194
Reamy, Octavius, 298, 308
Rebecca, 213
Rebels, 64, 65
Red Coats, 160
Red Rock, 22
Redfield, William C., 292
Reed, Mr., 243
Reed, Captain Charles W., 185–188
Reed, Commander Sherman W., 207, 208
Reekast, Augustus, Sr.. 226
Reekast, Mrs. Grace, 224
Regatta Week, 254
Regiment, 1st, 196
Regiment, 9th, 112, 113, 204
Regiment, 11th, 171
Regiment, 14th, 171
Regiment, 20th, 73
Regiment, 32nd, 195, 181
Regiment, 32nd, 181
Regiment, 55th, 156
Regiment, 241st, 157, 204
Regulator, 28
Resolute, 290
Resthaven Cemetary, 109
Restless, 232
Revenge, 118
Revere, Mass., 101
Revere, Paul, 65
Revolutionary War, 49, 77, 80, 92, 96, 103, 109, 127, 147, 155, 160, 232, 265, 293, 296
Rex, 33
Reynolds, Chief of Police, 156
Rhode Island, 60
Rice, Caleb, 166
Richard, Sam, 291
Richards, Mr. Thomas, 99
Richenbach, Mr., 226
Richmond, Va., 200
Rider, Mrs. Albert L., 200
Rinaldo, 180
Rio, Grisiano, 144
Risk, Corporal Thomas H., 194
Risk, William, 194
Roanoke Island, 200
Robinson, Charles L., 200
Robertson, Archibald, 64
Rochford. 77
Rock, Elizabeth, 111
Rock, Joseph, 111
Rockland, Me.. 292
Rogers, Prof. A. A., 134
Rogers, Llewellyn, 298
Roman, 126

Romance, 208
Romer, Col. Wolfgang William, 61, 78, 126
Romney, 63
Rose, 271
Rose Standish, 195
Rotch, Owner, 47. 48
Round Island, 157
Roustone, Captain, 27
Rowe, Edward, 264
Rowe, John, 27, 48
Rowe, Owen, 148
Rowe's Wharf. 27, 196
Rowson, Mrs., 213, 278
Royal Engineers, 64
Royall House, 49
Russ, Augustus, 221, 222
Russell, 100
Russell, Major, 23
Russell, George W., 142
Rutland, Mass., 97, 152
Ryan, John J., 153
Ryan, Peter, 75

Sacchetti, Dr. James V., 114
Sacred Cod, 235
Saddleback Ledge Light, 250
Safarina, Jose. 144, 145
Sailor's Bethel, 50
Saint Nicholas Magazine, 268
Saint Petersburg. 233
Salem, 112, 231–239, 241, 243, 244, 249, 259, 297
Salem Bay, 244
Salem Cadets, 182
Salem East India Marine Society, 232
Salem Harbor, 232, 233, 237, 239, 241–243
Salem Heights, 70
Salem Marine Society, 232, 241, 242
Salem Street, 126, 127
Salem Willows, 244
Sally, 254
Saltonstall. Gov. Leverett, 141
Sampson, Ernest, 299
Samuel Little, 108
San Francisco, 51, 52, 98
San Jacinto, 180
Sand Heads, 236
Sand Spit Sentinel, 217
Sangston, Lawrence, 172, 177–179
Sarah's Island, 164, 165
Saratoga, 74
Sargent, 127
Saunders, Major Reid, 185, 187, 188
Saunders, Robert, 273
Savage, 99
Savage, 243
Sawyer, Private, 188, 189, 192, 198, 203, 204
Sawyer, Timothy, 100
Say, Brothers, Will You Meet Us, 170
Scandinavian ship, 59
Scarlett's Wharf, 117
Scilly Isles, 263, 264
Scituate, 254, 260, 265, 267, 268, 302
Scituate Harbor, 265
Scituate Lighthouse, 265, 266, 268
Scotsman, 51, 170, 171
Scudder, Horace E., 44
Scully, John, 153
Sculpin Ledge, 144
Sea-Fencibles, 81
Sears, Professor, 243
Seaver, Captain Eben, 152

Seaverns, Dr., 193, 194
Seavey, Sumner D., 153
Seattle, 262
Second Baptist Church of Boston, 221
Secretary of Commerce, 292
Sedgwick, Captain Robert, 58
Seige of Boston, 277
Senate, 279
Sergeant's Wharf, 101
Seven Seas Spray, 295
Sewall, Samuel, 25, 26, 60, 61, 99, 100, 101, 117, 118, 167
Seymour, Major Truman, 195
Shade of Alden, 168, 214, 280
Shag Rocks, 177, 286–289
Shannon, 259–261, 279
Shaw, historian, 43
Shaw, Sergeant, 82–84
Shaw, Hugh, 83, 84, 88
Shaw, John, 102
Sheaf Island, 163
Shean Island, 163
Sheep Island, 157, 163
Shenandoah River, 172
Shenandoah Valley, 181, 182
Sherman, Thomas, 186
Sherwin, Mrs. Ann Winsor, 146
Ship Island, 163
Shirley bastion, 67
Shirley, Gov., 62
Shirley Gut, 32, 35, 36, 39, 41, 102–104, 109
Shirley, Mass., 154
Shoe Machinery Building, 88
Shrimpton, Captain, 103
Shuldam, Admiral, 64
Shurlock, James, 103
Shurtleff, 124, 205, 213, 214, 227, 271, 296
Silsbee, Captain Nathaniel, 235, 236
Silver Oar, 117
Simpkins, Nicholas, 57, 78
Sioux, 295
Skillman, Isaac, 221
Skull Head, 155
Slate Island, 163
Slidell, John, 166, 178–180, 200, 204
Small, Albert, 284, 293
Small, Judson B., 110
Small, Tom. 110, 219
Small, Zebedee, 285
Smallpiece, Mrs. Olive, 146
Smith, Captain, 160, 161
Smith, Fitz-Henry, Jr., 27, 274, 293
Smith, Dr. J. V. C., 27, 28, 34, 149–151, 205
Smith, Nancy, 152
Smith, General T. B.; 190
Snake Creek, 40
Snake Island, 92–94
Snetind, 146
Snow, Captain Ernest L., 295
Snow, Joe, 206
Snow, Joshua, 280
Snow, Silas, 142
Snow's Island, 121, 206
Soldier's Home, 152
Somerset, 65
Somerville, 82
South, 190, 195, 200, 205
South America, 54, 238
South Battery, 275
South Boston, 32, 52, 74, 76, 78, 82, 128, 133, 137, 148
South Boston Yacht Club, 162
South Carolina, 62, 184
South Shore, 160, 301
South Station, 47
Southern, 190, 200, 201, 204

Southern Metropolitan District, 148
Southack, 99
Sovereign of the Seas, 51, 54, 98
Spain, 196, 197
Spanish, 43, 251, 252
Spanish-American War, 75, 82, 198, 199
Spanish cigar factory, 283
Spanish Main, 123
Spanish Pirates, 59
Sparrow, Captain, 294
Spear, George, 149
Spear, Thomas, 149, 215, 216
Spears, John R., 54
Special Libraries Assoc., 136
Spectacle Island, 65, 88, 129, 131, 133, 143–146, 149, 159, 293
Spectacle Island Range Lights, 111
Spit, The, 218, 275
Sproul, Captain Ernest D., 262
Squantum, 33, 277, 291
Squantum Air Meet, 291
Squirrel, 118
St. John, 188
St. Joseph's A. A., 83
St. Lawrence River, 96
St. Paul, 232
Staghound, 51
Stamp Act, 62, 63
Standish, Captain Myles, 124
Stansbury, Thomas, 111
Staples, Captain, 304
Stark, 155
Stark, General, 96
Starlight, 180
State House, 271
State of Maine, 172
State Street, 90, 171
Station 12, 74
Stephens, Alexander Hamilton, 166, 190–194, 200, 204
Stephens, Linton, 194
Stephenson, Captain. 181
Stewart, Benjamin, 250
Stigmatine Fathers, 164
Stiles, Warren E., 204
Stone, Dirke, 122
Stony Beach Life Saving Station, 294
Storms and Shipwrecks of New England, 27
Stoughton, 61
Stoughton Hall, 60
Stoughton, Mass., 112
Stoughton, William, 60
Strong, Governor Caleb, 97
Strong, Dr. Thomas, 158
Sturgis, 107, 259
Suffolk County, 102, 108, 128
Suffolk Deeds, 111
Suffolk Record, 59
Suffolk School for Boys, 153
Sullivan, John L., 162
Sumatra, 231, 234
Sumner, 96
Sun Island, 163
Sunken Ledge, 163
Sunnyside, 39
Sunset Point, 157
Surf City, 244
Surprise, 51
Susanna Island, 94, 99
Swallow's Cave, 256
Swampscott, 21
Swasey, Paul Francis, 135
Sweetser, 79, 158, 165
Swift, Captain William H., 301

Tacony, 184–186, 288
Tailer, William, 61

Tanner. Captain, 40, 41
Tansill. Captain, 179
Tarr. Keeper Edwin, 114
Tarratines, 251
Taylor, Father Edward, 50, 51
Tea Wharf, 33
Teach, "Black Beard," 118
Temple, Sir Purbeck, 112
Temple, Robert, 111
Temple, Sir Thomas, 95, 102, 111
Ten Pound Light, 286
Tenedos, 242
Tenney, Mrs. Frank, 219
Tetlow, Helen Ingersol, 268
Tewksbury, Abijah, 103, 104
Tewksbury, C. P., 151
Tewksbury, William, 103, 104, 107
Tewksburys, 93
Thayer, Lt., Sylvanus, 69, 78, 80, 81, 87, 169, 178
Theodora, 179
The Blue and the Gray, 200
Theopold, Philip H., 141
Thermopylae, 167
Thimble Island, 146
Third Corps Cadets, 197
Thomas, Raymond, 141
Thomas W. Lawson, 262-264
Thomas, Mrs. Wilhelmina B., 142
Thompson's Island, 25, 33, 70, 88, 94, 124-243, 146
Thompson, David, 94, 124, 125
Thompson, Mrs. David (Amias), 125
Thompson, John, 125, 126
Thoreau, Henry David, 165
Thorndyke, Israel, 233
Thorwald, 149
Thurston, Lt. James, 185, 187, 188
Tigar Battalion, 169-171, 198
Tigers, 170, 171
Tilghman. General Lloyd, 184
Torrey, William, 163
Tower, David, 280
Toulouse, 162
Tousard, Lt.-Col., 67
Tourist, 197
Towle, Captain, 298
Town Records, 116
Town River Bay, 146
Townsend, Colonel, 99
Tory. 160
Treasury Department, 303
Treaty of Ghent, 81
Treaty of Paris, 80
Trelawny, Robert, 125
Trent, 180
Trent Affair, 178, 179
Trevore, William, 124
Treworgy, 93
Trimble, General I. R., 190
Truesworthy, Charles, 108
Truesworthy, Philip, 108
Truro Beach, 50
Tucker, Commodore, 190
Tudor, 278
Tudor, Frederick, 256
Tudor, Deacon John, 26
Tudor, Wiiiam, 97
Tupper, Major, 126, 277, 278
Turner, Captain, 219
Turner, Francis, 219
Turner, James, 223
Turner, John, 241
Tyler, Thomas, 239

U.S.S. Alacrity, 292
U.S.S. New Orleans, 33

U.S.S. Weehauken, 184
Underwood, Colonel, 152
Ut ion, 242
Up in Mabel's Room, 87
Upton, Captain Benjamin, 238
Upton, Mr. Charles, 245
Upton, Mrs. Charles, 245
United Daughters of the Confederacy, 200
United States, 74, 75, 93, 97, 101 180, 188, 198, 206, 226, 231, 233
United States Army, 102, 142, 227
United States Engineers, 197
United States Government, 279, 301, 302, 304
United States Maritime Service, 207
United States Navy, 102, 180, 186

Valjean, Jean, 193
Vaubaird, Admiral, 213
Vaughn, Engineer Hiram, 75
Vermont, 135
Very, Mrs. Nathaniel T., 244
Vestal, Colonel S. C., 156
Vienna, 184
Virginia, 67, 136, 172, 190, 200
Vision, 129
Vose, Major, 277

Wakefield, Joseph, 82-84
Walker, Captain, 74
Walker, Sir Hovendon, 61
Walker, Obediah, 147
Walsh, Richard J., 32
Walsh, Judge Richard M., 32
Walter, Rev. William, 126, 127
Waltham, 182
Wampatuck, 102
War Department, 153, 202, 217
War of 1812, 81, 128, 236, 237, 242, 259, 265, 268, 278
Ward, Francis J., 144
Ward, Sergeant James F., 199, 200
Ward, Kate, 74
Ward, Nahum, 143, 144
Ward Plant, 146
Ward, Samuel, 157, 164
Warren, Dr., 64
Warren, Director Frank L., 138, 141
Warren, Joseph, 80, 202
Washington, D. C., 113, 171, 180, 181, 266
Washington, George, 65, 67, 277, 278
Washington Light Guards, 198
Washington Street, 46
Webster, Fletcher, 170
Webster Regiment, 171
Weeks, John S., 223
Welch, Dr. T., 151
Wells, Rev. E. M. P., 128, 129
Wells Memorial for Workingmen. 128
Wendell, Oliver, 100
Wessagusett, 124
Westboro, Mass., 129, 154
West End, 84
West Head, 148, 151, 155, 213
West Indies, 160
West Point, 69, 70, 190
Weymouth, 163, 168
Wharton, Thomas Kelah, 169
When the Roll is Called Up Yonder, 289
White, Lt. Francis B., 98, 152

White, Lt. Horace Stockton, 152
White, John, 99
White, Major, Moses, 98, 152
White, Wilfred O., 263
White, William, 118, 119
Whitman, Walt, 50
Whitney, Richard S., 222
Whiton, Colonel, 152
Whittier, John Greenleaf, 73
Wightman, Mayor, 112
Wilber, Mrs. Herbert L., 283
Wilkes, Captain, 180
William, Alfred, 289
William and Henry, 232
William (of Orange), 111
William Starkey, 288
Williams, Captain, 286-288
Williams, Henry Howell, 96, 97
Williams, John D., 127, 135
Williams, Payson, 128
Wilson, Joseph, 302
Wilson Line, 144
Windmill Point, 155
Winissimett, 40
Winnie-Egan, 249
Winsor, Sarah, 268
Winthrop, Adam, 79
Winthrop, Ann, 79
Winthrop bastion, 67
Winthrop Board of Health, 93
Winthrop Highlands, 260
Winthrop, James, 80
Winthrop, John, 25, 58, 59, 78-81, 85, 86, 94, 116, 122, 148, 239, 241, 296
Winthrop Junction. 101
Winthrop, Mass., 25, 39, 41, 70, 78, 88, 89. 91-93, 100, 101, 103, 107, 154, 162, 194, 199, 298
Winthrop, Robert C., 111
Winthrop Street, 25
Woburn, 95
Wollaston, 146
Wood, William, 102
Woodman, Lt. William H., 191, 192
Woodroffe, Mr., 143
Woodrow Wilson Chapter, U. D. C., 200
Woodruff, Major C. A., 196
Woodward, James, 111
Woodworth. Stewart C.. 147
World War, 109, 114, 123, 147, 156, 198, 224, 296
World War II, 157, 204, 217
Worthylake, Benjamin, 166
Worthylake, George, 208, 272, 273, 293
Wray, John, 74
Wrentham, Mass., 216
Wyatt, Roy E., 145
Wyke, James E., 156

Xerxes, 167

Y. O. West End House, 156
Yale, 184
Yankee, 36, 39, 40, 169, 242
Young, Mr., 225
York Records, 95

Zanetsky, Fred, 223
Zanzibar, 231, 238
Zoo Ship, 298

THE BOSTON TEA PARTY.—DESTRUCTION OF